BETTER DAYS WILL COME AGAIN

BETTER DAYS WILL COME AGAIN

The Life of **ARTHUR BRIGGS**
*Jazz Genius of Harlem, Paris,
and a Nazi Prison Camp*

TRAVIS ATRIA

CHICAGO REVIEW PRESS

An A Cappella Book

LONGWOOD PUBLIC LIBRARY

Copyright © 2020 by Travis Atria
Preface copyright © 2020 by Barbara Pierrat-Briggs
Epilogue copyright © 2020 by James Briggs Murray
All rights reserved
Published by Chicago Review Press Incorporated
814 North Franklin Street
Chicago, Illinois 60610
ISBN 978-0-914090-10-6

Library of Congress Cataloging-in-Publication Data

Names: Atria, Travis, author.
Title: Better days will come again : the life of Arthur Briggs, jazz genius
  of Harlem, Paris, and a nazi prison camp / Travis Atria.
Description: Chicago : Chicago Review Press, 2020. | Includes
  bibliographical references and index. | Summary: "By the 1930s, Briggs
  was considered "the Louis Armstrong of Paris," and was the peer of the
  greatest names of his time, from Josephine Baker to Django Reinhardt. In
  1940, he was arrested and sent to the prison camp at Saint Denis. Based
  on groundbreaking research and including unprecedented access to
  Briggs's oral memoir, this is a crucial document of jazz history, a
  fast-paced epic, and an entirely original tale of survival"—Provided
  by publisher.
Identifiers: LCCN 2019029238 | ISBN 9780914090106 (cloth) | ISBN
  9780914090113 (pdf) | ISBN 9780914090229 (mobi) | ISBN 9780914090236
  (epub)
Subjects: LCSH: Briggs, Arthur, 1901-1991. | Trumpet players—Biography. |
  Jazz musicians—Biography. | Concentration camp
  inmates—France—Biography.
Classification: LCC ML419.B744 A75 2020 | DDC 781.65092 [B]—dc23
LC record available at https://lccn.loc.gov/2019029238

Interior typesetting: Nord Compo

Printed in the United States of America
5 4 3 2 1

For Kathy and Drew Atria,
with all my love and gratitude

Contents

Preface

by Barbara Pierrat-Briggs

WHEN I WAS BORN IN 1960, the first and only child of Arthur Briggs, my dad had already lived a full, eventful, and even extraordinary life. He was fifty-nine years old. He was recognized as a master trumpeter in both jazz and classical music. He had been accepted into the fraternity of pioneering jazz musicians in Harlem, New York, and Paris during the first golden age of jazz. He had forged a career as a hot trumpeter, vocalist, bandleader, and educator in Europe. And he had survived a Nazi prison camp during World War II.

Despite this astonishing life, my dad's story—the true story—was never told. The few attempts to do so were full of useful fictions and protective suppressions that my dad thought necessary. Throughout his life, these fictions and suppressions facilitated his growth and even ensured his survival, but they left jazz scholars scrambling to find the truth. Additionally, because he spent most of his ninety years in Europe, he was largely left out of America's historical record of jazz, leaving him unknown despite his massive achievements.

That is, until now.

Some years ago, author Travis Atria contacted me for permission to write an authorized biography on my dad. He was not the first person to approach me about my dad's story, but generally the long procession of writers, producers, and filmmakers over the years seemed more interested in their desire to tell the story than they were in my dad having lived it. Travis seemed different, particularly because he'd already done so much independent research. So, I phoned my cousin James Briggs Murray, a retired curator of music, film, and broadcasting at the New York Public Library's Schomburg Research Center, asking that he investigate Travis's professional background and give me an opinion. My cousin researched and read Travis's previous works, had a meal with him, and reported back that, among other publications, Travis had authored the essential book on R&B singer/songwriter, Curtis Mayfield, *Traveling Soul: The Life of Curtis Mayfield* (Chicago Review Press, 2016), with whose music my cousin was very familiar. He reported that Travis's treatment of Mayfield was accurate, thorough, insightful, respectful, musically analytical, and done with the appropriate social, cultural, and political context. In my mind and heart, these were exactly the characteristics I wanted in any book about my dad.

I met Travis in Paris in August 2017. Along with cousin James and our families, we spent a few days in serious conversation as we enjoyed good French food and wine. After those meetings, I decided to let my father's story, which I had protected so carefully since his death in 1991, finally be told. This book project, intended to fill an important gap in the documented history of jazz, is the result of Travis's tenacious investigation and James's and my added historical and family insights. But, for me, and for our entire family, this was not just a book project—it was an opportunity to tell the full and true story of our beloved Arthur Briggs at long last.

My dad was a gentleman and a modest man who had no tolerance for unfairness and wickedness. As a religious man, he prayed every day, but he was open-minded in accepting people and their belief systems. When I was two years old, after nearly a half-century of nonstop touring and performing, he retired in order to take care of me. My mom, thirty-four years his junior, was in the early years of her working career. So, it was my dad who got my day started and who picked me up from school in the afternoons. Unlike my classmates, who were taken straight home after school, my dad and I would normally stop at the baker's for cakes and hot chocolate before heading home. When we reached home, not only did my dad help me with my homework, he also cooked for me and played with me. He even knew all of my dolls by name. My dad was the fulfillment of my mom's life. He was a husband, somewhat of a father, and especially a friend to her—despite, and perhaps in some ways, because of their significant difference in age. They were inseparable. When he passed away, she was never the same.

My relationship with my dad was always loving, caring, and respectful, from my earliest childhood memories to my still vivid adulthood memories with him. I shall always remember our closeness together, our honesty with each other. I was full of admiration for him as a father, as a human being, as a musician, and as a man. That love, now extending and manifesting itself in the love I share with my husband, Denis, and our son, Stanley Arthur, remains at the core of my being.

Today, as a schoolteacher, I work five kilometers from the Nazi detention center in which my dad was held for nearly four years. I sometimes try to imagine what it took for him, after such a prominent musical career, to withstand the horrors of detention, to play Beethoven for the Nazis who hated jazz, and to play jazz for his fellow detainees— all while he was a prisoner of those who thought him inferior because of his skin. How did he emerge from years of wicked detention, never knowing if each day would be his last—how did he emerge from that hell with his mind, heart, and spirit so intact that he spent the next several decades as a respected professor of music, a devoted husband, and a loving father?

When your journey through this book is complete, I hope you will have come to understand the answers to these questions, and to appreciate the man who was a giant in my eyes—the man who was indeed a giant of jazz music—my father, Arthur Briggs.

Part I

How shall we sing the Lord's song in a strange land?

—Psalm 137

1

Winter, 1942

THERE WERE TEETH IN THE SOUP AGAIN, horse teeth. It was repulsive even to a starving man, and Arthur Briggs was a starving man. Hunger was a song stuck in his head as he shivered in a filthy hut, lice crawling on his skin. Evenings were once filled with jazz and risqué dancing, with gaiety and tumbling laughter, with champagne and fine cuisine. Now it was winter. He was hungry. And there were teeth in the soup again.

Briggs was trapped in Stalag 220, a Nazi prison for British citizens and other enemies of the Third Reich. Six miles south was Paris, where he had made his reputation as the greatest jazz trumpeter in Europe, earning the nickname "the Louis Armstrong of France." But isolated here in this camp, he might as well have been on the moon.

He could have fled the Nazis. He had family in Harlem, and his reputation as the greatest trumpeter in Europe was known in America. African American newspapers had followed his every move for years, including his work with Coleman Hawkins, Django Reinhardt, and Josephine Baker. Both Duke Ellington and Louis Armstrong wanted to hire him. But he remembered the sting of American segregation, and he hated it. He chose to stay in Europe.

Briggs believed he could hide in his Montmartre apartment until the trouble passed, but the trouble did not pass. Hitler now controlled Austria, Czechoslovakia, Belgium, Poland, Luxembourg, and half of France. He installed puppet governments in Denmark, Norway, the Netherlands, Algeria, Morocco, Tunisia, and the other half of France. He counted Italy as an ally, and his armies had penetrated so deep into the Soviet Union, they threatened to do what even Napoleon couldn't do.

While the Nazis stormed Europe and Russia, internment camps like Stalag 220 sprung up to house their prisoners, some held captive as forced labor, others as enemies of the state. As a black jazz musician and a citizen of a British colony, Briggs was an enemy twice.

To forget his fear and loneliness in captivity, he turned to the only thing the Nazis hadn't taken from him: music. Camp guards allowed the prisoners to form a makeshift orchestra, and Briggs led its brass section, honing it into a unit capable of tackling Beethoven, Strauss, and Mozart. He played to save himself but also to soothe the men's souls, ending each concert with an old Negro work song. In a previous age, the song gave harbor amid the horrors of slavery; now it kept the cold ember of hope alive for Briggs and two thousand men amid the horrors of World War II. If the Nazis understood what the song meant to their wretched prisoners, the punishment for playing it surely would have been severe. Briggs played it anyway, blowing life into the melody, while the lyrics rang in his bruised heart:

> *Don't be sighing, little darling,*
> *Sunshine follows after rain;*
> *Though the shadows now are falling,*
> *Better days will come again.*

Then he climbed from the bandstand and walked to his hut, aching, shuddering, wondering, *How did I get here?*

Arthur Briggs never told the truth about his birth, not even to his only daughter. He claimed to have been born in South Carolina in 1899, and his memoirs begin with dozens of pages of handwritten memories of Charleston, all of them fabricated. His dishonesty, as we'll see, came from a rather touching sense of honor and an understandable desire for self-protection, but it leaves most of his life until age sixteen a mystery.

Historians have tried to pinpoint his birth for decades without success, but new research shows conclusively that Briggs was born in St. George's, Grenada, on April 9, 1901.

Born to Louisa Wilkey and James Richard Briggs, James Arthur was the youngest of eleven children, including sisters Constance Amelia, and Edith Inez, as well as brother Warren Sinclair. Briggs was the baby of a large clan that included at least seven aunts and uncles on his father's side, as well as his paternal grandparents, Peter Harte Briggs and Dorothy Ann Bourne. Briggs's father was a sanitary inspector and perhaps also a preacher. He used the house as a meeting place for Bible study. Briggs's family was upper-middle class. His father owned land in Grenada, and although birth records are hard to trace past his mother's mother, Celia, it is almost certain Briggs's lineage on his paternal grandmother's side goes back to the great London Bourne.

London Bourne was born into slavery on the island of Barbados in 1793. He was of unmixed African ancestry. His father, William, was also enslaved but became politically active after gaining freedom, signing a petition in 1811 to let free people of color testify in court against whites. William also bought his son's freedom for $500 and eventually freed his wife and other children.

London was an iconoclast. By 1830, he worked as a sugar broker, owned three stores, and was worth between $20,000 and $30,000. This success made him unique among freed slaves. The fire of conviction made him important. Though he was socially conservative by nature, Bourne supported radical causes. He joined several antislavery organizations, some of which sought to establish settlements for Barbadians who wished to return to Africa. He also served on the governing body of the Colonial Charity School, established for the children of slaves and free people of color.

Bourne's biographer called him a precursor to Marcus Garvey and W. E. B. Du Bois, "in their continuous espousal of pride in being African, and in their actual involvement in African affairs, including emigration movements to Africa."[1] Bourne loved education, charity, and culture. He hated racism, violence, and ignorance. These traits were passed unchanged to Arthur Briggs.

It is strange, then, that both Bourne and his wife owned slaves. Barbadian records show Bourne owned six slaves in 1826, and five in 1834. It isn't clear what to make of this. Perhaps Bourne was an abolitionist *and* a slave owner—a bizarre combination to be sure—or maybe he took a lesson from his father and bought members of his own family to protect them. As with much of Briggs's lineage, this remains a question with no answer.

Briggs's family had deep ties to Barbados, likely stretching far beyond London Bourne. It must have been a major event, then, when they moved to 43 Green Street in St. George's, Grenada. Christening records show Arthur was the second and last child born there.

Grenada is a speck of sand, its landmass roughly half the size of Harlem. Christopher Columbus first sighted the island in 1498, and Europeans spent the next century and a half trying to beat the native Island Caribs into submission. The Caribs fought ferociously but fell to France in 1650. Within fifty years, Grenada was home to more than five hundred enslaved Africans.

England and France spent most of the seventeenth century ripping control of the island from each other, until England finally prevailed in 1784, making Grenada a British colony. Consequently, Briggs was born a British citizen. After England's Slavery Abolition Act of 1833, British masters tried to keep their former slaves in captivity through a system of apprenticeship. Like America, Grenada made no room for freed slaves in its economy or its society. Unlike America, the island had no physical room either. Slaves and masters executed an intricate social reconfiguration in extremely close quarters, as if they were ballroom dancing in a closet.

After apprenticeship came métayage, a sort of sharecropping that kept ex-slaves in perpetual poverty. In addition, they now had to compete with imported indentured labor. By Briggs's birth, the tiny island was home to Maltese, Spanish, Indian, French, English, and Portuguese laborers, and hundreds of African ethnic groups.

This creolized cultural stew was Briggs's incubator.

Briggs was raised in the Christian church, and though he quickly dispensed with its formalities, he never lost its lessons. Despite everything he experienced in life—from racist club owners, to corrupt bandleaders, to political executions, to a Nazi prison camp—he always believed in honesty, charity, humanity, and brotherhood. These traits remained remarkably steady throughout his life. He was moral but not moralizing; upright but not stuffy; rigid but not hard-hearted. He was formal in speech, impeccable in dress, and obsessed with dignity. From an early age, he was accustomed to the spotlight but not beguiled by it. He possessed enormous self-confidence, but not arrogance. He was quick to forgive, but when slighted, often because of his deep black skin, he made sure he was given restitution.

He had rough spots too. He was impulsive and quick to take offense, and he was known to abandon friends and break contracts with no warning when he felt his dignity was in question. But above all, Briggs refused to bend his principles to fit an unprincipled world. This set him on a difficult path, for those who do not bend often break. But he did not break. Though it never ceased to hurt and shock him when the world abused his ideals, he did not abandon them. He was the rare steadfast man.

He was also the rare straightlaced man. In a profession filled with drunks and addicts, Briggs was the soul of discretion. But beneath his conservative façade, he possessed an artist's fire. This fire propelled him around the world, from Grenada, to Harlem, to Paris, to Cairo, to Constantinople. It drove him to make some of the greatest jazz records in Europe, and it saved his life in a Nazi prison.

The fire was ignited when Briggs began taking trumpet lessons as a child. He immediately excelled. One of the first pieces he learned— he called it his "workhorse"—was "The Carnival of Venice," a showoff piece featuring dizzying scales and dazzling displays of double and triple tonguing, all at astonishing speeds. It demanded virtuosic ability, which Briggs had.

Though the music of Grenada was Calypso, Briggs's training was classical. As a young black man in a British colony, he had to be fluent in European culture, though Europeans knew nothing of his culture. This fact dogged him throughout his life, but it gave him an advantage that served equally well in the world's finest cabarets and in a Nazi prison. Briggs could please any audience. He didn't separate Beethoven from bebop. Music was music.

Like any normal kid, Briggs loved the pop music of his era—an early form of jazz called ragtime. Popularized by artists such as Scott Joplin, today most famous for writing the immortal rag "The Entertainer," ragtime was, as one historian described it, "White music played black." It was the result of European instruments in the hands of musicians who carried Africa's rhythms in their bones. Perhaps no one described it better than seminal jazz clarinetist—and one of Briggs's close friends— Sidney Bechet:

> It comes out of the Negro spirituals. . . . The only thing they had that couldn't be taken from them was their music. Their song, it was coming right up from the fields, settling itself in their feet and working right up, right up into their stomachs, their spirit, into their fear, into their longing. . . . *Rag it up*, we used to say. You take any piece, you make it so people can dance to it, pat their feet, move around. You make it so they can't help themselves from doing that. You make it so they just can't sit still. And that's all there is to it. It's the rhythm there. The rhythm *is* ragtime.[2]

Bechet came from New Orleans, which is generally accepted as the birthplace of jazz. In Storyville, New Orleans's seedy red-light district, black Creole musicians took European instruments such as the tuba, clarinet, trombone, and trumpet, and added their own traditions of syncopation and improvisation to create something new. Bechet recalled hearing the bands tear down the street blasting this irresistible sound: "It was laughing out loud up and down all the streets, laughing like two people just finding out about each other . . . like something that had found a short-cut after travelling through all the distance there was. That music, it wasn't spirituals or blues or ragtime, but everything all at once."[3] These were the first nonmarching, instrumental, blues-oriented groups, and they played a rougher, more fluid version of the Creole marches and quadrilles. It was first called "jass," a dirty sexual reference, which like rock 'n' roll fifty years later, sneaked into common usage.

Jazz lived in the notes between notes, the soulful wails that defied notation on a staff, the rhythms that lived, as the phrase went, between the cracks. Improvisation was the heart of this new music, a conversation between instruments that had no equivalent in European music. "The purity of tone that the European trumpet player desired was put aside by the Negro trumpeter for the more humanly expressive sound of the voice," wrote the poet-historian LeRoi Jones (later Amiri Baraka). "The rough, raw sound the black man forced out of these European instruments was a sound he had cultivated in this country for two hundred years. It was an American sound."[4] Briggs wanted this American sound, but he also valued purity of tone. He'd spend his life perfecting both.

We know two more facts of Briggs's youth in Grenada. In 1913, his sister Inez moved to New York to marry a man named Thomas Hall (Briggs often claimed to have accompanied Inez on the trip, but there is no evidence of this). Four years later, Briggs's father died. Arthur was only sixteen years old. If not for this tragedy, he might have stayed in Grenada and become a classical trumpeter. Instead, perhaps to ease the burden on his mother, perhaps to make his way in the world, he decided to leave his island and join Inez in New York. In November 1917, James Arthur Briggs boarded the S.S. *Maraval* and sailed away from home, never to return.

2

"The music is . . . a lost thing finding itself."[1]

—Sidney Bechet

NOVEMBER 22, 1917: FROM THE DECK of the S.S. *Maraval*, Arthur Briggs gazed at the Statue of Liberty. She filled the sky above his head, her coat covered in frost, her torch glinting in the cold sunlight. It was one of the coldest winters ever recorded. He was sixteen years old and alone at the doorstep of America. In the distance, Manhattan stretched like an open hand. The Registry Room at Ellis Island swarmed with bodies bent from the voyage at sea. Briggs waited in line for his medical and legal inspection, and sat patiently as a customs official questioned him.

"Profession?" the official asked.

"Musician."

Briggs had plans.

His entrance to America was a lesson in extremes. After the thrill of arrival came the shame of being herded onto a segregated subway car. He recalled the journey to Grand Central Terminal with typical formality and understatement: "[It was] tiresome . . . due to certain unsocial railway methods of segregation of which I was not aware."[2]

Then there was Grand Central Terminal itself, a perfect marriage of artistry and machinery. Briggs had never seen anything so magnificent. He walked through halls of imitation Caen stone and polished Botticino marble to the Express Concourse, where the turquoise ceiling seemed as big as the sky. He picked his way past red-hatted porters pouring through the terminal like ants from a toppled anthill; past women in tiered skirts and velvet hats festooned with ostrich feathers; past men in derby hats and fur-trimmed Ulster coats. The size and speed of New York was dizzying. Finally, a familiar face: Inez.

She took young Arthur to her apartment at 24 West 134th Street, where she and her husband roomed with another couple—the Spooners—and several tenants. They lived under a common Harlem agreement: the tenants helped Inez and the Spooners with rent, and in return, they received affordable rooms and use of the kitchen and other amenities at certain hours. The big apartment impressed Briggs, who had only known the cramped embrace of a tiny island.

In bed that first night, Briggs dreamed he was in a concert hall listening to Chopin's "Heroic Polonaise." In fact, the bold, passionate strains came from down the hall. Mr. Spooner was a trained pianist who dreamed of performing at Carnegie Hall. "Unfortunately," Briggs said, "although being qualified for such a task after years of intense studies, he realized that such an event must be discarded, maybe forever."[3] Spooner was the first musician Briggs had met whose color barred him from his dreams.

He was not the last.

Arthur Briggs found Harlem at the exact moment it became *Harlem*. It was the beginning of the Great Migration, a massive demographic shift, during which six million African Americans fled the Jim Crow South and moved to northern and western cities, changing America's face forever. Meantime, black immigrants from Africa and the Caribbean joined this flood, Briggs among them, causing tension between black Americans and black foreigners. As a child of Grenada, Briggs knew complex racial hierarchies, but the lines separating black and white on the island were permeable enough that Briggs was related to two black slave *owners*. He had never faced anything as limiting and dangerous as American segregation. As the great writer and activist James Weldon Johnson explained it, segregation was "the dwarfing, warping, distorting influence which operates upon each colored man in the United States. He is forced to take his outlook on all things, not from the view point of a citizen, or a man, or even a human being, but from the viewpoint of a *colored* man."[4]

Harlem enforced segregation by custom rather than by law. As black migrants crowded in, white property owners tried to deny them housing. When that became impossible, many owners threatened to accept black tenants; this, they hoped, would scare white neighbors into buying their property at prices higher than market value. Others, known today as blockbusters, placed blacks in a property and then bought the adjoining properties as whites fled and prices fell. Still others signed restrictive agreements, refusing to rent to black tenants at all. One such agreement read, "Each of the parties does hereby covenant and agree [not] to . . . cause to be suffered, either directly or indirectly, the said premises to be used or occupied in whole or in part by any negro, quadroon, or octoroon of either sex whatsoever."[5] These agreements, known as covenant blocks, appeared in every city where black migrants settled. All of these strategies were used to prevent black neighborhoods from developing and retaining wealth. Arthur Briggs's new home was the beginning of the American ghetto.

Within this crucible brewed an artistic explosion. Briggs arrived in New York at the beginning of the Harlem Renaissance, a period when writers such as Zora Neale Hurston and Langston Hughes, painters such as Laura Wheeler Waring and Aaron Douglas, dancers such as Florence Mills and Bill "Bojangles" Robinson, and musicians such as Louis Armstrong and Billie Holiday redefined American culture. Briggs would soon play a part, however small, in this Renaissance.

In the way of teenagers everywhere, Briggs quickly fell in with a group of friends. He awaited them on Inez's stoop in the morning and walked home from school with them in the afternoon. These friends eased Briggs into the first major transition of his life. He began to shed his identity as a child of St. George's, Grenada, losing his island accent in learning to speak like the other boys.

Briggs's school was connected to St. Mark the Evangelist Catholic Church on West 138th Street in Harlem, and when he discovered the church's brass band, he approached Mr. Spooner about his musical ambition. Spooner knew Gladius Marshall, St. Mark's conductor, and he promised to make an introduction. "To me," Briggs said, "that was a God-send."[6] Marshall was impressed by Briggs's sight-reading and his tone. The latter was no small feat—a trumpeter's tone comes from embouchure, the strength in the small muscles surrounding the mouth and lips. Embouchure can only be achieved over time, through persistence and pain, by pressing the soft flesh of the lips into the trumpet's small metal mouthpiece and practicing until the tone becomes clear and steady. Briggs had not only achieved superlative tone, he also knew how to use solfège (do-re-mi-fa-sol-la-ti-do) to identify the pitch of any note in a piece of music. Having such a musical background was crucial, for as Briggs said, "In my time, if you couldn't read, you didn't have a chance."[7]

When Briggs played "The Carnival of Venice," the showoff piece he had learned in Grenada, Marshall knew he had found a child prodigy. He immediately enrolled Briggs in the Martin Smith School of Music on West 136th Street, where Briggs joined the forty-piece symphonic orchestra, received three hours of tuition each week, practiced every Saturday, and played a concert every other Sunday. He and fellow trumpeter Elmer Edwards became natural allies, and here was another Briggs trait: throughout his life many of his best friends were trumpeters. That he didn't feel threatened was a sign of his confident, magnanimous spirit. He boasted of himself and Edwards, "We dominated the classical trumpet section."[8]

Briggs was now immersed in classical music, but he still loved ragtime. He recalled hearing it played on an early form of the player piano called the pianola. The music spoke to him, but he didn't know how to play it—not yet. "Most of the guys were aiming at a straight musical career," he said. "We *never* played the blues."[9] Still, he could feel it. He knew it was his music, and he knew something else: he was different from his bandmates. None of them impressed the older folks the way he did; none intended to become a professional musician, as Briggs knew he must.

Marshall began using Briggs as a regular replacement at the St. Mark dance school, and in a short time, Briggs was earning four dollars a week. This was a fortune, and Briggs spent it on the thing that mattered most. His trumpet, the one he presumably brought from Grenada, was so old and battered he had to stuff wads of chewing gum in the cracks to keep the air from leaking out. "The other kids had brand new horns and would often say insulting words concerning the gum, and my fifteenth-hand cornet," Briggs recalled.[10] With his new income, he went to the East Village and bought his "first real horn." With this new horn, Briggs began performing at funeral parades for local dignitaries.

These performances became so popular he was called to perform in New Jersey, Philadelphia, and Connecticut.

As Briggs discovered more of America, he realized how unwelcome he was outside the cocoon of Harlem. As an old man, he still remembered the restaurant in New Jersey that proudly displayed a sign reading: "Colored men are not served."[11] At the tender age of sixteen, he was faced with experiences he could not fully understand. In one year, he had left home and become a professional musician. Even he must have felt surprised how quickly it happened. Part of it was luck—he came to Harlem at a time when talented, reliable players were in high demand—and part of it was talent. For most artists, the climb from amateur to professional demands the tedious work of many years. Briggs scaled that mountain in a few giant leaps.

3

"I have done my best to put a stop to this discrimination,
but I have found that it was no use."[1]

—James Reese Europe

EVERYTHING THAT COMES NEXT RUNS through James Reese Europe. As
a founding architect of the New York jazz scene, Europe directly and
indirectly shaped the lives of hundreds, if not thousands, of musicians,
Arthur Briggs included. Europe was a man of rigid military bearing with
a wide-eyed glare that smoldered from behind circular wire-frame glasses.
He moved to New York in 1904 looking for work as a musician, only to
find the local chapter of the American Federation of Musicians segregated. When black musicians in Harlem did find jobs, they were treated
as menial labor and expected to work for tips.

Europe singlehandedly changed that.

He founded two clubs—the Clef and the Amsterdam—that func-
tioned as trade and booking agencies for black performers. These clubs
demanded better working conditions and better pay from venues, and
they enforced standards of conduct and a dress code on members.
Europe was also the first musician to bring ragtime to Carnegie Hall.
Jazz pioneer Eubie Blake called him the Martin Luther King of music.

In World War I, Europe was lieutenant of the famous 369th Infantry Regiment, better known as the Harlem Hellfighters. He directed the
Hellfighters' regimental band, which introduced France to an early form
of jazz. Europe's band already used many of the techniques jazz soloists
would make popular in coming decades, including the use of mutes
and a tonguing technique that produced a growl from the horn. Europe

called these effects a "racial musical characteristic," and he had to keep his band in check to be sure they didn't take it so far out the French wouldn't recognize it as music. Whatever the music was called—jazz, ragtime, or something indefinable—it worked. The Hellfighters became stars throughout France, and drum major Noble Sissle wrote to a friend back home: "Jim and I have Paris by the balls in a bigger way than anyone you know."[2]

In the spring of 1918, the Harlem Hellfighters began recruiting musicians to replace the men fighting overseas. Briggs had already joined Europe's Amsterdam Club and was working at movie theaters accompanying silent films. Though he was underage, his reputation had begun to spread, and the Hellfighters' stand-in conductor wanted him in the regimental band. So began a lie that followed Briggs for the rest of his life. In order to join the 369th 15th Brass Band, Arthur Briggs claimed to have been born in 1899, making him eighteen years old and eligible for military service. The second part of his personal transformation was complete.

Now a military man, Briggs began filling jobs vacated by deployed soldiers. He ran an elevator at the Latham Hotel on East 28th Street, and when that job went bust, he became a rivet catcher. The latter was grueling, unforgiving work. The warmer or "cook" would heat the rivets in a furnace until they glowed red-hot, then toss them to Briggs, who caught them in a solid tin bucket, climbed a scaffold, and passed the sizzling rivets to the bucker. The bucker worked in tandem with the riveter, the riveter using an air hammer to pound the rivets into place on a ship's hull, the bucker using a block of metal to provide counterpressure. It was hot, loud, and dangerous.

At lunchtime, his hands burnt from handling hot rivets, Briggs attended band rehearsal. The first day, he had to prove his mettle with a sight-reading test. Though still a teenager, he had the confidence to withstand the scrutiny of grown men. He played an overture, a medley of folk songs, and "naturally, the Stars and Stripes." After passing this test, his job was to play one hour per day as the men ate lunch and then spend the rest of the day rehearsing. Briggs enjoyed the work and signed on for six months "at a nice fat salary."[3]

This new work came in addition to his already full schedule, thrusting Briggs into the hectic lifestyle he'd maintain for the next twenty years. The St. Mark's Brass Band still put on a concert every two weeks, at which Briggs now received double pay, and in 1918, they played a political rally in the Lenox Casino, which later became the Nation of Islam's Temple No. 7, led by Malcolm X. The speaker that day was Marcus Garvey, a Jamaican immigrant who ignited a movement that presaged the Black Power movement of the 1960s. Briggs must have known of Garvey—his apartment sat a few hundred feet from Garvey's headquarters in Harlem—but that day was the first time he heard the man speak.

Garvey's ideas were radical for the time. He promoted global African solidarity, black self-determination, and black self-acceptance long before these ideas had traction in the culture. Garvey's ideas put him at odds with the two other leading thinkers in black American life: Booker T. Washington, who accepted the reality of segregation and urged black Americans to focus on building their own wealth in their own communities; and W. E. B. DuBois, founder of the NAACP, who supported integration, believing black people could achieve equality by proving themselves equal. Though Briggs rarely spoke of race, his few statements on the subject show he had more in common with DuBois than with Washington or Garvey—he believed his people could achieve equality by proving the value of their culture, and he often took his fellow black musicians to task when they failed to do this. At the same time, there was always a streak of Garvey in him threatening to burst forth when his dignity was challenged.

Briggs also joined the Theatre Owners Booking Association, an infamous organization that controlled black vaudeville. The TOBA had a reputation for grinding musicians down, earning it the wry nickname "Tough On Black Asses." Briggs worked for the TOBA at Lincoln Theatre on 136th Street and Lenox Avenue, filling in for the usual trumpeter when the man was too drunk to play. Soon, Briggs replaced the besotted trumpeter permanently. Said Briggs, "This was a great lesson for [the drunk trumpeter], as he finally stopped being juiced and thanked me." It was also a great lesson for Briggs, and he'd never forget it: beware the cheap thrills of liquor.

Despite the crush of constant work, Briggs still found time to duck into a theater most days and watch his favorite vaudeville comedians: Sandy Burns, who owned a stock company that toured the TOBA in at least five different shows, and someone Briggs called "Turkey Bosoms." As an old man looking back on his life, Briggs remained delighted by the memory of these performers. "No matter what people would say, these two black comedians were and still are the world's greatest," he said.[4]

Imagine him giggling his head off in a vaudeville theater. He was only a kid. Despite the natural cockiness of youth, he was vulnerable. Between ages sixteen and seventeen, he had lost his father, left his family, and moved from a tiny island to a big city full of temptations he had never felt and dangers he could not imagine. In that city, he pursued a competitive, ruthless profession and became successful, all before the world had stolen the softness from him.

Luckily, two older musicians from the Clef Club liked the kid. They became a surrogate family, guiding Briggs through danger. One was William Smith, a man Briggs called uncle. Smith, alias Cricket, alias Sweet Papa Too Fat, was an inventive trumpet player who played with James Reese Europe in 1913 on some of the earliest ragtime records ever made. Briggs recalled, "The first time I saw his way of working, I couldn't help laughing. . . . He wore a gray suit with a gray undertaker's hat that he used as a mute on his trumpet, which gave surprising sounds. With his dexterity, it seemed like people who were arguing or quarreling. The dancers stopped dancing to look at him and listen to him, applauding like madmen. He was [a] born comedian, changing his physiognomy: sad and languorous for some songs or jovial, depending on the moment."[5]

It was through "Uncle" Cricket that Briggs met his second mentor, the most important musical influence of his life: Will Marion Cook. Cook was assistant musical director of the Clef Club, and he taught at the Martin Smith School of Music, where Briggs studied. Like James Reese Europe, Cook was a towering figure of early jazz.

Cook cut a striking figure, with his tarblack waxed moustache stretching from cheek to cheek and his dark black hair, turning gray at the crown, throwing his light skin into relief. As Briggs said, "He was the closest thing to a white, to see him. You had to be a professional to know that he was colored."[6] And yet, much like Spooner, Cook's skin barred him from his dream of playing in a classical orchestra.

As a young man, Cook studied to become a concert violinist, first at the Oberlin Conservatory, and then in Berlin for several years, finishing his training with the great Czech composer Antonin Dvořák. But when he auditioned for a violin scholarship, he was passed over in favor of a white man. The judge later told him he would have won if he weren't black. Cook smashed his violin in disgust and stormed out of the room. "That broke his heart," Briggs said.[7]

Cook decided if he couldn't be a concert violinist, he'd at least try to get rich. He began writing for the theater, beginning with 1898's *Clorindy: The Origin of the Cake-Walk*, with words by seminal black poet Paul Laurence Dunbar. The Cakewalk was a high-stepping strut descended from a dance slaves invented to covertly mock white slaveholders; it became one of the first dance crazes to sweep America. Cook's next hit was *In Dahomey*, a show that featured actors dressed as West Africans, who periodically broke into tribal songs and dances around their authentic-looking huts. In the era of blackface, when even black performers darkened their skin with burnt cork, Cook refused this humiliating tradition, making him one of the first artists to challenge racist portrayals of black people in art. As one reviewer noted, "Reactions . . . ranged from amusement to revulsion."[8]

Shortly after Briggs's seventeenth birthday, he met Cook in dramatic fashion. Before a concert with the 369th regimental band, Uncle Cricket took ill and didn't show up. The conductor, Lieutenant Alfred Simpson, pointed to Briggs and ordered, "You take over."

"Lieutenant, you're making a mistake," Briggs pleaded.

"I asked you to take over," Simpson answered, unused to having his command questioned by a teenager.

Briggs choked down his fear and picked up his horn. He was "trembling and everything" as he performed, not knowing that Cook was in the audience watching. "We played a medley of folk songs," Briggs recalled, "and there were three sentimental coronet solos where you had to play the way you feel, you know, not just the notes."

Afterward, Cook approached the bandstand. "Son, you got plenty heart," he said.

"Well, I'm scared to death," Briggs replied.

The seasoned veteran smiled at the nervous young man. "No, you played wonderfully well. You had a nice tone, and your feeling just thrilled me."

Cook was assembling a band for an American tour, and he asked Briggs to join. After discussing the offer with Inez, Mr. Spooner, and Gladius Marshall, Briggs became a member of Cook's New York Syncopated Orchestra. "When Cricket came back," Briggs recalled, "he grabbed me and kissed me, and he said, 'Son, I hope this will be a stepping-stone in life for you.'"[9]

Inez had one condition before allowing her little brother to join a group of grown men on a monthlong tour: Arthur must have a guardian. Cook volunteered. Briggs already had an uncle in Cricket Smith; now he had a more important surrogate family member. The magnitude of the relationship, especially for a young man who had recently lost his father, was evident in the name Briggs called Cook for the rest of his life: Dad.

4

"There was something wonderful in the spirit of the Syncopated Orchestra."[1]

—Arthur Briggs

WAITING FOR HIS FIRST REAL TOUR to start, Arthur Briggs spent six months working odd jobs around New York City. On July 4, 1918, he performed in a brass-band competition at Madison Square Garden. Briggs and his band "were ever so proud" dressed in tailor-made suits and fit-to-measure uniforms.[2] They played directly before world famous composer Edwin Franko Goldman, who was second only to the great John Philip Sousa in the quality and popularity of his marches. It was a tough slot, but exciting too, and out of fifty competitors, Briggs's band won sixth place. This success earned the band three days' furlough and a barbeque picnic in their honor.

The furlough made Briggs realize just how overworked he was. Every day he faced a "steady grind, getting up at 4 a.m. to make the subway and ferryboat trip (two hours) to Port Elizabeth, starting to work at 7 a.m."[3] He requested three months leave from the Hellfighters and got it, but he didn't know how to relax. Immediately he found a "wonderful but hard job" at the Skating Rink on 181st Street and Broadway, where the band toiled twelve hours a day, from ten in the morning until ten at night, with three hour-long breaks for meals. "This did not prevent me from taking on a ball at the Manhattan Casino occasionally," Briggs said.[4]

The working vacation ended when "Dad" Cook began rehearsals in December. Cook honed his horn section first, training them in his unorthodox methods. "He knew how to impose the normal nuances: pianissimo, fortissimo, crescendo and diminuendo," Briggs recalled, but Cook also invented "special African effects that he did not write [because] he did not want to be copied." These African effects included tongue rolls, lip slurs, and glissandos, and they were part of Cook's attempt to inject the freedom of jazz into classical structure.

Briggs soon learned to follow Cook's unorthodox conducting. "He directed the orchestra with facial expressions and slight movements of his anatomy," Briggs said. "We were looking at him most of the time, because the parts we almost know by heart, and we can see the embellishments that he wants from his face . . . I never seen anyone else like him."[5]

Cook was a taskmaster, drilling his musicians after rehearsal each time they stumbled. One of his close friends called him "hot-tempered and argumentative" and "sure enough plumb crazy."[6] Yet it was just this craziness, born at least partly of bitterness, that gave Cook's work such fire. Luckily, Briggs had a knack for handling fire. Of Cook, Briggs said, "He had obviously taken a liking to me, and although he was an uncompromising and slightly irascible man, I did not give him the opportunity to reprimand me."[7]

Whatever Cook's idiosyncrasies, his gift was to make orchestrated music seem improvised. As the band picked up his methods, their virtuosity expanded. "We started taking liberties ourselves," Briggs recalled. "The violinist might do something that sounded good to us all and we'd all rave about it, you see. And then someone else would think of doing something else in the same number, or in some other number. It was a competition without being a vulgar competition, without being unpleasant."[8]

From this style of competition, jazz was born.

5

"Brass bands were my paradise."

—Arthur Briggs

IN LATE JANUARY 1919, BRIGGS set off on tour with a ragtag, multicultural group of thirty musicians and twenty singers from America, Africa, and the Caribbean Islands. To handle the challenges of mounting such an ambitious operation, Cook turned to George Lattimore, a Columbia-educated lawyer who founded and comanaged the Smart Set Athletic Club of Brooklyn, the first independent African American basketball team. The partnership would prove calamitous.

The band, "50 Players and Singers—All Star Soloists" as Lattimore's press advance called it, opened in Hagerstown, Maryland, playing a diverse set featuring many of Cook's compositions, along with Negro spirituals, light classics, popular songs, ragtime medleys, and waltzes. Cook hoped to use this blend of classical, popular, and ragtime, with all of its racial implications, to uplift and promote black culture, while striking a blow at the heart of segregation.

Unfortunately, the heart of segregation was not so easily struck. After leaving the first concert, Briggs heard the chilling sound of "dogs barking furiously behind us." Next came the police, who "cursed us with dirty words that I will not repeat, reminding us that we had to respect the curfew or pay the consequences." Lattimore, a dapper, cultivated man, calmly explained that the band had to catch the first train in the morning and thanked the officers for their hospitality. This softened them up—apparently they didn't recognize sarcasm. "Keep moving," the officers said. Under his breath, Lattimore muttered, "We are counting the minutes to move out of this burg."[1]

The next sign of trouble came in South Bend, Indiana, where the band arrived barely a day after Lattimore's advance publicity, and as a result, played to an almost empty hall. "The thing was all a question of . . . bad management [and] publicity," Briggs said. "The public was few and the costs were very heavy."[2]

During another of the coldest winters on record, the group slogged through Baltimore; Washington, D.C.; Dayton; Cleveland; Detroit; Milwaukee; Cincinnati; and dozens of small cities in between, giving Briggs a lesson in American culture beyond Harlem. Meanwhile, the Spanish flu pandemic of 1918 killed nearly 5 percent of the world's population. "We'd . . . travel by train—you couldn't travel by bus—and get into town, you'd have snow that high," Briggs said. "Business was awful."[3]

At the tour's lowest point, the band couldn't afford train tickets to their next date in Chicago. Cook took up a collection, but came up $200 short. Violinist Paul Wyer, alias Pensacola Kid, spoke up. He was a pool shark. With twenty dollars, he promised, he could make the money. Cook handed Wyer the cash, and they went to a nearby billiards room, where Wyer ran his con to perfection. "Wyer handled the billiard cue as well as his violin bow," Briggs said. "We were able to catch our train before the other players realized they had dealt with the Pensacola Kid in person."[4] This raised their spirits as they limped into Chicago.

The Great Migration had transformed Chicago into the jumping, jiving heart of the first great northern jazz scene. Where New Orleans had Storyville, Chicago had the Stroll, a series of clubs, cabarets, and brothels on the South Side. Bandleader Eddie Condon famously quipped that if you "held up a trumpet in the night air of the Stroll, it would play itself." It was the beginning of a scene that would produce jazz greats such as Benny Goodman and Gene Krupa, as well as a who's who of blues and R&B artists, including Muddy Waters, Buddy Guy, and Curtis Mayfield.

When Briggs arrived on the Stroll, Freddie Keppard and Joe Oliver, the two greatest jazz trumpeters in the world, were battling for the title of king. Back in New Orleans, trumpeter Buddy Bolden was the undisputed king (this title became the basis for jazz's royal hierarchy, which grew to include Duke Ellington and Count Basie). But when Bolden faded from the scene, his protégé Freddie Keppard took the title and split for Chicago. In Chicago, Keppard met his match in Joe Oliver.

Oliver eventually eclipsed Keppard and was the last man to hold the title of king. According to Louis Armstrong, who soon joined King Oliver's band, "No trumpet player ever had the fire that Oliver had."[5]

Briggs couldn't get into the clubs as a minor, so he went with Cook and saxophonist Mazie Mullins—one of the first women in jazz—to the Lincoln Gardens Café. He sat mesmerized as Oliver swung for two straight hours. Then Mullins and Cook chaperoned him down the Stroll to the DeLuxe cabaret, where Keppard held court. This was another revelation. Keppard made his horn growl, using a perfected version of the flutter-tongue technique Cook had taught Briggs. He was also a pioneer of the trumpet mute. "I believe [Keppard] really *found* the art of 'wa-wa' with certain tin cans and glasses that he used to get the weirdest sounds, which made one think that he was talking," Briggs said. "He was what you'd call a freak. [He] could play a top C." To hit a high C on the trumpet requires intense pressure and lip strength. As Briggs said, "A guy makes an A, he was pretty good, and a B-flat was better, you know. And if you ever make a top C, then you just, you know . . . I thought it was heaven."[6]

Though Keppard was, in Briggs's estimation, "far from the finesse of Joe Oliver," he gave a master class in the power of improvisation. Plus, Keppard had a hot band, featuring Tony Jackson on piano and Sidney Bechet on clarinet. Jackson was known as the greatest ragtime pianist in Storyville. His show-stopping trick was to dance a high-kicking cakewalk while bashing the keys. Rumor had it he could play any piece of music perfectly after hearing it only once, and he'd never forget it. He was an iconoclast, "openly, almost defiantly homosexual," and a massive influence on jazz pianists who came after him.[7]

If Jackson was great, Bechet was already the stuff of legend. Born and bred in the dives of Storyville, he was one of those rare geniuses who strike music's evolutionary tree like lightning, splitting off their own branch. As jazz historian Chris Goddard wrote of Bechet's early playing, "He is doing for a few moments exactly what an African master drummer does when he sets up a certain rhythmic pattern and then departs as far from it as possible without ever losing the original idea. As jazz evolved, it gradually adopted this concept, consciously or not, and developed it. To this extent, Sidney Bechet was already anticipating . . . something which Charlie Parker elaborated to such an extraordinary degree twenty years later."[8] Watching Bechet wring the soul from his clarinet, Briggs said, "It was the first time I really heard *the blues* played."[9]

Jazz was still an ensemble format; the soloist served the band, not the other way around. But Bechet's playing blazed a trail to the next era. As Goddard wrote, "Bechet could be regarded as the first really great jazz soloist . . . he had in essence a soloist's conception even before [Louis] Armstrong did."[10] Or, as Briggs put it, "Louis was not Louis at that time. . . . But Bechet was already *Bechet*."[11]

Cook recognized Bechet's brilliance. When the band went on break, he took Bechet aside and made him an offer. Before the next set began, Bechet mounted the bandstand and announced that he had just joined Cook's New York Southern Syncopated Orchestra. "He was applauded for a long time and the whiskey flowed afloat," Briggs said.[12] Afterward, Bechet came to Cook's table. Noticing the fresh-faced Briggs, and being well sauced, he shouted, "Hello, kid! I like you!" Just like that, Briggs had a new nickname: Kid. The alcoholic, violent, instinctive Bechet was strictly the opposite of the straight-laced, easygoing, classically trained Briggs; naturally they became best friends.

Briggs was now baptized in the mainspring of New Orleans jazz. Before Chicago, he had only heard a facsimile of jazz from the Original Dixieland Jazz Band, a group of white players that made the music nationally popular with "Livery Stable Blues," which sold one million copies in 1917. From that point on, the ODJB claimed to have invented jazz. Briggs enjoyed their records, but he had never heard anything like what Keppard and Bechet were blowing on the South Side of Chicago. It changed him.

It also scarred him. In a rare revelation of bitterness, he recalled, "After hearing recordings of the Original Dixieland Jazz Band, I could not understand why King Oliver's band did not record. As I grew older and observed the happenings, I began to realize that certain teachings of the Bible were not respected and that brotherhood was a hoax."[13]

It came as a harsh realization that in a segregated society the equal exchange of creativity was impossible. White musicians, to their financial gain and moral detriment, did little or nothing to change this. Briggs had no prejudice against white musicians—he hired many as a bandleader

later in his career—but it bruised his dignity to know that his contributions to music, no matter how great, would come second because of his
color. He watched brokenhearted as jazz rushed into the mainstream of
American culture, as LeRoi Jones put it, "without so much as one black
face."[14] Part of this was due to white critics who didn't understand black
jazz, and part of it was musicians like ODJB leader Nick LaRocca, whom
Goddard described as "an unscrupulous liar who gave interviews not
merely ignoring, but explicitly denying the black contribution to jazz."
Worst of all was the way the ODJB put on "a conscious snobbery of
low-browism, boasting that none of them knew music."[15] This played
on the racist assumption that black people were simple, childlike, and
primitive, and that music came to them naturally. It was the opposite
of everything Briggs loved and worked for, and it soured his opinion
of America.

Regardless, Briggs's ears were wide open in Chicago. Influences
poured in from every cabaret, dance hall, and vaudeville theater. On
his last day in town, the Harlem Hellfighters arrived. Fresh from the
war, they had just been honored with a massive parade in New York
and now were greeted as heroes in Chicago. Briggs talked shop with
these veterans as an equal. Watching the Hellfighters in concert, Briggs
had a crucial insight: "I realized, after the lift or swing of this African-
American rhythm, that they brought that *thing* which obliges one to
dance, not being able to stay still when it is properly played. People
argued that there were many other American brass bands . . . but as
Duke Ellington said later, they did not have that thing which *lifts you
off of your feet*."[16] Briggs, the child of Grenada, was now fully connected
to jazz as an expression of the African American experience.

It is likely here that Briggs found the final piece of his personal
transformation. He had already shed his accent and changed his birth
year; as he hung with the Hellfighters in Chicago, he crafted a plausible
origin story. Hellfighters subconductor Eugene Mikell had previously
taught at the Jenkins Orphanage in Charleston, South Carolina, and
many members of the Hellfighters orchestra had started in the orphanage's brass band. The orphanage band toured extensively in America and
overseas, and Briggs recalled seeing them on the streets of Harlem. After
leaving Chicago, Briggs rechristened himself an American, claiming he

was born in Charleston and that he began his musical studies there under Eugene Mikell. He continued telling this tale for the rest of his life.

On the way back to Harlem, the NYSO played Indianapolis "with a full house and an ovation without end," then Pittsburgh, Philadelphia, Syracuse, and Atlantic City, arriving home on March 31. Ahead of the London tour, Cook had booked a seven-day run at the Lafayette Theatre in Harlem, and another seven days at Hurtig and Seamon's New (Burlesque) Theater. The latter had a strict whites-only policy; black patrons weren't allowed until 1934, when the theater reopened as the Apollo. During this run, Briggs turned eighteen.

Back in New York, as Briggs prepared for his first European voyage, Inez worried for her little brother. She had good reason. "They were a pretty rough crowd in that band," recalled trombonist Ted Heath.[17] Inez insisted that Cook and Lattimore take on legal guardianship of young Arthur. She went to City Hall and drew up the papers that would serve as Briggs's passport. The lie Briggs told about his birthday was now printed on a legal document signed by the mayor of New York City. On May 1, 1919, Arthur Briggs stood on the deck of the SS *Northland* and watched the Statue of Liberty recede over the horizon.

6

"Let's hope that men will change. They will change, I think."[1]

—Arthur Briggs

THE SS *NORTHLAND* WAS A German war ship seized by the Allies during World War I. On this ill-omened vessel, Briggs spent thirteen days at sea. "After two years on a shipyard, in theaters and in train transport, the sea air and relaxation were much appreciated," he said.[2] Cook ordered the brass section to practice one hour each day to keep their chops; the rest of the day, Briggs stood on deck gazing over the waves, making a game of spotting marine life in the ocean.

Strangers on an adventure together often experience a feeling akin to friendship or even love. During the fair voyage, the passengers of the *Northland* felt this unique camaraderie. Two days before arrival, the musicians played a concert for the ship's passengers and staff. Drinks flowed and feelings ran high. "It was a very warm moment," Briggs recalled.[3]

And then, like a champagne bubble popping, it was over.

When Briggs awoke on June 12, 1919, the sky was loud with seagulls. England hung on the horizon. Taxiing up the River Mersey, the ship passed half a dozen strange shapes bobbing in the chop. Though Briggs had become an expert at spotting marine life, he could not identify these shapes. Then spread an awful dawning. "They were human corpses!" Briggs said; "More exactly, the corpses of six black men!"[4]

Liverpool had just been rocked by a race riot. As white British soldiers returned from the war, many found their jobs filled by African and West Indian immigrants. Others found their wives and sisters in the company of black men. Outrage led to murder, and murder led to riots.

Briggs thought he had left such ignorant violence behind in America. Instead, white mobs patrolled the streets of Liverpool, and a report in the *Liverpool Courier* read:

> One of the chief reasons of popular anger behind the present disturbances lies in the fact that the average Negro is nearer the animal than is the average white man, and that there are women in Liverpool who have no self-respect. There is also the unemployment grievance—the fact that large numbers of demobilized soldiers are unable to find work while the West Indian negroes, brought over to supply a labor shortage during the war, are able to 'swank' about in their smart clothing on the proceeds of their industry.[5]

For the second time in two years, Briggs was in a country where the murder of a black man was no crime. As a British citizen, he expected a better welcome. But due to his color, he required a police escort just to get from the docks to the train station. It took the whole four-hour trip to calm his disgust.

Luckily, London soothed the sting. Briggs arrived to find porters at the train station waiting with cars to deliver the band to their pensions. Briggs stayed at 1 Grenville Street in Russell Square, an area teeming with artists and musicians, where a hot meal awaited him in his room. He ate, and then, "so tired and moved by all these fatal events," he dropped straight to sleep.

With several days until final rehearsals with the SSO, Briggs was a free man in London. He explored the city on foot with Bechet and lead trumpeter Bobby Jones. They meandered down Oxford Street, saw Piccadilly Circus, and marveled at the changing of the guard at Buckingham Palace. With a salary of seventy-five dollars per week, they had enough money to catch shows at the Palladium Vaudeville and dine at a favorite local Chinese restaurant "without being embarrassed."[6] Jones became such a close friend during this time that Briggs called him his "*frère de lait*" (literally "milk brother," meaning the brother who shares the mother's breast).

If Jones was a milk brother, Bechet was something else. He roomed next door to Briggs and soon pressed the "Kid" into service as a babysitter. "Bechet was a good friend and a fine fellow, but he just couldn't trust himself," Briggs said. "He was so impetuous. Despite being older than I was, he asked me to keep an eye on him, because he might get drunk or get in with the wrong crowd. But he was so easily tempted that, when the time came, nothing on Earth would stop him from doing what he wanted to do."[7] Even at such a young age, Briggs possessed uncommon self-knowledge. He knew why Bechet had chosen him. "Although younger than he, and the youngest of the orchestra, I was undoubtedly the most serious," said Briggs. To most of the band this made him a downer; to Bechet it made him the perfect companion. Bechet certainly tested the boundaries of Briggs's kindness—he'd get drunk and begin "snarling, growling, and refusing to go to work"—but the young man stayed steadfast.

Briggs's close relationship with Bechet put him on the forefront of jazz history. During one of their strolls, they passed a music store and saw a curious instrument in the window, small and straight like a clarinet but with pads like a saxophone. "We were perplexed," Briggs recalled. The store clerk took the instrument—a B-flat soprano saxophone—and handed it to Bechet. With a diagram of fingering, Bechet squeaked out a C-major scale and then bought the strange horn. He had forgotten his money, so Briggs advanced him ten pounds. A few weeks later, Briggs bought a soprano sax for himself, along with a method book. "It was a much easier instrument than the trumpet," he recalled, although he was careful with the mouthpiece lest it ruin his trumpet embouchure. Bechet didn't find the instrument so easy. After hours of fumbling around, he knocked on Briggs's door, sax in one hand, method book in the other, and asked for help. "For once, I became a saxophone teacher!" Briggs said.[8]

Bechet caught on quickly. He would be the first to make the soprano saxophone a feature of jazz, and although it never became a fixture the way the tenor saxophone did, it added a new color to the jazz palette. In later years, John Coltrane made notable use of the instrument, most famously on his tour de force recording of "My Favorite Things," treading the path Bechet blazed with Briggs's instruction.

After a few days, Briggs and the band settled down to work. Cook first rehearsed them in a small studio, but he needed to hear the music in its proper setting, so he took them to the Philharmonic Hall (known today as Brock House) on Great Portland Street, where they were to open in a few days. Inside the gorgeous hall, Cook cut and molded the show until every note was exactly how he wanted it. Natalie Spencer, a British musician who sat in with the band, recalled, "One day we had a preliminary run through a new and rather formidable 'Blues,' and the band, feeling pleased with itself that day, played it through with great gusto and as we thought, rather creditably. Mr. Cook stood quietly by and let us go right on to the bitter end, and then all he said was, 'Alright, now we'll do it my way.'"[9]

While Briggs learned jazz with Cook, he continued pursuing classical finesse. He met Edmund Jenkins, whose father was the founder of the Jenkins Orphanage in Charleston and who studied at the Royal Academy of Music. Impressed with the young trumpeter's playing, Jenkins introduced Briggs to John Solomon, founding member of the London Symphony Orchestra. It was the first gesture among many that made Jenkins second only to Will Marion Cook as an influence on Briggs's career. In the soaring language Briggs often used when speaking of music, he credited Cook and Jenkins with giving him an "initiation into this international musical brotherhood, speaking just one language, a music score on a rack."[10] Only in music did Briggs find this brotherhood.

Briggs delighted in his new teacher. "He taught me everything— every single thing," Briggs recalled. From Solomon, Briggs learned to produce his tone without forcing it and to use his instrument without fighting it. He acquired theoretical training that put the entire world of music at his fingertips. The knowledge served him in good stead. Proper technique is more important to a trumpeter than almost any other musician. Without it, the lips simply will not hold up, especially under the repeated pressure of soft flesh buzzing against hard metal. Briggs was always gifted, but now he achieved world-class chops. "I'm not trying to boast of myself," he said, but "it seems to say as if the instrument and I were just one thing."[11]

7

"It is an entertainment which all would feel better for seeing and hearing."[1]

—The *Times* of London

JAZZ HIT LONDON AT THE RIGHT TIME. Hungover from the horrors of war, scarred by four years of destruction and deprivation, the city grasped for pleasure. "There was, if one knew where to look, opportunity for wild abandonment embracing drugs, alcohol and sex," wrote jazz historian John Chilton.[2] Jazz fit this mood; it was raucous like a bomb blast, exotic like an invading army, joyful like sunlight piercing the shadow of death.

A cult of jazz had grown in London, due in large part to the Original Dixieland Jazz Band, which arrived in London in April 1919 and was the talk of the town by July, when Briggs arrived. Precisely for these reasons, Cook refused to use the word *jazz* in any press descriptions or show bills. He had come to prove not just the worth of his own music but also the worth of his entire race; he didn't want either one associated with a fad. He did, however, make one concession to the ODJB's success: playing on the theme of Dixie, the New York Syncopated Orchestra became the Southern Syncopated Orchestra.

On July 4, Briggs and the SSO debuted at Philharmonic Hall. The concert began with "Sally Trombone," a novelty rag that veers between somber orchestral strains and madcap marching fanfare, directly followed by Brahms's intricate "Hungarian Dance no. 5" and the Negro spiritual, "Go Down Moses." This breakneck changing of styles was part of Cook's plan, and it continued throughout the show, combining such odd bedfellows as Dvořák's seventh "Humoresque" with the popular throwaway tune "Mammy o' Mine." For Briggs, it was a master course on crafting a concert, broadening his ear, and teaching him to play all styles. This musical dexterity would become a hallmark of his career, whether leading a small combo in a Parisian café or performing with a makeshift orchestra in a Nazi prison.

After intermission, drummer Buddy Gilmore took a solo. The modern drum kit was in its infancy—depending on the drummer, it might include a snare, tom-toms, wood blocks, cowbells, horns, or anything else that made noise. Few Londoners had seen or heard drums played this way, especially not in the presence of a full orchestra. They gave kits such as Gilmore's the derogative nickname "traps," after the English slang word for contraption. As the *Times* of London wrote: "One has grown used to associating syncopation with musical fireworks and jazz drummers who hurl themselves at a dozen instruments in their efforts to extract noise from anything and everything." But Gilmore did more than make noise. He was a showman. Again, from the *Times*: "The Southern Syncopated Orchestra . . . has a drummer who fascinated yesterday's audience—and more important still, the Coliseum's drum expert—by his lightning dexterity and his knack of juggling drum sticks."[3] The schtick became so popular that Lattimore hired another drummer, George Hines, alias "Bobo," who immediately stole Gilmore's spotlight with his antics. When Gilmore became jealous, Cook solved the problem by keeping Hines behind a curtain.

The undisputed showstopper of the SSO was Sidney Bechet. Cook composed the show's penultimate piece, "Characteristic Blues," specifically for him, giving him the freedom to change his solo from night to night as the spirit moved. This was the only true jazz of the program, and it introduced London to authentic New Orleans playing. Even Briggs, who put so much importance on proper tuition, was blown away. "We had various players who could embellish melodies and play variations in the symphonic style," he said, "and we also had musicians who could reinterpret a melody with ragtime phrasing, but Bechet could and did play pure jazz and blues. He was sensational."[4]

With Bechet's mastery, Gilmore's tricks, and Cook's professionalism, opening night was a smash. "The management had to refuse many people," Briggs said. "The ovation was second to none . . . all that remained was to wait for the opinion of the press." The opinion came with the next morning's paper. Most reviews were positive, if bemused. One reviewer wrote, "Some of the playing of the band was often more noisy than musical but . . . we have had so much imitation colored music that it is refreshing to hear the real thing."[5] The most important review of the SSO in London was by the Swiss conductor Ernest Ansermet, who gave the new music the stamp of classical approval. "The first thing that strikes one about the Southern Syncopated Orchestra is the astonishing perfection, the superb taste, and the fervor of its playing," Ansermet wrote.

> This is the birth of syncopation . . . We have shown that syncopation itself is but the effect of an expressive need, the manifestation in the field of rhythm of a particular taste, in a word, the genius of the race. This genius takes a trombone, and he has a knack of vibrating each note by a continual quivering of the slide, and a sense of glissando, and a taste for muted notes which make it a new instrument; he takes a clarinet or saxophone and he has a way of hitting the notes with a slight *inferior appoggiatura*, he discovers a whole series of effects produced by the lips alone, which make it a new instrument.

Not everyone was so impressed. One reviewer called the SSO "nightmare music." Another wrote a particularly nasty review that Briggs recalled sixty years later like a man reliving the agony of his first broken bone: "A columnist of high society, Mr. Gilbert Frankau, published a paper saying that he had never heard anything so awful in his life," Briggs said. "When we read this paper, arriving in the evening at work, we were shattered. We were convinced that it was over for us."[6] In these recollections, one feels how desperately Briggs wanted to succeed and how much it meant to his sense of self. Not only did he remember the reviewer's name after six decades, he took uncharacteristic pleasure in the man's downfall, saying, "A few days later we read an article in this famous chronicle of high society informing us that Mr. Frankau was suffering and had to resign. It must be so when one wants to be more royalist than the king!"[7] This was as huffy as Briggs got.

Success is the only antidote for the venom of a bad review, and the SSO had enough of it that Briggs survived. "We worked tirelessly in July and August, and reservations were always full a fortnight ahead," he said. "Work was getting very tiring, it was hot, we ran out of air, but morale was good, because as we say in the trade: when you have clients, you earn money!"[8] And they were about to get the biggest client of all. After several weeks at the Philharmonic Hall, the SSO was invited to perform at Buckingham Palace. At eighteen years old, Arthur Briggs had an appointment with the King of England.

8

"I had pretty good control of my instrument."[1]

—Arthur Briggs

THE PRINCE OF WALES LOVED JAZZ. It was one of many traits that made him an odd heir to the throne. At his urging, King George V, Queen Mary, the royal family, and more than one thousand guests gathered on the afternoon of August 9, 1919, to watch the Southern Syncopated Orchestra perform. They heard a scaled-down version of the orchestra: Cook had taken four musicians and formed a quartet around the star, Sidney Bechet. Handpicked to play trumpet for the King of England was the serious, studious Arthur Briggs. As the youngest of the band, Briggs's inclusion in the quartet is evidence both of Cook's feelings for his protégé and the magnitude of Briggs's talent.

That afternoon, four "magnificent buses" bearing the royal seal picked up the musicians in front of the Philharmonic Hall and spirited them to Buckingham Palace. Nervous excitement panged in Briggs's stomach as he passed the gilt bronze Victoria Memorial statue and entered the gates where, just weeks before, he watched the changing of the guard as a tourist. Inside the palace, Bechet recalled, "it was like Grand Central Station with a lot of carpets and things on the walls. Only it had more doors. By the time we got to play I was thinking I'd gone through enough doors to do me for a month."[2] A liveried butler led them to the theater—it was the bed of the recently drained royal lake—and they took the bandstand to the strains of "God Save the King."

The group performed a shortened version of their normal set, beginning with Cook's "Swing Along." Silence followed this first song, as the audience waited on the king's reaction. "The king pretended to applaud," Briggs said, "then it was a deluge of applause."[3] When Bechet launched into "Characteristic Blues," Briggs snuck a glance at the royal family, trying to gauge the effect of the "weird tones" on the king and his entourage. Seeing the royals whispering among themselves, Briggs panicked. *Uh-oh,* he thought. *What's going to happen?* He relaxed when the royal family began tapping their royal feet.

The concert at Buckingham Palace was a high-water mark for the SSO. Within weeks, Briggs learned how quickly the tide of success could ebb. By the end of August, the orchestra struggled to fill a room. Many times there were more people in the band than in the audience. After playing two hundred shows in three months, Cook had no choice but to reduce the schedule to four matinees per week. "Success was running out," Briggs said.[4]

Tired of the cumbersome challenge of mounting a fifty-piece band, Lattimore wanted to split the group into small formations. Cook refused and was fired in October. He returned to America, bitter and alone, and the SSO played its final concert at the Philharmonic Hall without its leader. Briggs lost more than a leader; he lost his dad.

The band picked up work where they could, including a performance at the Royal Albert Hall to celebrate the first anniversary of the armistice, and these side jobs led Briggs to the vanguard of black global politics. The king had recently invited notables of the empire to London, including many Africans and British West Indians, to thank them for their support in World War I. After putting them off for weeks, he finally invited them for tea, but instead of attending, he had a government representative read a message of thanks. "Their reception was ice cold, as we'd say," Briggs recalled.[5]

Edmund Jenkins formed the Coterie of Friends, a combination book club, study hall, political organization, and support group. The club's ambition was nothing less than unifying black people around the world into one political bloc.

The Coterie of Friends threw a party to honor the dignitaries, with guests including the president of Liberia and members of the South African Native National Congress delegation. This delegation, later renamed the African National Congress, was instrumental in tearing down apartheid, finally succeeding in 1994 with the election of Nelson Mandela. The event started with several speeches, including one from host Judge Thomas McCants Stewart, who said, "There must be more brotherhood, unlimited by race or color, if the world is to avert the greatest calamity it has ever experienced, namely a war of races."[6] The message was similar to the one Briggs had heard from Marcus Garvey, only it touched a more personal place. For the first time since leaving Grenada, Briggs was in a room full of West Indians. Perhaps he slipped back into his accent during the evening.

In December, Briggs performed again with the Coterie of Friends at a tribute to composer Samuel Coleridge-Taylor, alias "The African Mahler." Coleridge-Taylor was a hero to many black Americans for his mixture of traditional African music with classical composition. In a way, he was living Will Marion Cook's dream. Here was another lesson for Briggs: unlike Cook, whose color limited his opportunities in America, Coleridge-Taylor spent most of his career in Europe and realized his full potential as a composer.

Briggs played the tribute concert on December 7, 1919, at the grand but intimate Wigmore Hall in the heart of London. Jenkins conducted a band of fifty-three musicians, putting Briggs on the bandstand elbow to elbow with professors of the Royal Academy. Coleridge-Taylor's widow and daughter attended the performance, and although Briggs remembered being "scared to death," he said, "There was not a place left, even standing, in the room. It was a triumph."[7]

Music gave Briggs the key to this world. It put him in the same orbit as Samuel Coleridge-Taylor, Sol Plaatje, Marcus Garvey, Edmund Jenkins, and Will Marion Cook—men whose views on race were revolutionary. Briggs didn't need them to tell him about racism and segregation; he felt it on Manhattan's segregated subway cars, felt it when the *Times* of London ran an item about the "Nigger jazz band" at Buckingham Palace, felt it when he and Bechet moved out of their boarding house in search of something more permanent, only to find no one would rent to two black men. But these mentors showed him a way to survive, and thrive, and battle for dignity in a racist world.

Briggs's feelings on race were complex. He said, "I believe that men are men and I judge men by their actions."[8] But he was no fool. His color would follow him from Harlem to Helsinki, and he knew it. As he warned his only daughter later in his life, "Don't forget you're black. It will be more difficult for you."[9] In that statement, Briggs revealed his inner soul. He did not want the baggage of race, but he carried its weight always. This surely took a toll on him, and he carried that toll too, carried it within himself, hidden from the world, rarely relieved, except in solitude.

9

"There's some who can be stopped by a scratch, and there's some who just can't be stopped so long as they're living."

—Sidney Bechet

THREE DAYS BEFORE CHRISTMAS, the SSO sailed to Scotland, where Briggs met Peter Wilson, trumpeter for the Band of the Irish Guards. "We spent hours and hours talking about instrumental technique," Briggs said.[1] Though their time together was brief, Wilson's influence was significant. Above all, he showed Briggs the importance of playing to the audience's tastes. This lesson became another hallmark of Briggs's career as a bandleader, and he would make good use of it in his prison-camp orchestra.

In February 1920, Cook returned to London seeking reconciliation with Lattimore, but the men parted again in anger. The SSO hobbled along, every day burying Lattimore in mounting debt. He began paying the band with promises. Before a show in Liverpool, half the musicians quit. "Having received no pay for more than a fortnight," flautist Bertin Salnave recalled, "part of the company, not including myself, refused to continue working in such conditions, and decided to leave for London without telling Lattimore.... When I arrived there, with some others who had refused to follow the runaways, the hall was already full to bursting for the first performance, which was to take place in the afternoon. Our manager tried to appease the public's annoyance by announcing that the orchestra had had to leave suddenly for London, where they were to give an unplanned performance, so that the afternoon performance in Liverpool would be cancelled ... Mr. Lattimore came and said to us: 'Above all, do not go out! You will risk being lynched. Liverpool is the most racist town in all England!'"[2]

It isn't clear if Briggs quit the band in Liverpool, but within a month, he joined Cook's new band at the Trocadero in London. Billed as Marion Cook's Syncopated Players—through legal wrangling, Lattimore won the right to the name Southern Syncopated Orchestra—they played in London, Bristol, and Liverpool for a month. But even Cook couldn't keep a band going. Before a performance in Sheffield, he took Briggs aside and explained they didn't have enough money to make it to the next city, but Lattimore's band was coming through town that same night. "Go join him," Cook said. "It will be better for you."[3]

Charged with ensuring Briggs's well-being, Cook executed his duty admirably. However, it forced Briggs to make his first adult decision: stay with his "dad" out of a sense of honor and risk almost certain failure, or join what he called Lattimore's "band of traitors" out of cold business sense and continue his career. Cook's insistence that Briggs leave surely helped him decide, but whenever Briggs had to choose between music and any other concern, he always chose music. He was a deeply moral man with an unbending sense of fairness, but his highest moral calling was summed up in that hoary cliché: the show must go on.

He joined the traitors.

Briggs had a companion in his defection. Trombonist Jacob Patrick was a Charleston native and former member of the Jenkins Orphanage. He and Briggs had become "inseparable friends." They even gave each other nicknames: Patrick was Trombonesky, and Briggs was Trumpetsky (Salnave would later become Flutsky). Trumpetsky and Trombonesky met Lattimore at the train station, trying their best not to seem too friendly. The fog of unease broke when Briggs saw an old friend from the St. Mark's Brass Band. "I was so happy to see [him] again," Briggs said, "that I forgot the grievances I had against the others for breaking the orchestra . . . and embarrassing 'Dad' Cook."[4]

Briggs quickly became disillusioned with Lattimore. As they toured through northern England and Scotland, he recalled, "The rooms were not full, but the pockets of Mr. Lattimore were."[5] Back in London, Lattimore booked the Kingsway Hall, which the musicians called a "white elephant"—a dive bar. Attendance was dismal at first, but the band was

so good management soon had to turn customers away, leading Lattimore to book six months of shows throughout England. But he couldn't
capitalize on the success. The tour turned into another slog, he was
overleveraged, and the musicians never knew when, or if, they'd be paid.
Before a show in November at the Philharmonic Hall, the band once
again refused to perform. Lattimore, who had entered a dark emotional
spiral, didn't care. Within a month he began bankruptcy proceedings.

For Arthur Briggs, 1920 floundered to a close and 1921 struggled to
open. The band didn't play much in the early months of the new year, as
Lattimore focused on his bankruptcy case. In April, the court suspended
his request for a discharge, meaning he still owed his creditors money.
Needing a quick infusion of cash, he filled the summer with concerts.
Briggs was as frustrated as the rest of the band, but he went along out
of innate respect for his elders. "Being the youngest, I was not satisfied,"
he said, "but I was following the majority, you see."[6]

Then came Scotland. Lattimore booked the band for late September
in Glasgow and Greenock, followed by a trip to Dublin, Ireland. Trombonesky had traveled this same route with the Jenkins Orphanage in
the winter of 1915, and he warned of currents that cut like rapids and
fog so thick you could hold it in your hand. Even shipping companies
weren't brave, or crazy, enough to test the seas that time of year. Patrick
begged Briggs to skip the journey, but Briggs knew this meant breaking
his contract, effectively resigning from the SSO. He trusted Trombonesky
and had hit his limit with Lattimore, but he had also abandoned his
musical father to seize this opportunity.

On October 9, 1921, the SSO embarked on the SS *Rowan*. Some-
where in the Irish Sea, the ship drifted into blinding fog and crashed
into a cargo liner. Fifteen ghastly minutes later, another ship appeared,
drawn by the distress signal. Fog blind, it collided with the very ship
it had come to save. The *Rowan* sank within minutes, taking all of the
SSO's instruments and nine of its members to the bottom of the sea.
In all, thirty-five passengers died in what newspapers called the worst
wreck since the *Titanic*.

Arthur Briggs was safe in London. He had quit the SSO.

10

"For every Arthur Briggs . . . there were several musicians who died within a year or two of leaving home."[1]

—Mark Miller, jazz historian

SEVERED FROM THE SSO, stranded three thousand miles from home, Arthur Briggs faced the world alone. There was no Dad Cook to ensure his safety, no Mr. Lattimore to arrange his bookings. Briggs had only his trumpet and his reputation, and with these assets, he had to make a living. He heard that Bechet had joined a band of ex-SSO musicians at the Palais de Hammersmith in London, and he started there. Briggs met club owner George Mitchell, who wanted a group to alternate with Bechet's band. Mitchell had named this new outfit the Colored Dixieland Jazz Band, but he had no musicians. "You have eight days to introduce me to a group that's on the way," Mitchell said.[2] At eighteen years old, Arthur Briggs formed a band for the first time.

It wasn't exactly *his* band—Mitchell helped form it, replacing Trombonesky with a banjo player—but the experience taught Briggs several lessons. Chief among these was the value of reliable musicians. Mitchell hired a clarinetist and pianist who were both hopeless drunks. Then there was Bobo Hines, "a wonderful drummer, but not for dancing." Hines delighted audiences with his shtick—he'd roam around the room pretending to give patrons a shave and a haircut with his drumsticks—but he couldn't make the music *move*. The crowd didn't know any different, but Briggs did. He had heard Freddie Keppard and King Oliver in Chicago. "People were not dissatisfied with us," he said, "but certain of us were dissatisfied with ourselves."[3]

After the band folded, Briggs joined another popular group, the Five Jazzing Devils, for an engagement in Oslo. In November, he suffered a terrible passage to Norway on a leaky old ship—Briggs used the French word "rafiot," which translates literally to tub. "We were tight like sardines, unable to move for twenty-four hours," he said. "We thought we were lost."[4] He arrived at the Bristol Hotel shaken and tired. Instead of the room and board he was promised, he was placed in servants' quarters. The manager assured him this arrangement would be only for the night, but two days later, still in servants' quarters, Briggs threatened to call the consul.

The engagement got worse when the hotel manager hired a white South African pianist named Peter Van de Voot and foisted him upon the band. Briggs had a big heart, especially for fellow musicians. "If you're not good, you have to live," he said. "You maybe don't make the grade, but you have to live as a human being, and if you try your best, you're okay." But he spoke of Van de Voot with uncharacteristic venom: "This damn pianist was not able to read music and could hardly play a scale."[5]

Briggs had good reason for his anger. Van de Voot tried to get the band thrown out of the country, and when that didn't work, he tried to hire white English musicians to replace them. "He was really the world's worst pianist," Briggs spat. "He smoked big cigars and had Southern ideas and did everything to imitate Southern Americans."[6] That Briggs associated Van de Voot's racism with American segregation rather than South African apartheid is significant. Briggs had never experienced apartheid, but he had met many South Africans at the Coterie of Friends concert in London, giving him a frame of reference for a man like Van de Voot. However, it seems his experience in America was so hurtful that it colored all other perceptions.

Before opening night, Briggs warned the manager about Van de Voot's utter lack of ability. The manager answered: "I've announced you as the Jazz Devils," with the implication that the word jazz covered all musical sins. "You're right," Briggs said. "It's going to be hell!"[7] To his credit, Briggs made the gig, but the band struggled to convince the clientele. Even worse, considering Briggs's competitive streak, a superior jazz band was playing down the road. Briggs would never let this happen again. For the rest of his career, if he led an orchestra, he chose his own musicians. If anyone tried to force a player on him, he refused the job.

After Oslo, Briggs and the band (minus Van de Voot) hurried back to London and auditioned for Jack May, proprietor of Murray's Club. May was a lightning rod in London. He was an American, for one thing. If that wasn't bad enough, folks whispered about his past in the cutthroat Chicago jazz scene and about his penchant for giving young girls opium. One person described him as "a very bad fellow"—quite an insult from an Englishman. Another pegged him as a "restless genius." Whatever he was, he gave Briggs a job.

Yet again, it wasn't Briggs's band. May chose the name—the Five Musical Dragons—and hired a Ghanaian pianist named Kaleb Quaye, alias Mope Desmond, giving Briggs no choice but to play with another stranger. This time, however, it worked. Desmond was so good the dancers stopped dancing just to watch him play. Bertin Salnave called him "the best blues player in England."[8]

Murray's Club catered to high-class clientele. Patrons rolled up in private automobiles and exited curbside, dressed like they had come to meet the queen. They'd linger before the club's regal doors just long enough to let the commoners on Beak Street catch a glimpse and then slide inside as slick as oysters. The club exuded elegance: a short stairway led to a large ballroom where sparkling chandeliers hung from a high ceiling; to the left towered several mirrored columns; between the columns sat circular tables covered with white linen cloths. The tables faced a dance floor, and at the far end of the floor was an ornate bandstand. On a good night, Briggs and the Five Musical Dragons performed for more than four hundred people.

Briggs played the dinner hour, which required some finesse, as the patrons weren't yet drunk enough for jazz. The band played folk songs from around the world—the Scottish ballad "Annie Laurie," the Neapolitan traditional song "Torna a Surriento," and a few of Stephen Foster's faux Negro spirituals, such as "Old Black Joe" and the antislavery lament "My Old Kentucky Home, Good Night!" The set was calculated to avoid causing indigestion.

Briggs genuinely enjoyed playing these songs, but as an artist, he needed to grow. Inspired by Peter Wilson's advice to cater to the audience's tastes, he had been experimenting with a solo arrangement of the popular song "Parted," and one night he stood in the spotlight and played his arrangement of the bittersweet melody. "I played it softly and simply," he said. "It was a triumph."[9] The crowd begged for more, and Briggs, the budding showman, led the band into the jumping spiritual "Samson and Delilah." It was Briggs's first experience as the star of the show, and it hooked him.

After dinner, the bacchanalia began. Pretty young girls in racy outfits showed off the latest dances, their lithe bodies glistening with sweat. The patrons loosened their collars and crowded the dance floor. Jack May installed a rudimentary air conditioner called the Ozonair to keep them cool. By the end of the night, Murray's Club reeked of sex and money and excess. Briggs, always the gentleman, never mentioned his love life, but it must have been an exciting time for a handsome young man who, at twenty years old, could make a room of rich Londoners erupt in ecstasy with the power of his trumpet.

Soon, invitations came from the countryside. On January 27, 1921, Briggs boarded a train bound for Wolverhampton, a city in the West Midlands of England, where the Dragons were to perform at an elite hunting club. Briggs settled in the window seat but switched with Mope Desmond at Desmond's request. In the tiny town of Blisworth, another train came speeding in the opposite direction, when an iron footplate tore loose from its coal car and shot through the air, smashing through the window where Desmond rested his head. Briggs heard a terrible noise, and then all was blackness. Something heavy fell on his lap. "I tried to get away," he said, "and I realized with horror that it was my friend Desmond." Briggs was pinned to his seat. He screamed for help until a doctor on board came and lifted Desmond's limp body onto a bench. Blood gushed from a large gash on the back of his head. He was breathing, but barely. Within minutes, the doctor pronounced Desmond dead.

The train struggled to the next station, where an ambulance waited. Police questioned Briggs, and somehow, despite his "shock and despondency," he answered them. Desmond's body was delivered to a funeral home to await burial, and Briggs and the band took the next train to Wolverhampton, where they still had a job to do. "I was overwhelmed with grief," Briggs said, "but as we say, the show must go on."[10] The Wulfranians (as people from Wolverhampton are called) helped find a replacement pianist, and the Dragons forced out the songs, but Briggs had never done a harder job.

On the bandstand that night, dazed with sorrow, Briggs realized that Desmond had saved his life by asking to switch seats. It was too absurd to comprehend, but it was true. Wracked with guilt, Briggs returned to London, where he now had the fervor of a higher calling: he had to succeed so Mope Desmond wouldn't have died in vain.

11

"That was my first continental venture."[1]

—Arthur Briggs

AFTER SPENDING THE BETTER PART of two years in and around London, Briggs had no permanent home and no unbreakable bonds. "In those days, American Express was our address," he said.[2] In April, just before Briggs's twenty-first birthday, he joined drummer Hughes Pollard in Brussels. Pollard, alias Black Lightning, was a handsome, stern man from Chicago who had survived being gassed in World War I. He was part of a thriving jazz scene in Brussels; according to Briggs, "Pollard and his orchestra were considered champions." Briggs was impressed with Pollard's musical ability but more impressed with the clientele in this new country. "What a contrast with the rigid character that we show on the other side of the Channel!" he said. "Everything was different—the atmosphere, the food, the hotel rooms, the staff, the cafes, the restaurants open all night. A dream."[3]

The band played at Le Perroquet, a bar and ballroom attached to the Theatre de l'Alhambra. The building was gorgeous and imposing, adorned with architectural filigree and four giant caryatids representing Tragedy, Comedy, Drama, and Dance, thought to have been sculpted by Rodin. Briggs performed at nightly dances and backed the French actress-singer Mistinguett, the highest paid female entertainer in the world. She had begun performing in the 1890s in French cabarets such as the Moulin Rouge, and her risqué routines captivated Parisian audiences. In 1919, her legs were insured for 500,000 francs. Performing with such a massive star was another step up for Briggs, who was making a name for himself as a hot trumpeter.

In Brussels, Briggs met Belgian jazz enthusiast Robert Goffin. Ten years later, Goffin wrote the first serious book of jazz criticism, *Aux Frontières du Jazz*, in which he called Briggs "the very backbone of transatlantic jazz," and wrote: "It was [Briggs] who explained hot or, as we then called it, New Orleans music to us. . . . Possessing an amazing technique, an exciting feeling for hot music, and a characteristic swing (long before the swing era began), Briggs was one of those great American pioneers who taught jazz to all of Europe."[4]

Of course, Briggs wasn't American, but it is significant that he let one of his good friends believe the lie. His reasons for changing his identity were complex, and they shifted throughout his life, but in 1921, he was just one of many Caribbean and African musicians in Europe passing as American. At the time, black American musicians got the best gigs and the most consistent work. In many ways, it was the opposite of the situation in America. And yet, European clubs and audiences treated black musicians as tokens, demanding black faces on the bandstand with little care for musical ability. As Briggs succinctly put it, "It was like an ornament, whether you were good or not."[5]

After finishing at Le Perroquet on July 3, 1922, Briggs went with Pollard's band to the Belgian coast for several gigs in Ostend, "Queen of the Belgian sea-side resorts." The band played at Maxim's Cabaret, run by an inveterate gambler named Rigamontti. A few days into the engagement, Rigamontti lost all his money in a dire night at the casino and closed Maxim's without alerting the band. Briggs arrived that night to find himself out of a job. "Decidedly, my adventure in Belgium, which had started so well, was going badly," he said.[6]

Briggs looked for work, but no one needed a trumpet player. He dusted off the saxophone method book he had bought in London and began practicing. Through a friend, he found work briefly as a saxophonist, but even this did not last. "At that time, the musicians lived from day to day, according to good and bad fortunes," he said.[7]

His fortunes were about to get worse. Pollard took the money he should have paid the band and spent it on booze. One night, he got drunk in a seedy cabaret and tried to pick up a barmaid. The bar's bouncer approached menacingly, and Pollard said, "If you are her husband, I'll leave. If not, the lady is a barmaid, and I'm paying!"[8] The man broke a glass and slashed Pollard's face, leaving him with a scar that would become his trademark.

Despite feeling bad for his friend, Briggs was embarrassed by Pollard's behavior. It abused his sense of propriety. He often took his black colleagues to task for the ways they handled themselves in Europe. As he said, "Some of us acted as human beings and others didn't. You're supposed to control yourself. There were certain facilities we had in [Europe] that we did not have in the States, and you're not supposed to take advantage of them. Those that couldn't control themselves, what you'd call drunkards, they respect nobody, not even themselves."[9] Respect was key for Briggs. It was hard enough living in a world that often seemed rigged against him. He didn't intend to make it harder.

Meanwhile, at another bar, Trombonesky got into a terrible fight over several bottles of champagne, and when police arrived, they nearly beat him to death. Briggs went to see his friend in the hospital, where he tried to defend Patrick to no avail. "It was impossible for us to explain ourselves," Briggs said. "No one understood us. Those who understood a little did not want to hear anything. They said it was Patrick who had attacked the policeman."[10]

Briggs was devastated and furious. It was an emotionally volatile time. He had just suffered through Desmond's death and several musical failures, and seeing his best friend bloody and broken in a hospital bed, surrounded by unsympathetic faces and stranded behind a language barrier, was too much to bear. He acted on impulse. In the late summer of 1922, "completely disgusted" with Europe, he boarded a ship bound for New York.[11]

12

"The white boys would come around and listen."[1]

—Arthur Briggs

TEN DAYS ON A BOAT brought Briggs back to Harlem, where the renaissance had begun to flower. Black theater exploded onto Broadway in 1921 with *Shuffle Along*, a show so popular it stopped traffic along West 63rd Street. It was "a record-breaking, epoch-making musical comedy," as James Weldon Johnson attested, and the cutting edge music, written by Harlem Hellfighter Noble Sissle and his partner Eubie Blake, was "up to the minute."[2] In the summer of '21, the Black Swan Phonograph Company began making "race" records, bringing black jazz and blues artists to a national audience, and in '22 Claude McKay published *Harlem Shadows*, one of the renaissance's seminal works.

Briggs arrived to find Harlem flush with musical riches: Bechet was back from Europe; Duke Ellington had just arrived from Washington, D.C.; Fats Waller had published his first piano roll and, along with James P. Johnson and Willie "the Lion" Smith, was perfecting the stride style—so called because the left hand must cover great distances across the keyboard. Meanwhile, Fletcher Henderson began working for Black Swan records and would soon form the best band in New York, featuring Louis Armstrong and Coleman Hawkins. These men stood on the cusp of worldwide fame.

But something was wrong.

Briggs went to the Amsterdam Club and couldn't get a job. The Clef Club was worse. The white musician's union had the city in a stranglehold. Meanwhile, James Reese Europe was dead—stabbed to death by his own drummer—and no one took up his fight. Adding to the insult, white musicians regularly rode the A train to Harlem and cribbed ideas from black players, bringing these ideas back downtown where the money was. "Damn right there was a lot of bitterness," said trumpeter Doc Cheatham, who played with Duke Ellington and Cab Calloway. "They'd come up to Harlem and steal everything you're doing. We knew we were being frozen out of those places. . . . And we knew that there was nothing we could do about it."[3]

Briggs wondered why he had returned to America. His life's purpose was to play music. He'd already crossed the Atlantic Ocean twice seeking this goal. But it seemed there was nowhere on earth where he could pursue his passion in peace. It's not clear what he thought he'd find in Harlem. Perhaps three years overseas made him forget how much he hated American segregation. Now he remembered. "There was little room for the colored musicians," he said, "and therefore, for me."[4]

Within weeks, the impulse that made Briggs leave Europe, now doubly powerful, made him return. Belgium was the natural place for him to go, since he had a reputation there, but he couldn't forget what happened to Trombonesky. Instead, he went to Paris.

The City of Light seduced Briggs on first sight. It offered the exact lifestyle he longed for, including more work than he could handle and less apparent racism than anywhere he'd been. Montmartre, a longtime haven for artists, intellectuals, prostitutes, and gangsters, was soon to become the capital of European jazz, and a small colony of black musicians and ex-soldiers had begun to put down roots there. They lived and worked in the Pigalle district, Paris's seedy answer to New Orleans's Storyville and Chicago's South Side.

Unlike Harlem, in Paris black musicians were in such high demand that many white players had to wear blackface just to get a job. Within hours of arriving, Briggs went to a ramshackle coffee house wryly called the Flea Pit, which served as an unofficial headquarters, business office, social club, and late-night jam spot for jazz musicians, and met his old mentor Edmund Jenkins. He explained the difficulties in America, and Jenkins understood, saying, "You can work with me until you find something of your own."[5]

Of course, Paris was not the heaven it seemed. Briggs was still young and naïve, with an ocean between him and his nearest kin, and a language separating him from his surroundings. And he was in a dangerous part of the city. Days later, walking to rehearsal with trumpet case in hand, Briggs heard someone shout, "Monsieur! Monsieur!" As he didn't speak French, he kept walking. The voice shouted, "Musicien! Musicien!" Briggs didn't need to speak French to understand that one. Briggs turned to see a man exit a horse-drawn hackney cab. In a flurry of French, occasionally Briggs heard the one word he understood: *musicien*. Nearby stood West Indian drummer Gaby Malael, who crept into the conversation like a hyena tring to steal a kill. Luckily for Briggs, a woman approached and asked in a heavy accent, "You speak English?" Then, pointing to Malael, she said, "He's trying to take your job from you." And pointing to the man from the carriage, she said, "This man wants *you*."[6]

Through the makeshift translator, Briggs learned the man owned a dance club in Liege, Belgium—the one place Briggs swore he'd never go again—and wanted to hire an orchestra. Briggs directed him to the Flea Pit, where he had friends who could speak French. Malael followed "without being invited."[7] At the Flea Pit, Jenkins acted as referee. The club owner from Liege offered a six-month engagement beginning in November, which Briggs accepted. Next, they formed the orchestra: Malael elbowed his way in as drummer; Jenkins recommended Bertin Salnave, late of the SSO, on saxophone and flute; Albert Smith, ex-Harlem Hellfighter, joined on banjo. Rounding out the band was an English pianist, whom Briggs only knew as "Kid." They drew up a contract "on a corner of the table" and signed. "This contract was not very well crafted," Briggs recalled. "In particular the question of the conductor was not clearly mentioned."[8] He was about to learn an important lesson.

With a few weeks to kill, Briggs joined Jenkins's band at Club Daunou. They played a tea dance from 5:00 to 7:00 PM, broke for dinner, and then played again from 9:30 until midnight. Then Briggs sauntered to one of a dozen Montmartre haunts and played until 4:00 AM, often ending the night back at the Flea Pit for breakfast and an early morning jam, after which, exhausted and sweaty, ears ringing, he walked home in the golden dawn. "It was a lot of work, but it was well paid, and as I was very young, there was no problem," said Briggs.[9]

On November 1, 1922, Briggs returned to Belgium, bloody memories fresh in his mind. "That's the business," he said, "and I must say that we had a really wonderful time." The band performed at the Regina Dance Hall in Liege, a "provincial tavern" with entertainment on three floors, where Briggs remembered having "good success right away."[10]

The Regina's alternate orchestra had never heard jazz before, and they watched Briggs with the wonder of children witnessing magic. During breaks, they bombarded him with questions: *Do you have a special trumpet? How do you make those lip slides?*

One of the Belgian musicians, perhaps trying to salvage a shred of self-respect, said that jazz was fine and all, but Briggs surely couldn't play a polka. "That was not a question," Briggs said, "but a challenge."[11] Turning to the pianist, he said, "Can you play 'The Carnival of Venice'?" It was a hotshot move. With no rehearsal, Briggs stood in the spotlight and played the song to perfection. "I did not tell them that [the song] was my workhorse when I was fifteen and that I played it solo in the St. Mark's Brass Band," he said slyly. His point made, he strutted off stage.

Briggs was showing off, but without knowing it, he was also developing skills that were vital to his future survival. The confidence he earned onstage in Belgium and dozens of other cities around the world defined his sense of self. As he matured, this confidence became the conviction that made him a successful bandleader and the most famous trumpeter in Europe. Finally, it became the courage that saved his life in a Nazi prison.

At Briggs's next performance the room was packed. "I can tell you that when I was announced, you could hear a fly fly," he said.[12] If there was a king of Belgian jazz, Briggs was now it. The other musicians did not begrudge him this title. Had he not been so gracious and kind, or had his love of the music not been so open and pure, perhaps they would have felt insulted or threatened by his competitive display. But Briggs had a way of endearing people to him. His words are telling: "Such a feat immediately creates a certain prestige and strong friendships."[13] It is important that he included friendship with prestige. Briggs was a deeply emotional man who truly believed in the brotherhood of all musicians. The friendships he made in Liege meant more to him than anything else he did there, and many of those bonds lasted until he died. And there was another typical Briggs trait—when he made a friend, he remained loyal always.

The rest of the residency in Liege went beautifully. In January 1923, Robert Goffin visited. Years later, he recalled these days with a starry-eyed ode:

> I came to hear you on a smoky winter night in this brightly colored tavern and I remember your dark hand on mine, and your beautiful eyes, whose look gave a sense of our blossoming friendship. Entwined by streamers, showered with colored cotton balls, the close-knit couples spun like in the ribbons of the spot-lights. I withdrew into a corner and listened to the Creole Five surrender to the rhythms of the time . . . standing and clutching [your] trumpet with both hands, [you] dominated the band.[14]

Everyone in the band knew Briggs was the leader, but when the contract ended in April, Malael snuck away to Brussels and stole the baton. He signed the band up for a residency at a restaurant–dance hall called the Savoy, and in the contract, he stipulated himself as bandleader. "I was very unhappy," Briggs said. "Salnave, for his part, was furious."[15] After a tense discussion, the orchestra decided to honor the dates, but Briggs thought back to the deal he had made on a table in the Flea Pit, and the lesson hit home: beware a bad contract.

The Creole Five opened at the Savoy in April, near Briggs's twenty-third birthday. The restaurant's head chef was so impressed with the band he took Briggs aside and offered him free dinner every night. "You know, Mr. Briggs," the chef said confidentially, "the price we pay you is much more than we've ever paid!" This was news to Briggs. When he learned the band's salary, he realized Malael was keeping most of the money for himself. Yet again, Briggs acted on impulse. When Malael took the stage that night, he was missing a trumpet player. "It was too much," Briggs said. "I left without notice."[16] He spent the next three months adrift in Europe nursing his wounded pride.

The years since Briggs left the SSO were full of painful but indispensible experiences. Not all musicians acted like brothers. Briggs's musical ability wasn't enough to keep him safe from a bad contract or a greedy bandmate. There were some honest, trustworthy, and decent musicians, and Briggs learned to cherish them. But the world was full of scoundrels and cheats. He refused to join them. Instead, he doubled down on his morals. "A real orchestra leader, when he gets a good job, he should make his men benefit by it and pay them," Briggs said."[17] He'd soon get a chance to try. Come July, he received word that his friends from the Creole Five had abandoned Malael and re-formed in Ostend. They needed a leader. So Briggs became one.

13

"It was an age of miracles, it was an age of art, it was an age of excess."[1]

—F. Scott Fitzgerald

FOR THE FIRST TIME IN HIS LIFE, Arthur Briggs had a band fully under his command. He called it the Savoy's Syncops Band, after the Savoy Hotel in Brussels, where they played the winter of 1923–'24. Crowds packed the Savoy Hotel every night. They came for the novelty of seeing black men in the flesh; they stayed for the novelty of the jumping, happy noise the men produced. Briggs's friend Goffin recalled, "Soon Arthur Briggs had the Savoy's revolving door turning very well indeed. Many times we had to stand outside, elbows on the windowsill, listening enraptured to the rhythms and syncopations he certainly was the first to let us hear."[2]

In appearance, Briggs was conservative but impeccable. His tuxedos were cut to perfection, his hair carefully parted down the middle. The pinky ring glinting on his valve hand was the only clue that this was no ordinary man. When he began to play, the room moved. Such was his talent. But he was also hungry and impulsive, and this made it difficult to keep a band together. Months after opening with the Savoys, Briggs put the group on hiatus to follow a hot tip in Spain. "I loved traveling," he said simply.[3]

In Spain, Briggs hardly had a chance to unpack his suitcase before he changed his mind again. During one of his first shows at the Hielo Palace, a man who "seemed tormented and upset" rushed the bandstand and smashed the trumpet into Briggs's lips. The music stopped. Briggs put his hand to his mouth, and it came away bloody. Then the man cocked his fist and took a swing. "I was amazed to see that no one inter-vened," Briggs said. "Not a single member of the orchestra . . . made a gesture to defend me." One of the waiters jumped in front of the punch and was knocked out cold. Briggs later learned that the disturbed man was a member of the Spanish royal family and thus feared no repercus-sions. This was exactly the type of behavior Briggs hated—disrespect-ful, entitled, childish, and violent. He protected himself fiercely, partly because it was his nature to do so and partly because he was alone in the world with no one else to protect him. "Disgusted, I immediately took my instrument and left without warning," he said.[4] Briggs never shirked responsibility without good reason, but given good reason, he was gone in a heartbeat.

He took a train to Paris and reformed the Savoys for Le Perroquet. As a contemporary reviewer noted, Le Perroquet featured "two strident bands, one of them composed of negroes" and was "always very lively about two in the morning, when, owing to the number of tables, there is usually very little room in which to dance. As, however, this seems to be one of the indispensable conditions of a successful 'Dancing' no one ever objects."[5] Club owner Leon Volterra made sure the place stayed packed by giving each woman a beautifully dressed poupee doll as a souvenir, and the Savoys, strident band though they were, kept the revelers hopping.

It was the beginning of the legendary Jazz Age in Paris, and Briggs was there to see it all. The old Paris was vanishing, elbowed out by what the *Defender* called the "Race Colony of Paris," made up of Afri-can American musicians and black soldiers who stayed after WWI. It is tempting to make too much of the black colony in Montmartre, and equally tempting to make too much of the music—the jazz in France wouldn't have made the cut in Harlem—but to their credit, the French always viewed jazz as a black art form. "It was like the style, the mode, the fashion to have a black orchestra at the time," Briggs said.[6] Add the vogue for African art, which enthralled Picasso and Matisse, and the result was what the French called *le tumult noir*: the Black Craze.

Like all social upheavals, the Black Craze caused problems. For the French, the problems were those of a besieged people struggling to incor-porate a new, foreign culture. Dozens of jazz clubs opened in Paris seem-ingly overnight, all glaring neon and frenetic noise. They were tourist traps, full of awful food and designed to cater to any fad that would make a quick franc. In a contemporary account, writer Ralph Neville huffed, "Now, in the night restaurants of Montmartre, one is glad to be able to get anything fit to eat, the Maitre d'Hotel and staff not manifesting much enthusiasm as regards providing supper, though preternaturally keen to see that every visitor should be kept well supplied with the acrid and sometimes poisonous liquid costing two or three hundred francs a bottle which every visitor is obliged to order if not to drink!"[7]

For black musicians like Briggs, the trouble was of a more familiar kind. The main engine driving Montmartre's nightlife was a steady flood of white Americans flush with cash and on a mission to drown the horrors of the Great War in hard liquor, loud music, and reckless sex. When they arrived in France, they assumed the segregation of races, on which they had built so much of their self-image, arrived with them.

French racism existed, but it was generally patronizing rather than violent, and to black Americans accustomed to segregation and lynch mobs this seemed like freedom. "Color means nothing over here," jazz singer Alberta Hunter wrote in an article for the *Defender*. "If anything they treat the colored people better. . . . The white Americans look positively silly over here. They do their utmost to start trouble—to start the color question—but to no avail . . . Paris, in fact, all of France, is a heaven on earth for the Negro man or woman."[8] Such exaggerated testimony lured a small but growing crowd of black Americans to this supposed Promised Land. These characters became Briggs's social circle.

There was Ada Smith—"One hundred and forty-four pounds of freckles, fair skin, lovely feet and legs," by her own description; alias Bricktop, due to her shock of red hair.[9] From Harlem, via Chicago, via West Virginia, she sailed across the Atlantic Ocean, spurred on by a siren song and an invitation to work at one of the hottest cabarets going: Le Grand Duc. Despite its regal name, the club was a dungeon. Upon seeing it for the first time, Bricktop burst into tears. The tiny room held "about twelve tables and a small bar that would feel crowded with six pairs of elbows leaning on it," she recalled.[10] *This* was the vaunted Montmartre? She wanted to go home.

Seeing a friendly looking countrywoman crying, the young dishwasher at Le Grand Duc carried out a plate of food and made her feel better. It was Langston Hughes, who had also been lured to Paris by the same fairytale only to find the same upsetting reality. After arriving in Paris, Hughes wrote to friend and fellow writer Countee Cullen:

> I have fallen into the very whirling heart of Parisian nightlife—Montmartre where topsy-turvy no one gets up before seven or eight in the evening, breakfast at nine and nothing starts before midnight . . . I myself go to work at eleven pm and finish at nine in the morning . . . The jazz-band starts playing at one and we're still serving champagne long after day-light. I'm vastly amused. But about France! Kid, stay in Harlem! The French are the most franc-loving, sou-clutching, hard-faced, hard worked, cold and half-starved set of people I've ever seen in life. Heat unknown. Hot water—water—what is it? You can pay for a smile here.[11]

Then there was Eugene Bullard, manager of Le Grand Duc and pugnacious pillar of the black expat community in Montmartre. Dark skinned, handsome, and compactly powerful, he left America as a teenager and tramped around the world, hopping steamships and earning his living with his fists as an amateur boxer. He settled in Paris just before WWI and enlisted in the French Foreign Legion. During the war, his biographer remarked, "Bullard fought in the company of other *pauvres poilus*, the term the French citizenry bestowed on their heroic but lowly foot soldiers, infested with lice, too exhausted to shave, living, fighting, and dying in mud. Eugene braved lonely hours at night crawling into no man's land trying to avoid exposure by enemy flares while bringing back a dead comrade."[12] A gashing wound at the Battle of Verdun sent Bullard to a military hospital, but six months later he volunteered for the French air service. No one believed a black man could fly a plane, so they threw innumerable obstacles in his way, but Bullard pummeled those obstacles like so many sorry boxing opponents. He joined the Lafayette Escadrille, flew in more than twenty air combat missions, and was awarded the Croix de Guerre. The French called him *l'Hirondelle Noire de la Mort*: the Black Swallow of Death.

None of that meant a Yankee dime to white American tourists in Montmartre. They'd swagger into a nightspot and try to get every black face they saw ejected, war hero or not. Bullard, like Briggs, protected his honor fiercely. One night, a trio of white American doughboys taunted him, so he whipped them all at the same time. Another night, a white American tourist noticed Bullard conversing with a Frenchwoman and went livid at "a damn nigger talking to women in his company." He started a fight and Bullard broke his nose. When the Paris *Tribune* reported on the incident, it blamed Bullard for starting the scene and sneered, "dozens of Negroes are now said to be infesting Montmartre."[13] Bullard sued the paper and won 10,000 francs and an apology.

Bullard developed a reputation as a fixer. Bechet recalled, "The cabarets, the clubs, the musicianers—when there was some trouble they couldn't straighten out by themselves, they called on Gene. He was a man you could count on."[14] A measure of Bullard's stature in Montmartre is provided by Briggs's opinion of him. Normally, a man who wound up in jail as often as Bullard would embarrass Briggs's sense of propriety. But since Bullard never went looking for a fight and only fought to defend his honor, Briggs understood him:

> Most of the cases of insults we had and things came from [white] Americans at the time. And if they happened to walk into a restaurant, first class restaurant, and a black is sitting having a meal they would object and be nasty. Bullard, he couldn't take it because he was given the French nationality on account of being an aviator. And he didn't take no for an answer. And not only that, he was also a Mason. And it's very hard for a Mason that has certain obligations to suffer inwardly for no reason at all. Naturally if I do something wrong I can suffer for it, but if I do nothing wrong it's not my fault if my skin is darker than someone else's. I didn't ask for it. I was born the same as everyone else. Bullard, he'd be in the police station almost every morning. But they never kept him.[15]

Briggs recalled the older musicians taking Bullard to task, afraid he was going to ruin their good thing in Paris, but their fears were unfounded. Le Grand Duc not only flourished—with an integrated clientele to boot—it became the most popular hangout spot for jazz musicians afterhours. Hughes recalled: "When all the other clubs were closed, the best of the musicians and entertainers from various other smart places would often drop into Le Grand Duc, and there'd be a jam session until seven or eight in the morning—only in 1924 they had no such name for it."[16] As the sun came up and the jam sessions continued, Bullard served home cooking Harlem style: corned-beef hash with a poached egg; creamed chicken on toast; club sandwiches.

At these all-night jams, Briggs fueled the revelry of the Lost Generation. Le Grand Duc was home away from home for Zelda and Scott Fitzgerald, the tragic couple. Fitzgerald was finishing his new novel, which he wanted to call *Trimalchio in West Egg* and Zelda wanted him to call *The Great Gatsby*. They'd get roaring drunk and make a scene, and Bricktop would often have to accompany them home in a cab. She felt a motherly affection for Fitzgerald. Fitzgerald soon befriended Ernest Hemingway—a wary friendship at best—and a crowd of artists followed the great writers to Montmartre.

On any given night, Briggs provided the soundtrack as the likes of Alice B. Toklas, Jean Cocteau, Marcel Duchamp, and Ezra Pound got drunk. Hemingway marveled at Scott and Zelda's drunken behavior, writing, "I have seen them become unconscious not as though they were drunk but as though they had been anesthetized . . . and when they woke they would be fresh and happy."[17]

It was hard work keeping all those sots in check, and Bricktop was the only one who could do it. Most nights, she'd sit near the front door at Le Grand Duc keeping the books. Occasionally she'd float around the room like a bubble in a glass of champagne, greeting customers, singing a song with the band, breaking up a fight, and then returning to her perch up front. As she wrote in her ledger, "The first lesson to learn in trying to run a joint is—keep the client in <u>his</u> place which automatically <u>puts</u> you in your place. Result if the client steps out of his place into your place all you haft to do is shove him safely back into his place. Nothing breeds credit like familiarity."[18]

Bricktop regularly threw Hemingway out of the club when he got zozzled. John Steinbeck once sent her a taxi full of roses to apologize for his behavior one besotted evening. Then there was the night Fitzgerald got himself sent home in a taxi and Bricktop refused to accompany him, so he kicked out every window in the cab. "I made him dig into his pockets and helped him count out enough francs to buy the whole taxi," Bricktop recalled. "Scott turned to me and said, 'See, Brick, I'm not responsible. I was just trying to teach you a lesson. You've got to take me home.'"[19]

These were the juvenile spasms of an exiled generation, and yet somehow from this hedonistic haze there emerged an unparalleled flowering of artistic brilliance. At the time, Hemingway was writing his first novel, *The Sun Also Rises*; Joyce was fresh off the gargantuan *Ulysses* and had begun work on *Finnegans Wake*; Man Ray had just made the experimental film *Le Retour à la Raison* starring Kiki; Cunard was writing *Parallax*, her third book of poetry; Picasso was painting *Mandolin and Guitar*, one of his greatest still lifes. There were others, too, including T. S. Eliot, who had recently published *The Wasteland*, and Gertrude Stein, who acted as den mother of the whole crowd.

Then there was Cole Porter, one of the greatest songwriters in American history. One night at Le Grand Duc, Bricktop recalled, "a slight, immaculately dressed man came in. . . . I got up to sing and could sense that the man was watching and listening with more than ordinary interest. He applauded when I finished." After he left, Bricktop discovered she'd been singing one of Porter's songs ("I'm in Love Again") to the composer. "Everyone in Paris knew that Cole was funny about people singing his songs," she said. "If a singer didn't do it just right Cole wouldn't embarrass him or her but he'd leave quickly—and that would be the most embarrassing situation imaginable for the singer."[20]

Porter reappeared the next night asking if Bricktop could do the Charleston. Watching her dance, he exclaimed, "What legs! What legs!" Then Porter told her, half as an invitation and half as an order, "I'm going to give Charleston cocktail parties at my house two or three times a week, and you're going to teach everyone to dance the Charleston." So Bricktop found herself at 13 Rue Monsieur, chez Porter, with its opulent décor and floor-to-ceiling mirrors. The Aga Khan was there, as were socialite Elsa Maxwell and about fifty other students, including the Rothschilds, Consuelo Vanderbilt, and the Duchess of Marlborough. "I was about to become the dance teacher to the most elegant members of the international set," Bricktop recalled coolly. These rich people didn't intimidate her.[21]

Bricktop and Porter had a platonic love affair. "Bricky," as he called her, saved a seat in Le Grand Duc, and later at her own club, just for him. Even when he was away spending half the year in America no one could touch it. Porter introduced her to the crème de la crème of worldly society and lavished expensive gifts on her. When she couldn't afford a gown for a ball at the Paris Opera, Porter took her to the great couturier Captain Edward Molyneux and announced that he wanted to order her a dress. As Porter's biographer wrote, "When Captain Molyneux inquired what type of gown he had in mind Cole suggested a duplicate of the one that had been made for Princess Marina of Greece, only still more lavish."[22] He got it, too.

Despite her success, or perhaps because of it, Bricktop was a tremendously conflicted woman. Throughout her life she wrote copious notes to herself, almost like diary entries, on any and every scrap of paper lying around. She wrote as she lived—to the margins and always in all caps. In one note she described herself as "dead asleep . . . with vanity, bigness, hardheadedness, Jack Daniels, and French champagne."[23] A staunch Catholic, she felt guilty about her hedonism in Paris. Later in life, she wrote, "In those early Paris years I had a lot of men—a whole passel of men—and I did it up and down alleys, in taxi cabs, in the bed, out of the bed, all around the bed. I slept with white men and black men."[24]

She wasn't the only one. It was a booze-fueled, sex-crazed, war-scarred age. The old rules didn't apply anymore; the new rules had yet to be written. As Porter put it ten years later:

> *The world has gone mad today*
> *And good's bad today*
> *And black's white today*
> *And day's night today . . .*
> *Anything goes.*

14

"I don't think I'm being arrogant in saying that I helped to push everything, 'cause I was there on the spot."[1]

—Arthur Briggs

PARIS SHUT DOWN DURING THE SUMMER MONTHS, so Briggs followed the crowd to the sea. He rejoined the Savoys for an engagement at England's lavish Kursaal Casino and then finished 1923 opening L'Abbaye, a new club at the Namur Gate in Brussels. Briggs's name now drew crowds everywhere he played. He made good money—shared fairly with the band—and spent it on the normal things for a twenty-three-year-old man: clothes, cigarettes, records, and, one can only assume, girls.

In Brussels, Briggs reunited with Robert Goffin, who wrote a typically misty ode to the Savoys at L'Abbaye: "Should we remember the days of the Abbey, in front of the doorway surrounded by a double line of cars? . . . Sitting on the piano, wearing a silver hat, like a naively learned lesson, you recited 'Last Night on the Back Porch,' [a popular Broadway song of 1923] while the ladies of the dawn shined the fires of their diamonds towards the dancers."[2]

The ladies of the dawn surely shined their fires at the handsome young trumpet player too, but Briggs kept those memories to himself. He was doggedly focused on music anyway, spending many nights at his hotel with Goffin, who always arrived with a stack of new jazz records under his arm. Goffin spun these records in Briggs's room, waiting for the young master to explain the confusing, exhilarating noise. They were two kids, staying up all night, deepening their friendship through their love of music.

Jazz was going through a crucial transition: the age of the soloist had dawned. Briggs recalled hearing one particular record, "Southern Rose" by the California Ramblers, on which "the saxophonist began to play in a totally free way."[3] As Goffin put it: "The saxophonist . . . possessed by a demonic fury, suddenly rejecting all the known interpretations, fluid and velvety, escaped in high speed into celestial acrobatics in which reason played no role, in the only true musical surrealism before the term existed. We listened to this strange miracle that we did not understand but that made us delirious." Goffin "called Briggs to the rescue," and though Briggs was "a little thrown off balance with wonder at first," he recognized the New Orleans style he had learned from Bechet, also known as "hot" jazz. Goffin and his Belgian friends became immediate converts. "From that day on," Goffin wrote, "it was only one way for us to accept jazz."[4]

During these visits, Goffin introduced Briggs to a major influence in Bix Beiderbecke. Bix was one of the great cornet players of the 1920s. He played for a time with the Wolverines, the most popular jazz band in the American Midwest, which cut "Riverboat Shuffle" in February 1924. It became a landmark record, in large part because it was the first song written by Hoagy Carmichael, who is best known for such classics as "Georgia on My Mind," "Heart and Soul," and "Stardust." Briggs was enraptured. He especially admired Beiderbecke's subtlety, and he began hearing new possibilities for his playing.

The Wolverines, like the California Ramblers, were white, which led Briggs and Goffin into a discussion of race. Briggs made sure to teach Goffin about the black pioneers of jazz—Bechet, Oliver, Keppard—and they talked about Fletcher Henderson's orchestra with Coleman Hawkins on tenor saxophone, which had just begun recording in New York. This was no small lesson: European audiences only knew jazz music through records, and the vast majority of records came from white bands. If not for Briggs, Goffin would have had no knowledge of the music's black roots.

Briggs had begun his life's work in earnest. He was now an ambassador of jazz, spreading the music to every corner of the globe. Sometimes he did this in coversation, as with Goffin, but mostly he did it with his playing, performing feats that made everyone stop and listen. In

Brussels at the time were the Georgians, a white American jazz band that had broken off from the famous Paul Specht Orchestra in New York. Bandleader Frank Guarante, a trained trumpeter, "was an arrogant man, very hard with his musicians," Briggs said.[5] He was particularly proud of his ability to play high notes on the trumpet, which requires a great amount of lip strength and technique. On one particular song, he hit a note that was an octave and a half step above the tonic. He thought no one on earth could match him.

Meanwhile, Briggs's showpiece with the Savoys was "Edmee," an Austrian ballad in which he finished two full steps higher than Guarante's highest note. Guarante's musicians came to see Briggs perform, and when they heard the high note, Briggs recalled, "they shouted like madmen, stamping their feet, and clapping their hands." The management asked for an encore, but the musicians, knowing the pressure it would put on Briggs's lips, told the manager, "We are delighted; it's enough."[6] They hurried back to Guarante and told him he had to come see this kid at L'Abbaye. "I don't need to waste my time," Guarante said. "Nobody can do that in Europe, let alone in Belgium."

The musicians persisted, finally enticing Guarante with a female companion, but he watched the Savoys with derision. "This is nothing extraordinary," he told his friends. "I would've been better in bed."[7] He hadn't seen the good part yet. In the middle of the set, the lights went down, and the Savoys began "Edmee." Briggs stood behind a curtain, hidden from Guarante's view, and allowed the drama to unfold slowly. His gorgeous tone and subtle phrasing emanated from the darkness as he inched forward from behind the curtain. He couldn't see the crowd, but his musicians told him later that Guarante craned his neck, desperate to locate the source of the sound. Briggs built to the climax, hitting center stage the moment he blew the final, impossible note. The crowd erupted. Guarante had enough training to know he was beaten; he fled the room, leaving Briggs triumphant on the bandstand. The night ended in wild revelry, champagne flowing freely on the house. Even Briggs took a few sips.

Briggs was now the toast of Belgium, and he invited all to share his cup. When Goffin created his own jazz band, Briggs watched them perform, giving advice and even lessons. "They were so passionate," Briggs recalled.[8] Two trumpeters of the Royal Guard came to see the

Savoys, drawn by the magnetic allure of jazz, and Briggs taught them exercises to increase their capability. Meanwhile, the Savoys brought so much business to L'Abbaye the other dance clubs struggled to stay open. Briggs had put it all together—his technical training, his classical tone, his jazz roots, his natural showmanship—to become the best jazz trumpeter in Europe.

15

Kemal Promises More Hangings Of Political Antagonists In Turkey[1]

—*Los Angeles Examiner*, August 1, 1926

IN THE SPRING OF 1925, Briggs was invited to perform at the Weihburg Bar in Vienna, where his list of fans grew to include many of the nation's preeminent musicians, including the great cellist Pablo Casals. Briggs also blew away the American jazz musicians that came to Europe to capitalize on the craze he helped ignite. American clarinetist Garvin Bushell recalled, "[Briggs's] trumpet made ours sound like beginners."[2]

Briggs became so beloved in Vienna he was asked to appear with the Savoys in the silent film *Das Spielzeug von Paris*, alongside Lili Damita in her first starring role. For Briggs, it was an auspicious debut: Damita would soon become internationally famous and marry Errol Flynn just before his meteoric rise to stardom; director Michael Curtiz would go on to direct more than one hundred films including *White Christmas* and *Casablanca*, the latter of which won an Academy Award.

Briggs and the Savoys appear in the film during a dance sequence. Damita pokes her head through a giant drum skin with a dancer painted on it and the word *Jazz* written in large block letters across its front. She looks out at Refurt, Salnave, van Gils, Hughes, and Scanavino, who are bouncing to the rhythm. Of special musical interest is Refurt's drum set, comprised of an oversized bass drum, a snare drum tilted at an impossible angle, and one lone cymbal (the modern jazz kit was still several years in the offing).

Damita rips through the paper drum skin, revealing Briggs and Hughes seated behind her, instruments in hand. She leads them to the dance floor, where she and Refurt cut a few moves, while Briggs plays behind them, his trumpet pointed toward the floor in a pose Miles Davis would make famous decades later. It is worth mentioning that a black man in America could be killed for even the rumor of dancing with a white woman. In Vienna, Briggs did it freely and on film.

Though the film did not capture the Savoys' sound, it gives a priceless look at the band as a visual entity. Under Briggs's command, they wore immaculate black suits with black bow ties and French-cuffed shirts. Hughes even wore sunglasses. Briggs clearly had the sharpest eye for fashion: his suit was cut to perfection, with a white pocket square peeking from his jacket pocket, and the ever-present ring glinting on his pinky finger.

Briggs's screen debut came at the moment film began exploding as a global medium—yet another instance when he was in the right place at the right time. That same year saw a flurry of groundbreaking films, including Charlie Chaplin's *The Gold Rush* and early versions of *Cinderella*, *Ben-Hur*, and *The Wizard of Oz*. America alone pumped out an average of eight hundred films each year. Stars like Clara Bow and Mary Pickford broke hearts while slapstick men like Chaplin and Buster Keaton busted guts. Briggs's contribution to this growing field, as small as it may have been, cannot be overlooked. Nor can the film's impact on his career. He still hadn't made a proper record, so *Das Spielzeug von Paris* gave the world at large its first chance to see him, if not hear him. It was a publicity boon.

The Weihburg Bar invited the Savoys back in September, just before the film's release, for the normal schedule—tea dances in the evenings and nightly shows until 4:00 AM. Briggs was in his midtwenties and had the stamina to treat life like one endless night. Though the band was again billed as a "Nigger Jazz Band," Briggs had earned the respect of both his Austrian crowd and the press. A newspaper at the time noted that "the audience listens to the band as if they were attending a concert performance," which was a rarity at the club. Of the band, the paper said, "Although everyone seems to play something different, the rhythm of the dance remains cohesive."[3]

There is much to unpack in those statements. First, the paper takes care to remark that the audience sat quietly *as if* at a concert. This seems strange, given that they were at a concert, by today's definition of the word, but Europe still possessed a symphonic mind-set. To call Briggs's performance a concert was to elevate it to the level of Debussy and Wagner. This was a bigger compliment than most reviewers in Europe would pay the new music. To be fair, many Europeans recognized the brilliance of jazz right away, including some adventurous classical composers, such as Ernest Ansermet and Igor Stravinsky. But most listeners and critics in Europe saw jazz as a fad that would happily pass.

Second, the newspaper mentions the cacophony of melody and the force of rhythm that propelled the music. Many Europeans were confused by jazz. The idea of every instrument soloing at once had no analogue in their music, nor did jazz's complex syncopation and emphasis on the backbeat—especially not in Vienna, land of the waltz. By introducing his audience to jazz, Briggs was not just spreading his love of music; he was helping an entire continent redefine its sense of rhythm.

From Vienna, Briggs went east, tearing through countries, languages, and cultures, bringing jazz to uncharted territory, until he landed as far from home as he'd ever be: Constantinople.

In its sixteen centuries, the city had played many roles: jewel of the Roman, Byzantine, and Ottoman Empires; resting place of Christ's crown of thorns; keeper of the remnants of the Library of Alexandria. Most recently, it had played the role of battleground. After World War I, the revolutionary soldier Mustafa Kemal Atatürk led a war of Turkish independence, becoming the first president of Turkey in 1923. His government enacted sweeping reforms, including renaming the great city. In mid-1926, Briggs received an invitation to perform not in Constantinople but in Istanbul.

Briggs's Viennese agent booked the Savoys at Maxim's Cabaret, a jazz club run by an American named George Thomas. "You're going to be happy," the agent told Briggs. "The owner of the cabaret is a black man." Briggs replied, "Color doesn't matter."[4] And yet he must have felt intrigued by this particular black man. Thomas had grown up in Savannah, Georgia, escaped the steel grip of Jim Crow, and fled to Russia. After the Russian Revolution began in 1917, he made his way to Turkey. Briggs didn't meet men like George Thomas every day. He'd come to see that as a blessing.

Turkey was the worst trip of Briggs's entire career. To get there, he suffered a harrowing train ride through a devastated countryside. "We were afraid to see the misery that was spreading before us in the Balkans," Briggs said. "All these poor people, ready to do anything to have a few cents." To make matters worse, the train stopped every half hour. The trip became "more and more painful" as it went on:

> What was served on the train wasn't edible. Just knowing where it came from, we couldn't touch it. . . . We had to give a lot of tips to the steward, who took the opportunity to scam us, bringing us some food from outside at the stops. We managed to get fruit, but at such a price! We finally discovered that we could find large salads at each station. We therefore took stops in the stations to wash these salads, and to wash ourselves because there was only just one water source: One pump for the whole station. . . . Then we had to eat lamb, which I personally don't like, but which at that moment seemed like a delicacy to me. We slept as we could—in the heat, the smells, and the misery, because there were no sleeping cars.[5]

Then came Istanbul. The customs officials spoke no English, and Briggs spoke no Turkish. His bags were searched, leaving his clothes strewn all over the dirty ground. The officials were baffled by a portable bidet in saxophonist Mario Scanavino's bag, and they questioned him about it for more than an hour, with more officials joining the fray, until a frustrated and exhausted Scanavino hissed through his teeth, "It's for hygiene!" Then, joining a gesture to the word, he mimed its use.

The ordeal continued. Briggs and the band had stuffed their luggage with records, unwilling to part with their beloved music for even a few weeks, but judging by how the customs officers examined these items, "one would have thought they had never seen records."[6] The recording industry was new enough that it is possible these men had indeed never seen records. On the other hand, there was a phonograph in the customs office. Exasperated, Briggs put one of the records on the turntable, and when the music began, the officers shouted, "Impossible!" When the singing started, they became even more suspicious, fearing that the Savoys were trying to smuggle in revolutionary propaganda. One officer spoke a bit of French and reprimanded his men: "You are crazy, you do not understand that they are songs? These are records sold worldwide."[7] Finally, the band was released.

No one waited to greet them at the station. Hours passed, with Briggs becoming more alarmed by the minute. "After a very long time," Briggs said, "Mr. Thomas's representative arrived, pulling a cart, but this cart could only take one or two trunks and we had a dozen." Briggs commanded the man to find Thomas and make him send adequate transportation to the hotel. The man answered, "There is no hotel." Thomas had rented cheap rooms, and after two hours of driving, Briggs entered his room to find "mostly cockroaches and other critters."[8] He spent the night breathing a cloud of insecticide, which he had to spray every few hours to keep bugs from crawling over his skin as he tried to steal some sleep.

The next day, Briggs visited Maxim's and was shocked to find the club still under construction. He asked to rehearse, but Thomas told him it was impossible because of leaks in the roof. Briggs prepared his band the best he could, but he began hearing whispers that Thomas was deep in debt and could not be trusted.

The Savoys opened at Maxim's in the summer. By contract, Briggs and the band were to be served dinner every night, but a few days in, their stomachs rewrote that clause. "Two or three of us got ill," Briggs recalled. "We had stomach trouble and everything else. And we realized that [Thomas] was doing everything to save money."[9] He wasn't doing enough. Within the month, Briggs arrived to find a notice on the door: closed by order of the government. Briggs was on the hook this time. It was *his* band that was stranded in Turkey with no money. He bought their return train tickets home.

Before leaving, Briggs met the owner of Taxim Garden, a man he called Mr. Lehman. Lehman sent his secretary to make Briggs a proposal, but as Briggs recalled, "It was so ridiculous that I did not even bother to answer: I simply showed him our return ticket."[10] Briggs was now a canny businessman, with a nose for a fair deal and the guts to get it. He called Lehman's bluff. As it turned out, Lehman had hired trombonist Herb Fleming, but Fleming, who happened to be a friend of Briggs's from the 369th regimental band, refused to perform if he did not have a good orchestra. Lehman returned to Briggs with a real offer, Fleming got his orchestra, and the Savoys stayed in Turkey.

Briggs enjoyed his time at the Taxim Garden. He especially remembered the Turkish Navy band that played next door: "In that formation I saw, for the first time, a Turk as black as me."[11] But the trip soon took another twist. One night, Lehman called Briggs into his office. Hulking in the corner was a Turkish soldier. "Mr. Briggs," Lehman said, "Tomorrow we have a very, very big gala evening." Confused, Briggs replied, "The show is rehearsed." Lehman continued, "Yes, but that's not the point. I have a command by the president of the republic asking to send my orchestra to Ankara tomorrow. But you can't make it."

Briggs realized Lehman was trying to pass the blame for rejecting the president of Turkey's request. "I have nothing to do with it," Briggs said. "No, Mr. Lehman, we're not responsible." Just then, the hulking Turk spoke in perfect English: "There's no question of disobeying the president. The president wants the band and you must accept." To make certain Briggs got the hint, he added, "We can't force you to go. But if you do refuse to go, you'll never leave Turkey."

After some tense moments, the officer said, "We'll take you to your hotels. You can sleep, and we'll awaken you early in the morning and take you to Ankara." Briggs and Lehman looked at each other. "There was nothing we could do," he recalled. "The orchestra wasn't so satisfied, but we had no choice. So we went."[12]

In Ankara, the band was whisked to an upscale hotel and offered refreshments. Then, an officer drove them to a military camp. The band waited in a room with more refreshments, until the officer returned and explained that when the lights turned off, they were to play "Ca, C'est Paris" until directed to stop. Two hours passed. Briggs and his friends muttered darkly to each other, nervously eating dates and drinking juice, waiting for the signal. Fifteen minutes later, the officer returned again and said, "Take your positions as though you're going to play." Briggs put his horn to his mouth. Fifteen more minutes ticked by.

At last the lights went off. The Savoys hit "Ca, C'est Paris," a number they knew by heart. After several minutes, the officer signaled to stop. "Everyone was screaming," Briggs said. "We wondered what had happened; we didn't understand anything." The lights came back on, and a Turkish orchestra began playing. Everyone danced. The officer came back and said, "You are done. You can do what you want except to leave the camp. Around four o'clock in the morning we will take your back to your hotel."

At the appointed time, a Greek driver arrived. Noticing the driver spoke English, Briggs asked what the party was all about, and that's when he learned the truth: twelve dissident politicians had just been hanged in the marketplace of Ankara. Briggs had just played the after-party for an execution. "We bribed the chauffeur to take us to the marketplace, because he said that the bodies were still hanging," Briggs said. Before they reached the scene, a soldier stopped their car and pulled the Greek driver from his seat. Briggs never saw the man again. One of the soldiers took the wheel and shouted at the band, "You have seen nothing, heard nothing!"[13] The soldier drove the Savoys to their hotel and shut them in their rooms. "Fortunately for us, we didn't get to the marketplace, because we might have disappeared also," Briggs said. He didn't see the bodies, but he now understood the power of a murderous autocrat.

Returning to Taxim Garden, Briggs marched the Savoys into Lehman's office and demanded they break their contract. Lehman relented, even offering to help the band purchase train tickets home. The Savoys went home, but Briggs had unfinished business in Vienna. He visited his booking agent, plunked down the commission from the disastrous Maxim's engagement, and said, "When you hire a foreign orchestra to work in a foreign country, you should take serious information and especially bank guarantees!"[14] Then, Briggs returned to the place that served as a home base, if not a home: Paris.

16

"Paris is the dance, and I am the dancer."

—Josephine Baker

ENTER THE GODDESS, JOSEPHINE BAKER. Sprung from the squalor of the St. Louis ghetto, she was a teenage runaway, married and divorced at age thirteen, and then again at sixteen. Between marriages, she went to Philadelphia and auditioned for Noble Sissle in *Shuffle Along*. He dismissed her with two words: too young. Undaunted, she joined the show as a dresser and learned the chorus line routine from the wings. One night a dancer took ill, and she seized her chance. Baker's first taste of the stage hit her like a shot of Prohibition liquor. Dazed by the klieg lights, she crossed her eyes until they seemed to spin in her head; she rearranged her beautiful face into a ghoulish grin; she danced in a way both sensual and funny. The audience saw nothing but her. She was a star.

One night, a jealous chorus girl tripped Baker during a performance, but Baker turned even a nosedive into a comedy routine. Wherever she went, critics followed in breathless adoration: "A revelation" . . . "Unique sense of rhythm" . . . "A born comic."[1] But America was too small for her, its color line too cruelly drawn. Like Briggs, she made her name in Europe.

Baker hit Paris like a meteor. In 1925's *La Revue Negre*, an all-black revue in the style of *Shuffle Along*, she danced the Charleston wearing nothing but a feather skirt and dancing shoes. "As she danced, quivering with intensity," an audience member recalled, "the entire room felt the raw force of her passion, the excitement of her rhythm. She was eroticism personified."[2] By midnight, Baker's name was on the cover of every Parisian newspaper; by morning it was on every Parisian's lips.

When Briggs returned from Turkey in 1926, Baker wasn't just a star; she was a galaxy. Crowds gasped when she strolled down the Champs-Élysées dudded up, with her menagerie in tow—swans, monkeys, a boa constrictor—looking for all the world like the bee's knees, the duck's quack. "You couldn't get within blocks of her," Bricktop said. "Everything stopped cold."[3] Wedding proposals poured in, thousands of them, and a cult of personality amassed around her like a planetary disk. There were Baker dolls and Baker costumes, Baker perfumes and Baker pomades. Trouble getting your hair into that inimitable, gender-bending wave? Try Baker hair curls. White Parisiennes even darkened their skin with walnut oil to look more like her. It was a long way from Broadway, where the light-skinned chorus girls gave her a nickname that doubled as a dagger: the Monkey.

Baker transformed herself in Paris. She jettisoned her ungrammatical English and began speaking only French. No one mocked her for making mistakes in a foreign language. She spelled her name in the French way—Joséphine, with an accent. She loved that French audiences found her beautiful, and she began to believe herself beautiful. She loved French attitudes toward sex and that European men found her body as magnetic in bed as it was onstage. She even earned a new nickname: Black Venus.

She also began showing up several hours late to her own shows and throwing epic temper tantrums. She treated money and men with voracious nonchalance. During costume fittings, she'd grow bored and wander away, saying, "I don't have the calling to be a pincushion."[4] One evening she was late for a cue, and the stage manager found her sitting naked on the floor of her dressing room eating a lobster with her fingers. Many lamented this behavior; few appreciated that she was only twenty years old and had transformed nearly overnight from a poor St. Louis girl to the world's first black female superstar. As a hypersexualized black woman in a foreign country, she was subject to pressures no one could imagine. She had no peers.

To some extent, her antics were a way of letting everyone know, as her biographer put it, "who now held the whip hand."[5] It was an assertion of power, akin to Briggs's habit of quitting the instant his dignity was challenged. Like Briggs, Baker had been scarred by American racism at a young age. Unlike Briggs, this scar left her with a tragic quality and a compulsive need to protect the vulnerable and innocent, especially animals. Later in life she adopted twelve orphaned children from around the world, which she deemed her "Rainbow Tribe." Perhaps the vulnerable, innocent creature she was trying to protect was herself.

At the end of 1926, looking for a place to flaunt her newfound money and fame, Baker opened Chez Joséphine, her own nightclub on rue Fontaine. She made an entrance every night, usually in the wee hours, leading a group of hangers on and her menagerie of animals. Her pig, Albert, grew so fat on kitchen scraps he got wedged under the boiler and couldn't get out. They had to break the kitchen doorway to free him. "*Pauvre cochon*,"* was Baker's response.

In the *Folies Bergère* of 1927, Baker went from a star to a legend. During a jungle scene in Africa—almost anything involving black performers had a jungle scene in Africa—Baker slinked onstage, bare breasted again, wearing a skirt made of plastic bananas, sixteen of them to be exact, each looking like an erect penis saluting the ceiling. Her body seemed carved of marble; her legs put the great Rodin to shame. She danced, every motion erotic, libidinous, carnal. She danced, pelvis surging and serpentine, breasts rejoicing in freedom. As she quaked and quivered and swung and swayed, each pump of her derrière flung the bananas around her waist in phallic fits. It was called the *danse sauvage*, and it made her the biggest black female star in the world. She transcended gender. She was beyond mores and morals. She was undeniable, like ecstasy.

---

* "Poor pig."

17

"My memory of Germany is terrific.
One could never have imagined what happened after."[1]

—Arthur Briggs

IN NOVEMBER 1926, ARTHUR BRIGGS RE-FORMED his band and took them to the one place on earth more riotous, more decadent, more uninhibited than Montmartre: Berlin. The war had ravaged Germany, and so had the peace. At the end of World War I, the Treaty of Versailles forced the nation to cede vast swaths of territory, disarm its military, and pay 132 billion marks in reparations (roughly $450 billion in today's US dollars). Impoverished masses fled the countryside looking for work in Berlin. By 1923, the city was full of "innumerable beggars, paralytics, shell-shocked soldiers, and starving people of good family," wrote Robert McAlmon. "There was no gaiety or joy, only recklessness."[2]

For the poor, Berlin was a slum where the main industries were drugs and prostitution. But for everyone else, the city offered a cornucopia of cultural delights: the Bauhaus movement revolutionized architecture and design; German Expressionists produced the best films in the world, including Fritz Lang's classic *Metropolis*; Carl Jung developed his theories on archetypes and the collective unconscious; and Albert Einstein won the 1921 Nobel Prize for discovering the photoelectric effect. It was the *Goldene Zwanziger** of the Weimar Republic, a period of artistic freedom, progressive reform, and economic stability.

---

* Golden Twenties.

Jazz was the great equalizer for Berlin's rich and poor. They pressed against each other in the city's wild, decadent nightclubs. Bricktop, who tried to open a club there in 1927, recalled:

> It was a circus. . . . At night the sounds of music and singing and laughing made a steady joyful din, and there were so many lights that you could hardly see the sky. Anything went in Berlin, and I mean anything. All the dope-taking and homosexuality that was done in a light-hearted sort of way in Paris was serious business in Berlin. Some people said it was depraved, but I think it was just a way to forget the humiliating war defeat, to block out what you couldn't help seeing when the sun came up in the morning.[3]

One person who found the city depraved was Adolf Hitler. He believed the Weimar Republic to be a stain on Germany's culture. In 1923, he attempted a coup in Munich, along with two thousand supporters of the National Socialist Party, which he had recently revitalized. Though the uprising was suppressed, it made Hitler a minor celebrity. As his message spread, chapters of the Nazi party opened throughout Germany. Joseph Goebbels was appointed local party leader in Berlin, and days before Briggs arrived, Goebbels led a march through the city that turned into a riot.

Briggs likely knew none of this, and he avoided the city's seedy side, as was his wont. The Savoys were booked at one of Berlin's premiere clubs, the Barberina. With its red plush carpeting and mirrored walls, Briggs said, it was "unique in the world by its location, its clientele, its direction, and decoration."[4] It was connected to a vegetarian restaurant called the Kakadu, where trained cockatoos sat in cages above each table. When the diners were done, they'd tap the table and the bird would fetch the bill.

In re-forming the Savoys, Briggs inadvertently made himself the only black man in the band. When he arrived at the Barberina to rehearse, Ellie Glasner, the emcee of the show, stood at the bar casting a wary eye at him. He approached her.

"I present you Mr. Briggs and his orchestra," he said.

She answered in German: "A black conductor! It's not possible. Not at the Barberina!"

Briggs's German was basic, and drummer Chappy Obendorfer had to explain the problem: "She's not satisfied."

"Well, what about?" Briggs asked.

"You."

"I acted as if nothing had happened," Briggs said. It was a surprising response from a man used to storming off bandstands. Instead, he decided to answer these slights with music. When the Savoys began to rehearse, Briggs recalled proudly, "I can say that there was not the slightest clash." Glasner saw that Briggs's professionalism was beyond reproach, his mastery beyond question. At the end of the rehearsal, she sent a waiter to invite Briggs to the bar, where he found a table set with "coffee, tea, pastries and everything." Glasner said, "I'm awfully sorry. I hope you'll excuse me. I haven't been very polite." As a token of her sorrow, Glasner told Briggs she'd give him the same spread during intermission every night. "It happened," Briggs said. "And that person, Mrs. Glasner, she became my best friend."[5]

Briggs had already proven himself willing to quit a job at the slightest challenge to his honor. And yet, because Glasner apologized, he forgave her and even befriended her. This bigheartedness balanced his sensitivity. Had he done nothing but flee when his honor was injured, stranding bands like he did in Ostend and Spain, he would have been merely impulsive (and rather selfish). But he proved himself able to forgive, and in this ability shone his decency and humility.

The decision to stay paid off; Briggs called his debut at the Barberina "unforgettable."[6] He prepared a version of "Ça, C'est Paris," the song he had performed at the Turkish execution party, making it into a "funny sketch." For the serious Briggs, this was a departure—as he admitted, humor was "not my kind of work at all"—but he wanted to give his audience something special. His intent was to unite American, French, and German styles to make the appeal as broad as possible. "My band members, who were very intelligent, immediately understood and began to participate enthusiastically," he said. "Each member of the band brought their strength, an idea, or a particular talent." Trombonist Jean Naudin sang the first chorus in French, doing a comical imitation of Mistinguett. Then, the tuba and drums kicked into a German march "with very jolting inflection. . . . One-two, one-two, one-two."

This transitioned seamlessly into ragtime, "imitating New York's 15th infantry regiment, but with a very exaggerated style." Briggs led his musicians from the bandstand to the dance floor. They circled the room, doing a sort of cakewalk dance "imitating American nonchalance and relaxation." As Briggs recalled, "This had a tremendous effect . . . the room could not stop laughing for three quarters of an hour. . . . It was impossible to present the [other] attractions."[7]

After two weeks, Briggs received an option on his contract for another three months. "We played good music," Briggs said simply.[8] And yet little of it was jazz. Briggs knew that the Germans lagged far behind the French in their appreciation for his music. When a player strayed too far from the melody, the Germans called it *Katzenmusik* (cat music). To succeed in this situation, Briggs had to learn to read a room. "It was more or less a psychological judgment that I used," he said. "I could almost see by the expressions of certain clients what I should play for them. . . . That was one of the main points an orchestra leader had to think of. You were playing for a certain type of people. If you're playing in a dance hall, you're far away from the public. But if you're playing in a cabaret where you're right next to them, you have to try and find out what they want, and give it to them. . . . We played 'Bugle Call Rag.' We had another very, very fine number. It was called 'Up and At 'Em.' Those numbers you would choose when to play them. If you had some youngsters in the place, you'd know when you could use them, you see. But in general, the Germans loved authentic music, melody. Melody with a little beat."[9]

For Briggs, music was communication. When he was with a hip crowd, he'd cut loose and play as hot as he liked, but if his audience had square tastes, he'd play them square music. And in truth, he liked playing it all. No matter where your musical taste lived, he'd meet you there and play you something worth hearing.

This sensitivity served him well. Early in 1927, the owner of the Barberina opened a new club called the Valencia and hired a French jazz band to perform. The band had a disastrous opening, and Briggs was called in to help. He arrived to find the dance floor empty and the band confused.

"I don't understand," conductor Jean Yatove said to Briggs. "We played our best repertoire."

Briggs looked at the band's scores and saw nothing but American jazz. "Have you thought of playing the song 'Valencia'?" Briggs asked. The club had been named for the song, and Briggs knew it would go over well. But "Valencia" was a puff piece, a pasodoble recently recorded by Paul Whiteman, one of the biggest and squarest musicians in America.

"Arthur, you know we don't play that kind of stuff," Yatove retorted.

"My little Jean, when we play for the public to make a living, we play what the public wants and not what the musician wants."

One can practically see Briggs patting Yatove on the cheek as he said this. He was the elder master, all of twenty-five years old, teaching the fiery youngster how to put the audience's needs before his own. As Yatove's band played "Valencia," Briggs sang a few choruses into the microphone. He left Yatove with more words of wisdom: "Drop the arrangements of the songs you made, because no one knows them. If you see that the customers fill the whole room to dance and even go outside, continue as long as possible to tire them, and after, play a set of slow pieces so that they can rest." As soon as he returned to the Barberina, Briggs received a phone call from the Valencia's manager telling him that the "customers had applauded as never before" and inviting the Savoys and Glasner to the Valencia for a drink after work.[10]

Glasner was so impressed with Briggs's professionalism she invited several of Berlin's top bandleaders to the Barberina to watch him perform—men such as Marek Weber, Dajos Béla, Ephraim Schachtmeister, and Norbert Fraconi. Knowing these men would be in the audience, Briggs decided to perform an "ambitious piece with a big solo to dazzle them a little."[11] He never could resist a chance to show off.

During his days in Vienna, he was introduced to "The Trumpeter of Säckingen," a virtuoso piece for trumpet but in a different way than the "Carnival of Venice." The melody of "Säckingen" is pretty and languorous, requiring the trumpeter to hold out repeated long notes with feeling and then, eight bars before the end, execute an interval of a tenth. To understand how difficult this is one must consider that the slightest change in lip pressure can produce several different notes on a trumpet, regardless of the fingering. After tiring the lips with repeated long notes, to hit such a wide interval required a master's precision.

According to legend, only two trumpeters had ever played the piece successfully. Briggs intended to make it three.

At the end of his set, he quietly stood at the back of the room. The Savoys played the introduction on the bandstand, and he joined them "very slowly, as an echo." Recognizing the melody, the audience burst into thunderous applause and didn't stop until Glasner called for quiet. Briggs noted the reaction. He played the melody with tenderness, caressing each phrase, and when he reached the interval of the tenth, he not only hit it, but he held it four counts longer than written "to prove that it's just a matter of flexibility and self-confidence."[12]

The applause came in torrents and didn't let up until an elegantly dressed man came forward and shouted, "Champagne for everyone!" The man bought dinner for the whole house, and the evening ended in bacchanal. The wee hours of the morning found Briggs back in his hotel room, ears ringing with applause, blood surging with adrenaline. "It was a feat," he said.[13]

18

"We were only interested in getting ourselves on wax."

—Arthur Briggs

AFTER YEARS SPENT IN CABARETS and dance halls, where the proof of his prowess existed only as echo and memory, Arthur Briggs finally etched his name on wax. In January 1927, Ellie Glasner helped set up his first recording date with Vox-Schallplaten-und Sprechmaschinen-AG, a German label that specialized in piano rolls and phonograph records.

Recording technology was primitive, and Briggs found the process tedious. At a typical session, one microphone was placed at the front of the room, and the band had to spend hours positioning and repositioning themselves around it, searching for the perfect mix. Softer instruments such as clarinets were placed closer to the microphone. Louder instruments such as trumpets were placed farther back. A full drum set was almost never used because it overpowered the other musicians. As the band played, the force of the music coming into the microphone vibrated a stylus that etched the sound onto a wax master record. The Savoys had to nail each song in one take. If anything went wrong, the whole thing was scrapped and started again.

Briggs and the Savoys cut two titles at their first session but released only one, a bouncing foxtrot called "It Made You Happy." When European jazz fans dropped the needle, they heard Briggs's voice, young and eager, saying, "How do you do everybody? This is Arthur Briggs and his band playing for you. The name of this tune is 'It Made You Happy When You Made Me Cry.'" On the cut, Briggs plays tunefully, but one senses a certain reservation, as if he and the Savoys are still holding back for a dinner crowd.

This reservation is even more pronounced when comparing it to Briggs's next recording, "Bugle Call Rag." Though the Savoys cut the song just two months after "It Made You Happy," they sound like a different band. Again, the record starts with Briggs's eager voice: "Hello everybody, this is Arthur Briggs and his band playing. Get ready to shake your hips to the 'Bugle Call Rag!' Are you ready boys?" to which the band shouts, "Yes!" Then Briggs blows a clarion call on his trumpet, an exhilirating three-note phrase repeated twice, and the Savoys drop in behind him. This time, Briggs dances around the rhythm, alternating bluesy lip slides with punchy bursts of sound. He has the *fire*.

Something had indeed changed while Briggs was making these recordings: black American jazz records began to be distributed globally. Briggs made a deal with the local record store to set aside all new records until he had a chance to hear them. "I went to visit [the store] at least once a week," he said. "I'd listen and buy those that were good."[1] In mid 1927, Briggs was particularly struck by Duke Ellington's "East Saint Louis Toodle-Oo," one of those rare works whose brilliance time cannot touch. Briggs asked the clerk to play it over and over again as he listened in fascination. Briggs also loved Fletcher Henderson, Frankie Trumbauer, and Red Nichols. Meanwhile, Louis Armstrong, "the king of us all" as Briggs called him, produced seminal recordings with the Hot Five and Hot Seven. On songs such as "Heebie Jeebies" and "Potato Head Blues" he showed himself to have no peers. As trumpeter Max Kaminsky said of Armstrong's playing, "I felt as if I had stared into the sun's eye."[2] Within a year Armstrong hit his peak, creating a body of work against which he and everyone who came after him would be measured.

As Briggs absorbed these cutting-edge records, he began to play differently. "It was not a direct copy," he said, "but it was just [a] certain influence. I was trying to find my path between what I heard and what I felt myself."[3] Briggs made eleven recording dates in the first three months of 1927, navigating this new artistic path, all while keeping his nights booked at the Barberina.

By June, he was back in the studio helping his German friends make their first attempts at jazz music. The records he played on with Dajos Béla in particular provide a fascinating contrast with the Savoys. As

Béla's band plays, one can hear the German classical sense of rhythm struggling to incorporate jazz's polyrhythmic feel. The musicians play the notes but not the spaces between the notes. Briggs's playing on these cuts is like sunlight breaking through the clouds.

Briggs knew the German bands weren't great, but he was happy to help his friends get better, happy to earn a living, and happy to help the music get born. No gig was too small—Briggs even recorded a commercial record for the Bottina shoe company. On the record, a childlike voice praises Bottina shoes as *"gut, schick, billig"* [good, elegant, inexpensive], and Briggs kicks in with an instrumental called the "Bottina Shimmy." He'd soon do something similar for Dresden's Eg-Gü shoe polish.

In September, Briggs re-formed the Savoys for a gig at the Eden Hotel and signed a contract to record one hundred sides for Germany's largest recording company, Deutsche Grammophon Gesellschaft. Ultimately, sixty-four titles would be released, including excellent cuts such as "Hallelujah," "Miss Annabelle Lee," "Ain't She Sweet," and "Dulcinea." Briggs had also just heard Fletcher Henderson's recording of "I'm Coming Virginia," a hit song with lyrics by Will Marion Cook, and he decided to pay tribute to his old mentor with an excellent version of his own. Many of these records were distributed worldwide. As jazz historians Rainer Lotz and Horst Bergmeier wrote, "The discs are considered to be among the best jazz recorded during the Weimar Republic."[4]

Briggs might have made the best jazz in the Weimar Republic, but to gauge his place in jazz, one must judge him beside his American contemporaries. This is hard to do, especially because he was cut off from American talent for most of his career. But, listening to these early records, it is clear that Briggs had more in common with Red Nichols than he did with Armstrong or Beiderbecke. At the time, Nichols was among the most respected trumpeters in the world. Many early jazz critics considered him Armstrong's superior. Of course, this was a wild miscalculation, born in part from the effects of American segregation— many white jazz critics were ignorant of black jazz, and many others simply couldn't understand it. Nichols was undoubtedly a masterful player, but he did not possess Armstrong's genius or daring.

Briggs had the talent to compete with any player in America, but like Nichols, he never quite made the leap of vision to be considered an innovator. Had he stayed in America, it is possible he would have made this leap. Instead, despite making many remarkable recordings, his most important role was jazz ambassador, teaching European musicians and audiences alike to speak a new musical language. This role brought Briggs less personal glory, but it was more vital for the music as a whole, and the music was always his main concern.

Ultimately, Briggs's best playing was done live and never captured on recording. The only way, then, to truly judge him is to listen to a peer who saw him live in his prime. The American trumpeter and bandleader Doc Cheatham was one such man. He came to Europe in 1928 and became Briggs's close friend. Recalling Briggs in those days, he marveled, "He could do anything. He was upsetting. There was nobody like him."[5]

19

"You may not be interested in war, but war is interested in you."

—Leon Trotsky

SOMETHING WAS WRONG IN VIENNA. When Josephine Baker arrived in the city on a world tour scheduled by her lover-manager Pepito Abatino that took her to twenty-five countries in two years, she was greeted like a natural disaster. Every lamppost in the city was festooned and every wall was plastered with huge posters showing Baker, the Black Pearl, naked except for a string of pearls and an ostrich feather. Newspapers published lurid tales of her life in Paris, including details of her many sexual affairs. St. Paul's Catholic church announced it would ring its bells the moment she arrived, warning good Christians to stay off the streets so they didn't accidentally see this "demon of immorality."[1] Vienna's nascent Nazi party pressured the City Council to bar her from performing at her scheduled venue. She rented a new theater, but it wasn't ready for a month, during which time the Nazis took their complaints to Austrian Parliament and petitioned the minister of the interior, claiming to have received thousands of letters protesting Baker and her "brazen-faced heathen dances."[2]

Baker faced similar treatment all over Europe. In Hungary, a group of protestors threw ammonia bombs onstage and shouted "Go back to Africa!" She was contracted to appear in Munich, but the Munich press, which was largely Nazi controlled, demanded that she be deported as an undesirable alien, and the police barred her from performing. She returned to Berlin in a show that had two Jewish producers and appeared alongside the blond singer and actress Lea Seidl. On opening night, Seidl was onstage when a large group of Nazi sympathizers began to hoot and whistle. Her costar whispered, "This is terrible. Oh God, they will kill us." A Nazi critic wrote, "How dare they put our beautiful blonde Lea Seidl with a negress on the stage?" Between incessant Nazi heckling and vilification in the right-wing press, Baker was frightened. Three weeks into the show's run, she stood in the wings wearing an elegant chinchilla street coat and carrying a sack over her shoulder. Catching Seidl's eye, she whispered, "Don't say anything. I disappear."[3] She and Abatino fled, causing the show to close.

Baker wasn't the only one disrupted. Weeks before Baker arrived in Vienna, Arthur Briggs was scheduled to perform jazz adaptations of popular songs at the Konzerthaus, home of the Vienna Symphony. The Viennese Nazis saw this as an affront to their city's history as the home of Mozart, Mahler, Strauss, Schubert, and Haydn. They were still reeling from the appearance of Ernst Krenek's jazz-opera *Jonny spielt auf,* which depicted a black jazz violinist who boasted of his sexual power over white women. "Our State Opera has fallen victim to an insolent Jewish-Negro blemish," read a call for protest demonstrations when Briggs arrived.[4] Days later, the *Wiener Allgemeinen Zeitung,* a Viennese newspaper, ran a cartoon featuring a racist caricature of Briggs and Baker together. Instead of appearing at the Konzerthaus, Briggs was forced to accept another engagement at the Weihburg Bar.

For all the noise they made, the Nazis were a blip on Germany's political radar. In the national election of May 1928, they won less than 3 percent of the vote, and they fared no better at the state level. Briggs undertook a tour of Germany during this election, but he had no reason to note the machinations of a tiny fringe party in a foreign land. He enjoyed performing in Hamburg, Breslau, Leipzig, Stuttgart, Cologne, Düsseldorf, Nuremberg, and Saarbrücken. It was the most extensive tour he'd done since his days in the New York Syncopated Orchestra, but despite his wide travels, he did not see, as Baker had seen, the forces of chaos amassing on the horizon.

20

"Somebody had blundered and the most expensive orgy in history was over."[1]

—F. Scott Fitzgerald

AFTER HIS GERMAN TOUR, ARTHUR BRIGGS returned to Paris without the Savoy Syncopators. The band that had been his main concern for the past six years split up, never to re-form. In March 1929, he put together a new group called Arthur Briggs and His Black Boys, although half the musicians were white, and began a residency on Place Pigalle at L'Abbaye Thélème.

Named for the famous "antichurch" in Rabelais's *Gargantua and Pantagruel*, the Abbaye had been a hedonistic haunt of artists and misfits since the late 1800s, taking as its motto, "Do what you will." By 1929, it was among the most famous cabarets in the world. The room Briggs played formed a rough pentagon, with tables lining the perimeter and chairs situated with their backs to the wall looking out at the dance floor. The walls were painted a shade of lavender so light it was almost white; the carpet was of rich green velvet. Six imposing electric chandeliers hung from the ceiling, bathing the room in a ghostly glow common to churches and brothels. Ventilation was so poor Josephine Baker later blamed the Abbaye for a case of bronchial pneumonia that nearly killed her.

If Briggs ignored the rumblings of rising nationalism in Germany and Vienna, he couldn't help but feel them when he returned home. France had begun limiting the number of foreign musicians allowed in each band, and during one Black Boys rehearsal, Briggs noticed a labor inspector darkening the door. Seeing two Belgians in the band, the inspector ordered Briggs to stop the music. He had a band of French union musicians waiting outside, and he intended for them to take over Briggs's job. When they entered the room, the Abbaye's manager told them, "If you don't leave immediately, you'll end up in Pigalle Square with bruised asses." The union band left in a hurry. Then the manager told Briggs, "If you want to temporarily replace the three musicians in question, I will pay them more, but on the condition that they are not members of the musician union!"[2] It seems he didn't appreciate the intrusion any more than Briggs did.

Briggs always hated being told who to play with, but at least he got to choose his replacements. In April, he ditched the Belgians and recorded eight sides with the Black Boys for the French Azuréphone label. In May he was offered a second job when impresario Lew Leslie brought his hit Broadway revue, *Blackbirds of 1928*, to the Moulin Rouge. Leslie was a white man but was one of the first producers to present black performers on Broadway. In temperament, he was like Will Marion Cook, only more erratic. It was not uncommon for Leslie to jump into the orchestra pit in the middle of a show, oust the conductor, and take over, though he knew nothing about music. "His habits of changing the running order of his shows, hiring and firing his performers on a whim, and changing costumes and scenery for no apparent reason during a run were legendary," wrote one historian. "In fact, on his printed programs it was not uncommon to find his nota bene, PROGRAM SUBJECT TO CHANGE OWING TO MAGNITUDE OF PRODUCTION."[3]

Leslie's lead trumpeter, a man named Luke Smith, couldn't handle the workload, so Leslie asked Briggs to try out for the spot. One morning Briggs dropped by the Moulin Rouge for what he assumed was an informal audition. To his surprise, the entire company awaited him. Leslie plunked down the score for the third act and began to conduct. Twenty minutes in, Smith dropped his trumpet in exhaustion. As the band raced headlong toward the climax, going at a "crazy tempo," Briggs had to handle the lead trumpet by himself.

The final song was "Digga Digga Doo," a complicated piece played at a breakneck tempo. "I was sight reading," Briggs said. "I had never seen this piece in my life."[4] Near the end of the song, the trumpet had to play a note so high Briggs had never seen it written before. Not only that, he had to play it four times in a row and then hold it eight bars to the finish. "Obviously the whole orchestra was watching me," he said, "and I came out brilliantly." The entire production erupted with applause.[5]

Leslie might have come from New York, but he had never seen anyone like Arthur Briggs. He hired Briggs with four words: "Your conditions are mine." Handed a blank check, Briggs proved his belief in the brotherhood of musicians was more than empty talk. He refused to take more money than Smith out of solidarity, saying, "Arrange it with Mr. Smith; what he decides is fine."[6]

Blackbirds was the biggest revue Briggs had ever performed with, featuring dancers, singers, actors, musicians, and even magicians. Briggs especially enjoyed Peg-Leg Bates, a one-legged dancer who had a different wooden leg to match each costume, and the Berry Brothers, magicians "who could have taught you how to make thousands of dollars by pulling the Ace of Spades from your sleeve."[7] The undisputed star of the show was Adelaide Hall. She had taken her first steps onstage as a chorus girl in *Shuffle Along* in 1921 and quickly became a legend on Broadway. With Duke Ellington's 1927 hit "Creole Love Call," she began a recording career that spanned eight decades. When she arrived in Paris, she was thronged by a mob of fans and reporters, and her popularity grew to rival Josephine Baker's. When *Blackbirds* opened in June, a four-story-tall illuminated likeness of Hall towered over the Moulin Rouge. After a triumphant opening night, the cast caroused at Bricktop's, where Briggs said, "they tried to kill me with alcohol, but I wasn't drinking."[8]

Briggs stayed with the *Blackbirds* for three months, during which time he doubled at the Abbaye. He'd start his evenings at the Moulin Rouge, play until 11:30 PM, and then walk five minutes downhill on the Boulevard de Clichy to the Abbaye, where he and the Black Boys played into the wee hours of the morning. He cut a unique figure, dressed to the nines in a tuxedo and overcoat, trumpet case clutched under his arm, making his nightly stroll through the seedy red-light district where he had found, against all odds, a dignified, rarified life.

Just when he might have settled in Paris, however, Briggs received a telegram offering him $300 a week to conduct Noble Sissle's touring band. Briggs was happy to hear an old name—Sissle was James Reese Europe's lieutenant in the Harlem Hellfighters, as well as a cocreator of *Shuffle Along*—and happier to play for that kind of money. Everything was going his way. He took the job, not knowing he was going to need all the money he could get.

Days later, the London Stock Market crashed. Then, on October 29, the New York Stock Exchange experienced the single worst collapse in American history. Fourteen billion dollars vanished in one day. Grown men jumped out of skyscraper windows. The world plunged into panic. Just like that, the Roaring Twenties—the formative period of Arthur Briggs's life, with its travels and travails, its love affairs and friendships, its new languages and new countries, its record dates and cabaret nights—was over. It was a sudden disaster, as if an entire generation had suffered a stroke. F. Scott Fitzgerald, poet of the Jazz Age, gave voice to the grief: "Now once more the belt is tight and we summon the proper expression of horror as we look back at our wasted youth," he wrote.

> Sometimes, though, there is a ghostly rumble among the drums, an asthmatic whisper in the trombones that swings me back into the early twenties when . . . it seemed only a question of a few years before the older people would step aside and let the world be run by those who saw things as they were—and it all seems rosy and romantic to us who were young then, because we will never feel quite so intensely about our surroundings any more.[9]

Part II

*"Behold, He withholdeth the waters, and they dry up;
also He sendeth them out, and they overturn the earth."*

—Job 12:15

21

March 1, 1930

THE RAIN CAME. IN SOUTHWEST FRANCE, six weeks' worth fell in two days. At Montauban and Moissac on the River Tarn, the water was already high, as warm weather melted the snow on the mountains. Like a drunkard, the river consumed rain and snow. It swelled and shattered its levees and unleashed a wall of water as lethal and relentless as fire. When at last the flood receded, sixteen thousand people were homeless; one hundred and forty-five were dead. The destruction was unimaginable, as if God himself had accidentally stepped on the world and crushed it all to rubble.

In April, Arthur Briggs joined Noble Sissle and his Sissling Syncopators at the Théâtre des Champs-Élysées for a concert to benefit the flood victims, where the band stormed through a showstopping rendition of "The Battle of Jericho." The concert also boasted a fifty-seven-piece orchestra and an appearance by Cricket Smith, whom Briggs hadn't seen in years. Uncle Cricket had joined an old-fashioned minstrel band, which made an incongruous pair with Noble Sissle, who always refused to appear in blackface or to have any show of his associated with it.

Briggs and Sissle were cut from the same cloth. Sissle was proper, upright, and dignified. According to one historian, he blended the traits of "a sternish uncle, a jovial headmaster, and a conscientious sergeant major." He demanded his musicians be "as clean as the white gloves he always wore to conduct."[1] Briggs respected Sissle and bristled when recalling the way some musicians cast slurs on Sissle's name: "Sissle was one of our most fortunate boys," Briggs said.

He had a very, very fine education, and he knew how to take care of himself and how to treat people. He was a fine person. I had no difficulties with him at all. He was fair. When he promised you a certain sum, he'd pay you. . . . And I had heard of certain musicians—I won't mention the names—who made remarks, one of them wrote a book even, and he said Noble Sissle's band was Uncle Tom and that the music was awful. Well, having played with Sissle, I'd say that guy, I don't know how he got into Noble's band.[2]

True, Sissle wasn't a musician, but as Briggs noted, "he didn't try to say that he was." He was a performer, lyricist, and businessman. That's why he hired Briggs.

Briggs recalled his duties proudly: "Leading the attractions in an orchestra like Noble Sissle's is a very important role. It was necessary to have a sense of organization, memory, precision, and great feeling also." Briggs had spent the better part of a decade developing these skills. If anything, he was overqualified for the job.[3]

In June, the band opened at one of the most demanding cabarets in the world, Les Ambassadeurs. As a newspaper review noted, the cabaret had a "knowing and difficult clientele [of] multi-millionaires, statesmen, kings, prime ministers, diplomats, kings of commerce." This jaded crowd had seen it all, but the review continued: "Noble Sissle knows his business, and even to a psychologist it is astonishing to see the gathering at dinner change from a rather staid and even bored appearance at first to one of real gayety under his touch."[4] Perhaps the touch was Sissle's, but Briggs's fingerprints were all over it.

At the Ambassadeurs, Briggs was thrown into a world of elegance, performing for Lord and Lady Mountbatten, the Maharajah of Kapurthala, Baroness Eugene de Rothschild, and American car mogul George Dodge. He also headed a delegation sent to entertain the Prince of Wales at the French seaside resort Le Touquet, and he performed for Aga Khan III, imam of the second-largest branch of Shia Islam, who threw lavish parties at the impossibly posh restaurant Le Pré Catelan. As an old man recalling these days, Briggs still sparkled. According to his son-in-law Denis Pierrat, who transcribed his spoken memoirs,

"One hears while listening to the tape that Arthur is in paradise at that moment. All he likes is here: the beautiful world, the beautiful manners, the beautiful scenery, the magnificent gardens, the class." Briggs had come a long way from St. George's, Grenada. He now moved freely among what he called "the elite of the world."[5]

Briggs and Sissle also attracted a young crowd to the Ambassadeurs. One of these young men, an insolent jazz fanatic, approached Briggs and asked, "Why don't you play real jazz like Mezz Mezzrow?" Mezzrow was a middling clarinet and saxophone player from Chicago, more famous for dealing marijuana than for making music. He became a darling of white jazz critics who lacked the sophistication to know better. "The question seemed absurd," Briggs said.[6] He dismissed the young man.

Briggs had just met Hugues Panassié, who would soon change the history of jazz in Europe. Panassié was not a musician, but he was the next best thing: a tireless promoter. In later years, he led the Hot Club de France, a group of die-hard jazz lovers responsible for Europe's greatest contributions to the form. His methods were not without controversy: he was called "a jazz dictator" and "the self-chosen Pope of Jazz."[7] But as Goddard testified, "Even though France may not have been a country where jazz history was made, it was certainly the place where it was first written about. The man who, single-handedly, was responsible for this was Hugues Panassié."[8]

At the Ambassadeurs, Briggs also ran into his old friend Robert Goffin, who recalled the engagement with yet another misty ode:

It was you Briggs, who helped me to better love all those soaring airs: "Chili Bom Bom," "My Lovey Come Back," "Capitole," "My Buddy," "Minding My Business," "Who's Sorry Now," "Everybody Loves My Baby," and also "Maybe," that more than one abandoned lover sang mournfully with you. Dear Arthur Briggs . . . you were in Vienna where Lili Damita kissed you on the mouth; you were in Budapest, where the enchanted island of Saint Marguerite went down to the Danube; you were in Constantinople where the muezzins, terrified to have heard you, shouted louder in the night; you were in Berlin where a real countess wanted to sell her racing team to follow you from capital to capital; you were in Paris where I came to surprise you one evening while you played the "Japanese Sandman" . . . and it was at the little tobacco stand in the Place Blanche that we spoke again of all that we liked. Today, my dear Briggs you play with Noble Sissle, and I really want to hear you again. See you soon dear friend and do not forget the old "New Orleans" formula that we discovered together.[9]

Here Goffin gives the only glimpse into Briggs's relationships with women, showing the great trumpeter as a virile, famous, desired man, leaving melancholy lovers in his wake, being chased by a German countess and kissing a beautiful actress on the mouth. Only one other fact remains of Briggs's love life at the time: in 1930, he met a Belgian woman named Georgina Dageleer and fell in love. Little is known of Dageleer except that she lived with Briggs in France and befriended Bricktop. Less is known of their relationship. Briggs claimed in an interview to have married her near the end of 1930, but records show they actually married a decade later, for reasons we will see. During the '30s, the couple lived together in the kind of relationship artistic types are wont to have, considering themselves married in spirit if not by law.

Georgina soon learned that being married to a musician was a lonely life. In November, Briggs left to England for nearly two months of shows. It was a fitting bookend to his first trip a decade earlier: he came to London in 1919 with the Southern Syncopators as a kid trying to make his way in the world; he returned in 1930 with the Sissling Syncopators as the premiere jazz trumpeter in Europe.

Much else had changed since 1919. London was reeling from the collapse of its stock exchange, and the British musicians' union now cracked down on foreign bands. On a positive note, film technology had advanced, making it possible for the band to record for British Pathé, the famous producer of newsreels and documentaries. As the only footage of Briggs featuring sound, it is a crucial document. In the film, Sissle stands center stage wearing a sharply cut black tuxedo and tails. His nine musicians form an arc behind him, Briggs to his right. The music is a shade behind the times, at least compared to the vanguard of American jazz in 1929, but the orchestra is as tight as a drum skin. Sissle sings

"Little White Lies" convincingly enough, followed by an instrumental break, and then Jack Carter sidles from behind his drums and stands over Briggs's left shoulder to sing a rousing version of "Happy Feet." Carter rushes back behind his kit and the band kicks into double time as tuba player Eddie Cole steps out front for a furious tap-dance routine. Watching Cole, one understands the importance of dance in jazz history. Tap dancers taught drummers to syncopate the beat along with their feet, and this syncopated style became the hallmark of jazz drumming.

Unfortunately, Briggs does not take a solo during the video. In an orchestra like Sissle's, the lead trumpeter rarely did. As Doc Cheatham explained, "Playing lead in those days was a tough job. You needed all the rest you could get. The only opportunity you got to lay out was when somebody else was soloing. . . . There weren't too many trumpet players back then who could play lead. And out of those there were even fewer who *wanted* to."[10] This is part of why Louis Armstrong was so revolutionary. He combined soloist and lead trumpeter into one. Briggs had the ability to do the same: as trumpeter Bill Coleman said, "Briggs was a first-chair man, but he could play things at a jam session that made everybody know that he could also take hot choruses, a thing very few first trumpeters in a section could do." But in Sissle's band, Briggs was a standard lead man. He did the hardest work and got the least glory. It fit his temperament.

Despite his lack of solos with Sissle, Briggs became a star in England and began to gain fans in America. With Sissle, he performed on four live broadcasts for the BBC and cut four sides for Columbia Records, while the band's every movement was reported breathlessly in African American newspapers. To capitalize on the success in America, Sissle booked a six-month tour to start just before Christmas 1930. Despite Briggs's distaste for his former home, he left Georgina and boarded the CGT liner *Paris* in mid-December for another trip across the Atlantic Ocean.

Briggs reached Ellis Island three days before Christmas. For the third time, he gazed up at the Statue of Liberty. For the third time, he went through customs, this time listing his profession as "artist." His sister Edith had moved to the country, and he listed her address as his intended destination. For the third time, he took the ferry to Manhattan.

He was no longer the boy of sixteen, nervous and alone at America's doorstep. He knew what to expect—the segregated subway car, the glory of Grand Central Terminal, the sounds and smells of Harlem. But the city, and the country, had changed in ways he could not imagine.

22

"Working in America will kill you."[1]

—Arthur Briggs

It was Christmas Eve, and Harlem wore a mantle of white. Four inches of snow had fallen overnight, while Arthur Briggs awaited the biggest show he'd ever play in his old hometown. The band opened at the Rockland Palace, formerly the Manhattan Casino, where Briggs had performed as a teenager. The Palace was one of the first gay-friendly establishments in Harlem; it famously hosted the Hamilton drag balls, where a cash prize was awarded for best costume (Josephine Baker was a perennial favorite costume). It also hosted banquets thrown by Father Divine, a man who claimed to be God.

Opening night hummed with holiday spirit. Sidney Bechet joined the band at Sissle's invitation, adding a formidable weapon to an already powerful arsenal. Jelly Roll Morton showed up and tried to poach Bechet and trumpeter Tommy Ladnier for his band, and though he didn't succeed, his appearance gives testament to the level of talent Briggs was with. Morton claimed to have invented jazz, and he wasn't far from the mark. His "Jelly Roll Blues" is widely considered the first jazz composition ever published.

For Briggs it was a time of reconnection. He was back with his sisters, back with Bechet, back in Harlem. It was also a time to reflect on how far both he and Harlem had come. He wasn't the Kid anymore: he led the band, and Bechet looked to him for direction. Harlem wasn't the second city anymore: it had stolen Chicago's crown as the jazz capital of America, and clubs crowded the streets like racehorses jostling for position.

On Seventh Avenue—Heaven, as it was called—stood Smalls Paradise, the Club Hot-Cha, the Clam House, the Log Cabin, and the Yeah Man. On Lenox were the Radium Club, the Savoy, and the Cotton Club, where Cab Calloway and his band replaced Duke Ellington when Duke was touring. At the Theatrical Grill on 133rd Street, Garland Wilson pounded boogie-woogie on the piano. Near the corner of 131st Street and Lenox Avenue, the reefer man sold two joints for a quarter. Sitting silently like dark matter amid this scene were five hundred speakeasies.

On West 134th Street, if Briggs caught the angle just right, he could see two new skyscrapers rising in the distance above the Midtown skyline. The Chrysler Building had just been completed, and it held the title of world's tallest building for eleven months, until the Empire State Building, still under construction when he arrived, thrust its point 408 feet higher. By the time it was finished, no one had money to rent it. Floor upon floor remained empty. The building was a giant tombstone: Here Lies Roaring Twenties Excess.

During his days off, Briggs checked in at the Clef and Amsterdam clubs "to see if the situation was still as bad as in 1922."[2] To his delight, he found that black musicians in Harlem no longer struggled to find work, but this was a small relief. Everyone else was struggling mightily. One in four Harlem residents was out of work in 1930, compared to one in ten nationally. In coming years, Roosevelt's New Deal largely ignored black neighborhoods. A massive project in New York City resulted in the creation of 255 public parks; only one was built in Harlem. Langston Hughes wrote, "The Depression brought everybody down a peg or two, and the Negroes had but few pegs to fall."[3]

In the cold pit of winter, Briggs climbed aboard a bus and spent four months touring Depression-scarred America. The band stopped in Chicago, where Eddie Cole brought them to his house. Cole's father was a Baptist minister, and Briggs attended a service, where Cole's brother—an eleven-year-old Nat King Cole—played organ. "He really had the gift," Briggs said. After the service, minister Cole offered the band a "sumptuous banquet" of down-home cooking: corn, sweet potatoes, cranberry sauce, and turkey. "It was a wonderful day of rest for us," Briggs said.[4]

In late January the band swung back through New York to record several sides for the Brunswick label—the only recordings featuring Briggs and Bechet together—and then spent seven days in Philadelphia at the ritzy Pearl Theatre. There, Briggs heard of a young pianist named Count Basie, whose band "was said to be the hottest orchestra this side of hell." He stayed an extra day to see for himself and said, "It was a great moment, you can believe me."[5]

Briggs was connected to the mainspring of American jazz at another crucial moment in its development. *Swing* was the new word as band-leaders such as Basie, Armstrong, Ellington, and Glenn Miller pushed jazz into a new rhythmic era. The old two-beat style of jazz Briggs grew up with was all but exhausted. Swing was a four-beat music; it was more relaxed than the proto-march syncopation of ragtime. One thing hadn't changed, however. As swing passed into mainstream American culture, it was white musicians such as Miller who made most of the money and received most of the acclaim.

At least Miller was a great player. Briggs was shocked to see how many hacks abounded in America and saddened at what had happened to great men like his old mentor Edmund Jenkins. Briggs gave a rare glimpse of his emotions, saying,

> It broke my heart. Edmund Jenkins worked at the Queens Hall just to make some money, you know, playing clarinet with Jack Hilton and his piano player, a very bad one too. . . . I'm just telling you the way I feel, because those guys, what made me mad with them at the time, they were so what you call dicty and high-toned, you know, snobs. And if everything went together and they had the talent with it, it would be a different thing, but they had no talent at all. They were just taking all the money. One thing I could never understand: how the booking agents committed such robbery. . . . I don't want to criticize, but we were not [white bandleader] Guy Lombardo, 'cause those guys are hardheaded. They wouldn't learn. They didn't try to amelio-rate the situation. I imagine they still play the same way today. They're awful. I mean they have no feeling or nothing. . . . No culture, nothing. The majority of those booking agents were that

way. I don't want to say too much because if I really start picking show business to pieces it'll be an awful thing.[6]

As for Sissle's band, Briggs spoke with pride: "We had the top work; we were not conning."[7]

Seeing such suffering hardened Briggs's heart against America. When Sissle took the band through the Deep South this hardness calcified. Briggs thought he knew segregation, but in the North he had only seen a weak strain of the disease. In Miami, Briggs recalled hotels bearing signs that read FORBIDDEN TO JEWS and JEWS AND NEGROES, GO AWAY. In Atlanta, the entrance to a public park read YOU NIGGERS WHO READ THIS SIGN, RUN AWAY. IF YOU CAN'T READ, RUN FASTER![8] For Sissle, this was nothing new. During his army training in Spartanburg, South Carolina, he was viciously attacked in a hotel for failing to remove his hat in the lobby. For Briggs, however, it was a bitter experience. He later called America the "world champion of hypocrisy."[9]

The work was harder in the South too, where people "liked to dance and wanted their music loud." The band took extended solos, which Sissle encouraged. "He'd keep us swinging without ever knowing that your lip couldn't always take it," Briggs said. "He'd call on someone saying, 'Brother so-and-so, lead us in prayer.'"[10] The younger cats, like Tommy Ladnier, blew as hard as they could, believing technique to be the enemy of swing. Only when their lips split open did they come to Briggs, the technique master, for advice.

The band returned to New York near Briggs's thirtieth birthday. They played the Princess Restaurant on Fifth Avenue and doubled at the Hippodrome Theatre in Midtown Manhattan, where Harry Houdini once made an elephant disappear. Briggs started at the Hippodrome at 9:00 AM and worked seventeen or eighteen hours straight. After work, he and the band dined in Harlem, "and for those who liked it, [drank] prohibition alcohol." Briggs recalled, "It was dangerous because this alcohol could make you blind or paralyzed. The origin of the production was as dubious as four aces in a poker game; but despite that there were always some members of the orchestra who had a bottle on them all the time."[11] After dinner, they went to the "gin mills" to "drink and jam and drink some more."[12] After a few precious hours of sleep, they woke up and did it again.

Briggs did everything but drink. He had grown used to this lifestyle in Europe, but what seemed charming in Montmartre was unbearable in Manhattan. He described work in Europe as "human," saying, "We didn't need to make exhausting journeys like [America], where you have no choice, with impossible schedules and incessant travel without breaks."[13] He hated touring in America, hated living on a Greyhound bus, hated the endless distances traveling in a hostile land. Slogging through the snow reminded him of his first tour with Cook during the infamous Spanish Flu of 1918, only this time, in every city, lines of huddled, desperate men waited for bread. "I reckoned much more of that and my life would be considerably shortened," he said.[14]

Still, his last few days in New York were joyous. He met an old friend from the St. Mark's Brass Band and reminisced about Gladius Marshall, "that wonderful, very competent, humane man who accompanied us downtown (that is to say, in the rich, white Manhattan), to buy the props we needed: Desks, instrument boxes, etc."[15] He also ran into Cyril Mickens, his friend from the SSO and the *Blackbirds of 1928*, who greeted him in the French way—a kiss on each cheek. "We were like two brothers and so happy to find each other," Briggs said.[16]

As happy as he was to see his friends and family, Briggs couldn't wait to leave them. The trip had deepened his aversion to America, setting him up to make the most disasterous choice of his life. Had he not toured the States with Sissle, it is probable—perhaps even likely—that he would have escaped to Harlem ten years later when the Nazis threatened to invade France. As it happened, however, Briggs left America knowing he could not return.

Sissle took the band back to France in late April, and Briggs inhaled Paris like fresh air. For Sissle, however, Parisian air did not smell so sweet. French law now required half the musicians in every band to be French, and though Sissle worked out a deal with the Ambassadeurs to skirt the law, he ended the engagement early. He asked Briggs to return to America with him, but Briggs replied, "I can't go back. It's too hard."[17] Forty years would pass before Briggs set foot in America again. The final transformation of his life was complete. The man from Harlem, via St. George's, now belonged to Paris.

23

"Everybody came to Bricktop's."[1]

—Arthur Briggs

AFTER LEAVING NOBLE SISSLE'S BAND, Arthur Briggs bought a lavish villa in Bougival, a ritzy suburb of Paris akin to Beverly Hills in Los Angeles. Maurice Chevalier and Mistinguett lived nearby; Bricktop was a neighbor. "The dream of every performer was to have a place in the country," Bricktop said. "Maybe it was a need to have roots, because the performer's life was basically rootless."[2] With a wife and a permanent address, Briggs had roots for the first time in twelve years.

That summer, Bricktop took Briggs to her cabaret on the Côte d'Azur. He joined her band, which included two New Orleans players—the exceptional multi-instrumentalist Frank "Big Boy" Goudie, and Bricktop's husband Peter DuConge—as well as American pianist Freddy Johnson. Briggs particularly loved Johnson. "I consider him one of the best piano players I ever played with," he said. "It seemed like we worked like clockwork, without arrangements or anything else, without even saying anything to each other. We just felt each other, that's all."[3] Mabel Mercer, star of Parisian cabarets, also joined the band; she'd soon influence a young Frank Sinatra, who emulated her vocal phrasing. Then, of course, there was Bricktop herself, who always sang a few songs with the band. "We considered her our big sister," Briggs said. "I dare to say that [she] was the greatest hostess on the Place de Paris."[4] It was the most musically gifted band Briggs had played with.

No longer the girl from Le Grand Duc, Bricktop was now one of Montmartre's greatest attractions. In November she opened her own club at 66 Rue Pigalle in an intimate room that seated about one hundred people. The lighting was designed by fashion photographer George Hoyningen-Huene, who had just begun his seminal work with French *Vogue*. He lit the banquettes from behind and "created a cozy, kind of mysterious atmosphere." Bricktop chose red and black as her theme colors—the carpet was rich red, the banquettes red on black. "When it opened in November 1931," she recalled, "it was the talk of Paris."[5]

Bricktop's was a far cry from the juke joints in America. Briggs was again ensconced in an elite crowd of socialites and millionaires, including Ralph B. Strassburger, who often waltzed into the club and picked up everyone's tab, saying, "Brick, close the door; this is going to be my party tonight." Then there was Michael Farmer, Bricktop's favorite. If she wore a dress he didn't like, he'd rip it down the front and tell her to go to the finest store in Paris and buy a new one, saying, "I'll pay for it."[6]

These people "didn't have to play by the same rules as ordinary people," Bricktop said. "They did what they wanted when they wanted. If they wanted to smoke opium or sniff cocaine, they did it . . . [they] carried cocaine in little jeweled boxes. . . . They were all fooling around with each other. . . . It was all very incestuous, but of course that was the thing to do. They were having affairs and doing the same things people do now, but they had a more elegant way of doing it, my dear."[7]

The Prince of Wales regularly arrived with an entourage, got stoned, and dropped a pile of hundred-franc notes on the band. In return, they let him play drums on his favorite song, "I'm Putting All My Eggs in One Basket." Most nights, he waited to play until the other patrons left, but at private parties, he played all night if the mood struck him. Briggs had already performed for the future king twice, but now he became acquainted. "He was really wonderful," Briggs said. "His tempo was good. We didn't pay much attention to his left hand as long as he had what you call 'oom-cha.'"[8]

During these besotted nights, Briggs provided the soundtrack to one of the most famous love affairs in history, between the Prince of Wales and American socialite Wallis Simpson. Three years later, when the prince was crowned King Edward VIII, he informed the royal family of his intentions to marry Simpson, but they refused the match. In response, he abdicated the throne to marry "the woman I love."

No guest was more important at Bricktop's than Cole Porter. Bricktop reserved a table for him as she had done at Le Grand Duc, and when in Paris, he filled it nightly with friends. Porter was in the midst of writing the Broadway musical *Gay Divorce*, and one night, he arrived with the score for a new song under his arm. He handed it to the band and asked them to test it. When they finished, the club erupted with applause. Porter rushed the bandstand and kissed each musician on the cheek in the French way. The song was "Night and Day," today considered among Porter's greatest contributions to the Great American Songbook. Briggs was the first ever to perform it.

And yet, as heady as these nights were, something vital was missing. The Depression began to gut Montmartre of the artists, bohemians, and nouveau riche that propelled the Jazz Age. Hemingway and his crowd of geniuses vanished. Zelda Fitzgerald had to be institutionalized, and while Scott waited for her recovery, he wrote "Babylon Revisited," a fictional elegy to Montmarte following the loosely autobiographical protagonist Charlie Wales as he returns to his old haunts, including Bricktop's, to find them deserted. Fitzgerald captured the gaping sense of loss, writing, "[Charlie] was not really disappointed to find Paris was so empty. But the stillness in the Ritz bar was strange and portentous. It was not an American bar anymore—he felt polite in it, and not as if he owned it. It had gone back to France . . . he thought, 'I spoiled this city for myself. I didn't realize it, but the days came along one after another, and then two years were gone, and everything was gone, and I was gone.' . . . and he suddenly realized the meaning of the word 'dissipate'—to dissipate into thin air; to make nothing out of something."[9]

Only the super-rich could still grasp at the dream. Their revelry continued as before, but they didn't care about jazz. The music at Bricktop's was, as one historian described it, "audible wallpaper."[10] Even Briggs, who always enjoyed playing for the dinner crowd, found it difficult. "We had to control ourselves constantly and be careful to control our feelings," he said. "No question of being carried away by the love we had for certain pieces."[11]

There was also a sinister energy suffusing Europe. Its emblem was the Colonial Exhibition of May 1931, for which France gathered citizens of its colonies and shipped them to Paris to show off their beastly state and celebrate the good France had done in civilizing them. Many of these colonized citizens were displayed in the Human Zoo, sometimes half naked, in grand reproductions of their home countries.

Briggs came from colonized people. He left no record of his feelings about the exhibition, but he must have been aware of it, as it drew millions of visitors during its six-month run. The exhibition represented what many, if not most, people in France thought of Briggs and his culture. Meanwhile, a March 1931 article in *La Revue Musicale* called jazz the music of animals and sneered, "These savages must be suppressed."[12] Critics had been hurling racist jabs at jazz music since the beginning, calling the music a passing fad and worse. But now the fad was undeniably dead. As Briggs passed his thirty-first birthday, he had to work harder than ever to make sure the music didn't die too.

24

"To be a jazz lover in Paris . . . was like being an early Christian in Rome."[1]

—Charles Delaunay

HUDDLED LIKE CHRISTIANS IN CATACOMBS, a small group of believers gathered in Paris to profess their faith in jazz. They dubbed themselves the Hot Club de France. They were college students fueled by the zeal of youth, led by Hugues Panassié, a disciple baptized in the holy fire of *le jazz hot*. They proclaimed their mission in the November 1932 issue of *Jazz-Tango-Dancing* magazine: "First, organize the enthusiasts of hot jazz; and second, by spreading the word about jazz, aid it in becoming appreciated, defend it, and help it conquer the place it merits among the movements of artistic expression of our times."[2] They were voices crying out in the wilderness.

Meanwhile, Arthur Briggs had begun jamming with Bricktop's band after hours. They called themselves the Harlemites, and they played for three reasons: "To have fun, and stimulate each other, [and] to build a repertoire."[3] Panassié asked the Harlemites if they'd help the Hot Club, and though Briggs hadn't forgotten the young man who asked him the insolent question, "Why don't you play real jazz like Mezz Mezzrow?," he held no grudge. He agreed without hesitation.

The first Hot Club concert was held in the basement of a music store Briggs booked on loan from a friend. In the bitter cold, the Harlemites played to a mostly empty room. Rather presumptuously, the Hot Club issued membership cards: founder Panassié was member one, Freddy Johnson number two, and Briggs number three. Briggs loved it. He didn't care that he was considered the best trumpeter in Europe and was performing for a smattering of college students in a freezing basement. He didn't care that the Hot Club held concerts on Sundays at 9:00 AM, so he'd barely get to sleep after a night at Bricktop's before waking up and trudging to some dive to play for free. His love of jazz was unpretentious. He believed in the club's mission, so he donated his time and talent. He found it invigorating and fulfilling. "Now, just imagine how good we were," he boasted. "We were working at Chez Bricktop's every Saturday night, and at nine o'clock on Sunday morning we were in a concert hall playing. And for nothing. We were interested in the education of the public for our profession and for those who come after us, you see. The thing that we liked most was that we were totally free, and we could make the music we liked."[4]

At first the Hot Club struggled to find an audience. Panassié charged a nominal membership fee and rejected advertising. "There were ups and downs," Briggs said. "Either there were musicians who did not come, or we forgot to stick the posters and there was nobody. . . . The project was too idealistic." Soon, Panassié was joined by author and jazz fanatic Charles Delaunay, who became coleader of the Hot Club. Delaunay was born to the arts—his parents coinvented Orphism, an offshoot of Cubism—and in the early months of 1933, after "bitter discussions," he convinced Panassié to operate with a small budget, rent decent concert halls, and advertise their shows.[5] In May, they booked the Lafayette Square near Gare Du Nord, and more than one hundred people came.

Encouraged, the club sought to expand. Panassié rented the Salle Pleyel, a gorgeous concert hall on Rue Rochechouart that once hosted the premiere of Ravel's Sonata for Violin and Cello. The Harlemites filled it to capacity. They performed as the Hot Club Orchestra, featuring the great jazz singer and songwriter Alberta Hunter. "It was a beautiful moment," Briggs recalled.[6]

Days later, Briggs and Johnson were rehearsing when they caught the ear of music executive and talent agent Jacques Canetti. Briggs had met Canetti in Vienna nearly a decade before, back when Canetti "still wore short pants in the traditional Austrian fashion." He greeted Canetti as an old friend and explained to him in German who the Harlemites were and what they wanted to do. "The only thing that interested us," Briggs said, was "recording."[7]

Canetti was the artistic director of Brunswick Records. He extended an open invitation to Briggs and became the Harlemites' unofficial manager, drawing up a contract giving the band a percentage of their record sales. In June and July 1933, the Harlemites cut nine sides, eight of which were released. These included a fantastic, frenetic version of "Sweet Georgia Brown," a joyful Johnson composition called "Foxy and Grapesy," and two Fats Waller songs. On the recordings, Briggs is masterful, even playful. He alternates syncopated flurries of scales with dizzying lip slides and squealing high notes, his style more personal and mature than ever.

The greatest song from the sessions happened by mistake and showed how close Briggs and Johnson had become. One morning Briggs was warming up in a corner of the studio, when Johnson arrived and sat at the piano. "The funny thing is that we immediately started to play together," Briggs said. "I invented something and Freddy followed me without saying a word." From the control booth, Canetti caught Briggs's eye and made a motion to continue. Briggs finished the first chorus, and then nodded to Johnson, who took a chorus of his own. As the final note rang out, Canetti rushed into the studio and said, "My God, that's good." Briggs replied, "What's good?" As they listened to the playback, Canetti asked, "What's it called?" Off the cuff Briggs replied, "Grabbin' Blues."[8] It became a hit in Paris.

July was a busy month. On the eve of Bastille Day, the Harlemites played a benefit for the American Gold Star Mothers, a group formed to honor mothers and widows of soldiers lost in WWI. Then, in addition to recording their own material, they backed German bombshell Marlene Dietrich on two songs: "Allein in Einer Großen Stadt" and "Wo Ist Der Mann?" Dietrich had just begun her career in America with the 1930 film *Morocco*, in which she played a cabaret singer who dressed in a man's suit and kissed a woman—shocking for the time. It earned her an Academy Award nomination. Finally, at the end of the month, Duke Ellington arrived. Fresh from a triumphant tour of England, he performed to a packed house at the Salle Pleyel. "It was practically a national holiday," Bricktop said.

After the concert, Ellington came to Bricktop's. The music might have been wallpaper, but the club was like Mecca, drawing all the American jazz greats that came to Paris. A crowd of celebrities followed him, and at one point in the evening, he was sandwiched in a booth between Josephine Baker and Franklin Roosevelt Jr. While he drank and caroused, Ellington kept his ears trained on Briggs, and he was impressed with what he heard. Between sets, he asked Briggs to join his band. "I prefer to be here," Briggs replied simply. Briggs had several reasons for passing on the opportunity of a lifetime. Chief among them, he didn't want to return to America. Also, Duke's first trumpeter, Art Whetsol, was a friend. "Even if I was broke and out of a job, I would never take it, because it was Art Whetsol's job," Briggs said. Finally, he knew how hard Ellington was on his orchestra. "He writes puzzles. . . . He killed [Whetsol]! And he was ready to kill me, but I wasn't in for the killing."[9] Yet another opportunity to succeed in America went by unclaimed.

After the summer season in Biarritz, Briggs returned to Paris and cut three sides with the Harlemites. He was again superb, proving the effect a great band had on his playing. Two of Johnson's compositions—"Sweet Madness" and "Harlem Bound"—were issued as a single and, according to Briggs, won 1933's "Best Recording of the Year."

Two weeks later, the Harlemites played a Hot Club concert at the Salle Pleyel. A reporter from the *Philadelphia Tribune* attended, providing a detailed account of the evening to his American audience:

> Sunday night, despite the rain and dreariness that had continued throughout the day, 2,800 lovers of jazz music played by its originators—Negroes—packed the Grande Salle Pleyel, enjoyed the offerings and left with the happy satisfaction of being present to see a hot jazz leader "made." The occasion was the presentation of Freddy Johnson, the boy wonder at the keyboard, and his newly organized 14 piece orchestra, The Harlemites, in their first concert of the "Hot Jazz" music. . . . The audience was composed of men and women of all walks of life, and of all nations. Those of the humdrum existence that filled the top balcony to overflowing, like the elites that graced the boxes with their brilliancy

and splendor listened attentively and as the final note of each number faded, applauded wildly. It was a repetition of Duke Ellington's tremendous success under the same sponsorship and on the same stage exactly three months ago. . . . Every member of the orchestra rendered one solo or more, and the principal soloist, Arthur Briggs, who is a serious rival to the great Louis Armstrong, and well known to lovers of jazz music of this city by records made with Freddy Johnson for the Brunswick Co., was tremendously acclaimed and received prolonged applause for his every masterful execution.[10]

As the paper noted, Johnson had stepped out front as the band's leader. Sadly, there was something sinister in the move. Briggs's first inkling of trouble came when he received no royalties for "Sweet Madness"/"Harlem Bound." "We never got a dime," he said. "My satisfaction is to listen to the recordings."[11] Then, members of the band began whispering that Canetti and Johnson were in cahoots. Canetti booked a tour of Belgium and Holland, hoping to find a lucrative market there, but before the band left, guitarist Sterling Conaway overheard Johnson on the phone with his wife saying, "Darling, when I come back, that trunk will be stacked with 1,000 franc bills." The band got word, and a meeting was scheduled to discuss finances. Someone sent Briggs a copy of a contract Johnson and Canetti had secretly signed, giving them most of the money from the tour. Briggs was furious and hurt. He understood that Johnson wanted to make money, but so did everyone. Plus, the Harlemites had something more important than money on the line. "We were thinking of making a reputation," Briggs said. "But [Canetti] thought of one thing, just knocking out everybody and taking everything for himself. . . . Canetti was shrewd, and Freddy was with him. They worked together. I didn't want to think so, but I was forced to think so after that."[12]

Rancor spread through the group like cancer. Peter DuConge refused to let Johnson back into Bricktop's. He told his wife, "If you don't throw [Freddy] out, I'll throw him out." The band quit in protest, refusing to go on tour, and the venue in Belgium filed a lawsuit for breach of contract. "The atmosphere had become hateful," Briggs said. "The end of this adventure was really heartbreaking."[13]

That autumn the Depression hit Paris with full force, scattering the withered remnants of the Jazz Age. Bricktop's teetered on the edge of collapse. "Some nights the club was less than half full," she said. "People who never had a prayer of getting into Bricktop's in the big years had no trouble getting in now. . . . That Paris season was the worst I'd had since I'd been in business."[14] It wasn't just Bricktop's. Montmartre was empty. Night after night, nervous cabaret owners paced the floor while jazz bands played to a handful of customers. Despite Briggs's best efforts, jazz seemed to be dying. He faced 1934 not knowing if Paris held a place for him.

25

"Arthur Briggs . . . is considered to be the best trumpet player on the continent."[1]

—Jacques Canetti

IN MARCH 1934, FREDDY JOHNSON LEFT for the Netherlands, where the Dutch announced him as "the sensation of the season . . . including Arthur Briggs, a star like [Louis] Armstrong."[2] This was either a mistake in billing or, more likely, a ploy by Canetti and Johnson to hire another trumpet player and pass him off as Briggs. It was a backhanded compliment: Briggs was so famous Johnson couldn't tour without him. It was also a sign of Briggs's stature in Europe that he and Armstrong were mentioned as equals.

Jacques Canetti noticed. He had become Louis Armstrong's manager, booking him on a tour of Europe with a group of local players, including Bricktop's husband Peter DuConge, late of the Harlemites. When Armstrong became gravely ill in London, Canetti fired off a telegram to Briggs: "Louis very sick. Come to replace him!" The telegram reached Briggs in Bougival. Suspicious of Canetti, he showed it to Bricktop. "It's odd," she said. "I don't think it's Louis's idea, otherwise Peter would have known and warned me, and *he* would have sent this telegram."[3] Briggs wouldn't even consider replacing Armstrong without his consent. He left the telegram unanswered.

Days later, DuConge telegraphed Bricktop: "It's bad. We're finishing the tour and coming back in a fortnight."[4] As it turned out, Canetti had overbooked Armstrong, whose lips couldn't take the strain. Armstrong intended to finish the dates as a point of honor—"I found this very worthy of an artist," Briggs said—but his lips were split and bloody. He had no choice but to quit the tour.

Back in Paris, Canetti tried again to hire Briggs, wooing him with promises of fame and fortune. "Armstrong has broken his contract," Canetti said. "It's over with him. I'd like to lead you. We're going to put together a large band; you'll see, I'm going to boost your career!"

Again, Briggs declined.

"You could have made a fortune with me!" Canetti said angrily.

"Yes, with you, I would've won the whole world, but I'm not too pretentious," Briggs replied.

"You'll come back to see me one day," Canetti vowed. Then, softening, he said, "We're good?"

"We're good," Briggs said.

"I can't be angry with you, Mr. Briggs," Canetti said. "I can't!"

"We'll be in touch," Briggs said, and with that, he left.[5]

Briggs showed great restraint with Canetti, restraint he did not possess during his impulsive youth. After seventeen years as a professional musician, he had earned the wisdom of self-control. Canetti had approached him with two fool's bargains, but rather than slam the door in his face, Briggs coolly dismissed him. It was a subtler way of protecting his dignity, one that left bridges unburned.

Armstrong spent the spring of 1934 recuperating in Paris. He stayed several weeks at Bricktop's villa in Bougival, where he and Briggs hung out every day. "I thought he was a great guy," Briggs said. "I explained to him that I had seen him in 1919 with King Oliver's orchestra. He answered me: 'Nobody knew I was in Chicago in 1919 . . . but you are right, it was me.'"[6] Briggs's testimony flies in the face of decades of Armstrong scholarship, but he insisted it was true.

Briggs was horrified to see Armstrong's lips, which were "hard as a piece of wood" and bleeding.[7] "There was pus coming out of his upper lip," Briggs said. "I saw that myself." He blamed it on Armstrong's lack of proper technique. "Louis did not have the tuition that we had. That's the strong mouth playing. Pressing the mouthpiece to the lips. . . . They worked him to death. They worked him so hard that he had no other alternative but to press in order to get the results that he wanted. He thought by using pressure he would get the results that he wanted. By using pressure though, he just smothered his lips."[8]

Armstrong was notoriously competitive and cagey with other trumpeters, but he let his guard down with Briggs. "Sometimes he would take up his horn and try to do something for me and in my presence," Briggs recalled. It is a wonderful image—America's greatest trumpeter lazing around with Europe's greatest trumpeter on a beautiful estate outside of Paris, showing off for no other reason than their mutual love of music. According to Panassié, Armstrong even said of Briggs, "I would very happily make him my first trumpet in the orchestra that I will form as soon as I come back to the United States."[9] Briggs had now received offers from two towering bandleaders, but it wasn't enough to entice him back to America.

Armstrong understood why Briggs loved Paris. The city seduced him as it had so many others. "[Louis] acquired a stature in Paris that he had never attained at home," a biographer wrote. "Here he was an artist, not a 'colored entertainer.'"[10] Though it seems strange from today's vantage point, where Armstrong's name is hallowed throughout the world, in 1934, he struggled to prove his worth.

The problem was bigger than Armstrong. Jazz still staggered trying to find its footing as legitimate art. Gone were the days of novelty and danger; the rebellious youths of 1924 were now the responsible adults of 1934. With the Hot Club, Briggs tried to reach a new generation. He played a concert at L'École Normale de Musique, which ended in a fiery duel with his fellow trumpeters. Meanwhile, Delaunay started a record exchange, which became a veritable library of rare jazz records, and Panassié published *Le Jazz Hot*, the first comprehensive history of jazz, in which he singled out African Americans as the prime innovators of the form.

But a new age had dawned in Paris, with a new fad of its own—Cuban music. Anyone who wanted to work had to bow to commercial pressure. Briggs wanted to work. He started a Cuban band. He was lucky, in a way: Cuban music had its roots in Africa and was similar to the Calypso he heard as a boy in Grenada. His new band, Arthur Briggs and the American Cubano Boys, was more than a concession to the current style; it was an expression of the music bred into his bones.

For the summer season, he took the American Cubano Boys to Deauville on the sea in Northwest France. He then joined Cuban bandleader Don Barreto and his Cuban Orchestra, cutting southeast across the entire country for an engagement in Cannes. It wasn't exactly Briggs's scene. A picture of Barreto's band shows Briggs looking slightly out of place, dressed like a flamenco dancer in a puffy-sleeved shirt. But he gamely played along.

The job in Cannes was no different from working a chic club in Paris. The band was expected to perform quietly so as not to disturb the rich people at play. For the brass section, this meant playing with a mute, which was placed in the bell of the instrument to muffle the sound. It required more force from the trumpeter and was harder on the lips. Briggs's technique was so advanced he could control his volume without a mute and still produce a full tone, but the trumpeter in the alternate band was struggling. He came to Briggs for help.

"I am Mr. Aimé Barelli," the young man said.

"I've already heard of you, you know," Briggs responded kindly.

"Well, I'm only getting started," said Barelli.

"We're all getting started," replied Briggs.

"I wanted to ask you something," Barelli continued. "I'm forbidden to play without a mute and it's very tiring. What can I do to play softly, with a nice sound, as you do, without a mute, and without bothering the customers?"

Briggs advised Barelli to practice the exercises in the Arban trumpet method book, pointing him to the specific page on embouchure. "We would have to work on it for at least twenty minutes every day," Briggs said. "You have to have a lot of patience, and don't get nervous, because the development of the facial muscles is something that is done very slowly."[11]

Throughout the engagement, Briggs checked on Barelli's progress every week. Barelli found some of Briggs's suggestions too hard on his lips, and Briggs encouraged him: "Indeed, it hurts for a day or two or three; then the improvement happens. Don't give up! The world wasn't made in a day!" By the end of the time in Cannes, Barelli had mastered the exercises. He asked Briggs to watch him perform and began playing without a mute, wanting to show off his newfound prowess,

Louisa Augusta Wilkey, Briggs's mother. *Courtesy of James Briggs Murray*

Briggs's sister, Edith Inez (seated center) surrounded by her children Clarine (left), June (right), and Austin (standing rear). As a teenager, Briggs followed Edith Inez to Harlem and lived in her apartment. *Photo by James Van Der Zee, courtesy of James Briggs Murray*

James Richard Briggs, Briggs's father. *Courtesy of James Briggs Murray*

Will Marion Cook, pioneer of early jazz, leader of the Southern Syncopated Orchestra. Cook became a father figure to Briggs and the most significant musical influence on his career. Briggs even called Cook "Dad." *New York Public Library*

James Reese Europe, architect of Harlem's jazz scene, creator of the Clef and Amsterdam Clubs, leader of the Harlem Hellfighters regimental band. As a teenager, Briggs joined both clubs, as well as the Hellfighters' reserve band. *National Archives*

Briggs toured constantly for twenty years, traveling as far as Constantinople and Cairo. Note that his birth year is incorrectly listed as 1899. Born in 1901, Briggs lied about his age to join the Harlem Hellfighters reserve band during World War I.
Courtesy of Barbara Pierrat-Briggs

Seminal jazz clarinetist Sidney Bechet. Briggs met Bechet as a teenager and became a lifelong friend. From Bechet, Briggs learned true New Orleans jazz.
Photofest NYC

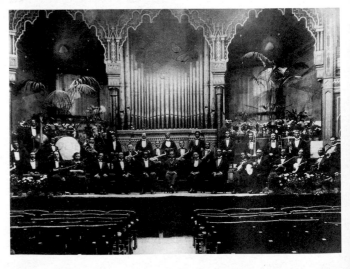

The Southern Syncopated Orchestra. Led by Will Marion Cook, the group was one of the first to bring early jazz to Europe, and it gave Briggs his first taste of international touring.
Courtesy of Denis Pierrat

Briggs on one of his first tours in Europe after leaving the Southern Syncopated Orchestra, ca 1922. From left to right, Bertin Salnave, Arthur Briggs, Al Refurt (seated), Mario Scanavino and his wife, two unknown musicians. *Courtesy of Denis Pierrat*

Briggs (second from left) with the 5 Musical Dragons in 1922, just before Mope Desmond (seated at piano) died in a train crash en route to a performance. *Courtesy of Denis Pierrat*

Arthur Briggs (second from right) and His Savoy Syncops Orchestra, Vienna ca 1925. *Courtesy of Denis Pierrat*

Briggs in a lighter mood, 1920s.
Courtesy of Denis Pierrat

Briggs (far right) in a still from *Das Spielzeug von Paris*, a silent film directed in 1925 by Michael Curtiz, who would later direct *Casablanca* and *White Christmas*.
Courtesy of Denis Pierrat

A series of stills showing Josephine Baker in kinetic motion, ca 1927. She earned several nicknames in Paris, including: Black Venus, the Black Pearl, and the Creole Goddess. *Photofest NYC*

Josephine Baker in her infamous banana skirt. Worn during the *danse sauvage* at the *Folies Bergère* in 1927, the outfit became a defining part of her legend. *Original photo by Lucien Waléry, 1926*

Josephine Baker and her iconic hairstyle, 1920s. Parisian women imitated her hair and dress and even darkened their skin with walnut oil to look more like her. *Photofest NYC*

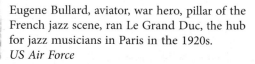

Eugene Bullard, aviator, war hero, pillar of the French jazz scene, ran Le Grand Duc, the hub for jazz musicians in Paris in the 1920s. *US Air Force*

Ada "Bricktop" Smith, legendary nightclub owner in Paris during the Jazz Age. Briggs joined the band at her club in the early 1930s. *© Carl Van Vechten Trust, National Portrait Gallery, Smithsonian Institution*

Briggs (standing second from left) with the Harlemites, the house band at the legendary Bricktop's club, a favorite hangout of jazz musicians and socialites, including Cole Porter. There, Briggs provided the soundtrack as the future King Edward VIII fell in love with Wallis Simpson, the woman for whom he would abdicate the British throne. Freddy Johnson, one of Briggs's closest musical companions, stands far left. Ca. 1933. *Courtesy of Denis Pierrat*

Briggs (far right) and his American Cubano Boys, ca. 1934. *Courtesy of Denis Pierrat*

Django Reinhardt, perhaps Europe's greatest contribution to jazz. Briggs helped Django's rise to fame with the Quintette du Hot Club de France, but his role was never recognized. *Photo by William Gottlieb, via Library of Congress, LC-GLB23- 0730*

Promotional poster for Briggs and the Hot Club, ca 1935. Seated beneath him from left to right are Alix Combelle, Georges Marion, Django Reinhardt, and Stephane Grappelli. *Courtesy of Denis Pierrat*

When Cuban music became the fad in Paris, Briggs followed the audience's taste. Here he is (seated far left) looking slightly out of place in Don Barreto's Cuban jazz band, 1937. *Courtesy of Denis Pierrat*

Briggs (bottom left) with his band in Egypt, ca 1937. The band worked four hotels in Cairo simultaneously. *Courtesy of Denis Pierrat*

Briggs (standing in white suit) leading his band, likely in Egypt, ca 1937. *Courtesy of Denis Pierrat*

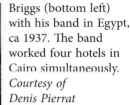

JOSÉPHINE BAKER

TOURNÉE MONDIALE 1938/39

GEORG HOHENBERG
KOPENHAGEN
ROSENFELDTSALLE 13
TEL : GENTOFTE 32 - 97

ORGANISATION:
PRIÈRE RÉPONDRE À /
ERBITTE ANTWORT NACH:

HERBERT TRAU
WIEN V.
MARGARETENSTRASSE 96
TEL : A 37-607

Copenhague le 2 mai 1938.

Cher Monsieur Briggs,

J'ai voyagé à Copenhague pour trouver un peu d'argent pour régler tous les comptes avec vous et les autres artistes. Malheureusement je vois que cela n'ira pas si vite comme j'ai pensais et au m. de la tournée Baker je ne peux rien encore recevoir, car elle commence qu'ue à notre malheureuse tournée en Suède, seulement le 9 oct. à la place d'aujourd'hui.

Comme vous cher Monsieur Briggs est le plus sérieux de la troupe je m'adresse à vous en vous priant de m'aider avec un règlement des tous les artistes.

Josephine Baker wrote Briggs this letter in 1938 apologizing for their disastrous tour of Sweden and asking for his help to rectify the situation. He refused. *Courtesy of Barbara Pierrat-Briggs*

A group of men at Stalag 220, the Nazi prison camp in St. Denis, captured here just days before Briggs arrived in October 1940. *International Committee of the Red Cross*

The barracks at St. Denis, hastily constructed to contain the overflow of prisoners. They were flimsy against the cold and full of lice. *International Committee of the Red Cross*

Members of the kitchen staff working in the prison camp, October 1940. Briggs was allowed to eat with these men in return for his musical services. *International Committee of the Red Cross*

Otto von Stülpnagel (right), commander of Nazi occupied France. Briggs performed his first classical concert in prison for Stülpnagel in January 1941. When the Nazi commander expressed his surprise that a black man could play Beethoven, Briggs replied in German: "Es gibt viel Sachen die man nicht kennen." (There are many things you don't know.) *German Federal Archives, 183-H29377*

A surviving flyer for a "Super Variety Concert," which Briggs and his orchestra held in the Nazi prison camp at St. Denis in January 1942.
Imperial War Museums

Another flyer for a concert, in which Briggs performed scenes from Mozart's *Don Giovanni*, an ambitious undertaking for an amateur orchestra in a Nazi prison.
Imperial War Museums

The St. Denis prison campgrounds. A tennis court can be seen to the right. Despite the dreadful conditions of the camp, the prisoners were allowed to play sports.
International Committee of the Red Cross

A group of visitors waits to be admitted to the prison camp, 1943.
International Committee of the Red Cross

A prisoner cleans his bunk bed, June 1943. The camp was full of lice and bugs, requiring frequent inspections and cleanings.
International Committee of the Red Cross

Prisoners walking near the barbed wire gates, May 1944. Outside the gates stood residential apartment buildings; the residents of these buildings created a rudimentary sign language with the prisoners to pass along news and other information.
International Committee of the Red Cross

A postcard painted by an inmate during the brutal winter of 1942, signed by Briggs and the orchestra. The first signed name is Tom Waltham, the pianist who requested Briggs's transfer to St. Denis and likely saved Briggs's life in the process. The last signed name is Gay Martins, with whom Briggs formed a vocal group that sang Negro spirituals in the camp.
Imperial War Museums

Another postcard painted by an inmate of the St. Denis Prison camp. Briggs and the orchestra signed their names on back.
Imperial War Museums

Josephine Baker singing the national anthem during World War II. Beginning in 1939, Josephine Baker worked as a spy for the French Resistance, until a miscarriage nearly killed her. After recovering, she spent the rest of the war performing for the troops and raising millions of francs for the Free French.
National Archives, 111-SC-175237

Briggs (far right) with Dizzy Gillespie and Charles Delaunay, 1950s.
Courtesy of Denis Pierrat

Arthur Briggs leading Sidney Bechet's funeral, 1959.
Courtesy of Denis Pierrat

Briggs's great-nephew, James Briggs Murray,
in the oral history tape vault at Rutgers
University's Institute of Jazz Studies. Behind
him is the tape of the longest interview
Briggs ever gave. *James Briggs Murray*

Briggs's great-nephew, James Briggs Murray
(left), with Wynton Marsalis and Jeannine
Bookhardt-Murray. Both Murray and
Marsalis have spent decades promoting the
history of jazz music. *James Briggs Murray*

After ending his career as a performer, Briggs became a teacher.
Here he is in the 1980s with his students.
Courtesy of Barbara Pierrat-Briggs

Briggs began to lose his sight near the end of his life.
By the time of this picture, at Paris's Café des Arts in 1985, he was blind.
Courtesy of Denis Pierrat

when a waiter rushed over to the bandstand and said, "Put that mute back immediately." Barelli pointed to Briggs in the audience. "Okay," the waiter said. "Since Mr. Briggs is here, give it a try."[12] It was good to have a name like Arthur Briggs to throw around and even better to have the man as a teacher. Barelli played beautifully, while Briggs sat in the audience beaming at his student's success. The ambassador of jazz returned to Paris a trumpet teacher.

26

"Django was very fine . . . a baby."[1]

—Arthur Briggs

DURING *LE TUMULTE NOIR*, the seeds of jazz that grew lush and wild on the Right Bank fell on rocky soil across the Seine. But as the Depression wilted Montmartre, Montparnasse and the Latin Quarter bloomed. When Arthur Briggs returned to Paris in September 1934, the Left Bank was ripe for harvest.

Briggs was approached by the owner of a failing club in Montparnasse called Stage B. "Knowing that I was number three to the Hot Club de France," Briggs said, "and that my work appealed to the youth, he asked me if I could find a new formula for this establishment."[2] While Briggs performed a winter residency with Don Barreto's Cuban Orchestra at the Chantilly, he also formed a band of his own. To get around French law, he became part owner of Stage B, which he renamed the Sweet and Hard Club. This allowed him to form the band any way he wanted.

He spent two months finding the musicians and getting them in shape. Briggs hired violin virtuoso Stéphane Grappelli, who took up piano in order to be heard above the din, as well as saxophonist Alix Combelle and drummer George Marion. Then, one night after work, Briggs went to La Brasserie Alsacienne, a musician's hang, and met the Romani guitarist Django Reinhardt.

Django had yet to make his name as one of the greatest jazz guitarists in history—and certainly the most important figure in European jazz—but he already had a reputation. "I hesitated to approach Django,"

Briggs admitted. "Not only was I unable to offer him a sizeable fee, but everyone I'd spoken to about signing him on had warned me against it. 'You're crazy, my friend,' Louis Vola had said. 'Django will never be there for work. He comes only when he feels like it.'"[3]

Django was difficult, temperamental, unfathomable. The stories of his inconsistency are legendary. Once, when he didn't show up to a gig, his bandleader found him outside on a bench, stoned out of his mind, staring into space. The bandleader shook him out of his reverie, and Django said, "How beautiful the moon is, my friend."[4] Sometimes he'd play for nothing; other times he'd demand as much money as Cary Grant was paid for his films.[5] Grappelli, who became Django's closest musical companion, said, "Though he was very well known musically, he himself was known by very few people. He was the most reserved fellow I ever met in my life. He almost never spoke, and his abruptness of manner didn't help."[6]

Briggs had dealt with difficult men before. Naturally, he had no problems with Django. He appreciated Django's genius and marveled at his superhuman speed and dexterity on the guitar even though only two fingers on his fretting hand worked, the others having been paralyzed in a fire during his youth. Briggs and Django shared a deeper understanding. Django's people—the Romani, known pejoratively as Gypsies—had been enslaved and persecuted since the fourteenth century. Django's experience of discrimination was surely different from Briggs's, but he understood, as Briggs understood, the pain of persecution. Briggs came to consider him a great friend. He even loved Django's antics. "On a Saturday night, when the place was packed and jammed, [he'd] not show up, but he'd phone and say, 'Art, I am having a good time.' You know where he's at? In Montmartre playing in a cafe for nothing. For nothing. Just playing in a cafe, having a good time. That's all."[7]

Briggs's new band began playing at the Sweet and Hard Club in November. "The work was hard," Grappelli said. "We played without a stop from ten until four in the morning for ninety francs a night, but we had a whale of a time. The music was good because we could play what we liked. The place had one of the best atmospheres I've ever worked in."[8] Briggs tried to start his own group in the style of the Hot Club, handing out membership cards and putting on free concerts Saturdays and Sundays, "to make swing known to the young people."[9] Just like with the Harlemites, he was playing music his way, with a band of close friends. "It was more like brotherhood than anything else between us," he said.[10] Sadly, he didn't foresee that this brotherhood would break up in almost the exact same way the Harlemites did, leaving him with the same grief.

Before joining Briggs, Django and Grappelli had staged informal jam sessions at the Hotel le Claridge, sometimes including Django's brother Joseph on rhythm guitar and Louis Vola on string bass. Briggs invited this loose conglomeration to perform between sets at the Sweet and Hard Club. "This was an immediate success," Briggs said. "The quintet really had the swing and the obvious enthusiasm to play together. For me it was perfect since I could rest for about half an hour. What happened was that these five musicians liked their work so much that half an hour was not enough for them. . . . So, I hired them on Saturday and Sunday, for the mornings."[11] Without realizing it, Briggs had helped start a revolutionary jazz band.

Up until this point, jazz was horn-based music. Instruments such as banjo, guitar, and violin were used mostly as rhythmic backing for the trumpet, saxophone, and clarinet. Django's quintet was perhaps the first in jazz history to feature only stringed instruments. It was a thrilling new sound, and crowds soon mobbed the Sweet and Hard Club to hear it. Even Panassié, who had been holed up in his provincial castle, bitter at the advance of swing music and desperate to keep the Hot Club focused on New Orleans jazz, came. One night, as Django's quintet fumbled toward a new musical statement, Panassié shouted requests from the audience. Briggs didn't appreciate the disruption. Being number three in the Hot Club, he felt comfortable enough with Panassié to chide him. When Panassié shouted for "Aunt Hagar's Blues," Briggs shot back, "Your parents weren't even born when that piece was written."

"Well, then play us something from New Orleans," Panassié retorted.

"They play what they like," Briggs said, protecting his musicians and their right to experiment. "You see how happy people are, you see the line, you see how happy they are to dance."

"Yes, but we want them to play for us, for the Hot Club de France," Panassié insisted.

"You are a guest," Briggs answered. "The bartender has already sent you a note to inform you that you won't have to pay for drinks. You didn't object. Well, then, you're welcome. But only people who pay for their drinks can make requests!"[12]

Briggs didn't mind giving his time and talent freely to the Hot Club, but after everything he had done, he was not about to let anyone come into his club and push around his musicians. He bristled at the arrogance of Panassié and his ilk to think that because they had fallen in love with the music, they owned it and could control it. "I knew I had shocked them," Briggs said, "but I didn't care. People don't help musicians make a living by accepting free drinks, and they don't get to give orders for anything."[13]

After the music ended, Briggs saw Grappelli in a deep discussion with Pierre Nourry, one of the Hot Club's leaders. "So, what do they want?" Briggs asked Grappelli.

"They think we are a beautiful quintet and want us to make records," Grappelli said.

"Very good; and you, Django, what do you think?"

"If your name is on the record and if it's a quintet with Arthur Briggs, it's okay. Otherwise, no."[14]

Briggs was in for a shock of his own. In September, and again in December, Django's band, now named the Quintette du Hot Club de France, cut several sides, beginning an iconic run that defined European jazz. Briggs was not included. Upset, he asked Delaunay why the alternate band at his club was recording under the Hot Club name without his knowledge and without financial compensation. Delaunay demurred. "Of course I can give the Hot Club label," he said, "but I have nothing to do with it!" Briggs then asked Django, "What's going on?" Django turned to Grappelli and said, "Why don't you tell him?"

"What do you want, Arthur, we were offered . . ." Grappelli began.

"No," Django cut in. "*You* were offered, not us."

"Well, it doesn't matter," Grappelli said. "We were offered to make a record, Django and me, in the name of the quintet of Hot Club de France. And I accepted."

"Not me," Django said. "It's Grappelli who arranged everything. I play for my pleasure, as long as I play with good musicians and friends. I don't even know what the financial terms are!"

Though Django tried to blame the whole thing on Grappelli, it seems the entire group saw a prime opportunity to make a record and took it. Briggs couldn't fault them for that, but he was hurt, and his pain only grew as he watched the Quintette become lionized as a groundbreaking, era-making group. Indeed, they were just that, but when the history was written, Briggs's role in the Quintette was almost completely erased. Worse still, Briggs's role in founding the Hot Club was never fully recognized. And worst of all, when Delaunay wrote a comprehensive jazz discography in 1936, he did not include a single recording from Arthur Briggs.

It isn't clear why Briggs was cut out so completely from the histories of the Hot Club and the Quintette. Members of the club had long complained that it was not French enough; perhaps the Quintette was an attempt to rectify that complaint with an all-French group. Or perhaps it was a simple oversight—the work of inconsistent memories after many decades. Whatever the reason, Briggs was unfairly forgotten. The pinnacle of his life as a jazz ambassador passed as if it had never happened.

As a younger man, Briggs might have acted on impulse and severed his connection from the Hot Club. Instead, he showed restraint. Perhaps he cared about the club's mission too much to abandon it. Still, while he held no grudges against Django and Grappelli, he began to feel resentment toward the Hot Club. His pure spirit was now tainted with cynicism. He especially began to mistrust writers, who promulgated the false story of the Quintette du Hot Club de France, making him a footnote at best.

It was now a recurring theme, from Gaby Malael in 1922, to Freddy Johnson in 1932, to the Hot Club in 1934: Briggs trusted other musicians too much. He cared more for music than for glory, with the assumption that everyone felt the same way. He seemed unable to accept that the brotherhood of musicians was also a cutthroat business. In the short term, these qualities made him beloved and brought him acclaim—at the end of 1934, a group of musicians in Paris feted Briggs at the Cabane Cubaine, a popular musician's hang. News of the event was broadcast far and wide, including in the *Chicago Defender*, which carried an item stating: "Arthur Briggs, the second [Louis] Armstrong—the one musician in Paris who is never without work—had a grand gala accorded him Thursday night."[15] In the long term, however, Briggs was eclipsed by others more unscrupulous, or more power hungry, or just better at playing the game than he was. Had he been the type to boast of himself, perhaps Briggs would have received the credit he was due. That was never his style. Instead, he spent the next sixty years watching his contributions get smaller and smaller each time the story was told.

27

"All the [bad] musicians had faded out of the picture in Paris entirely."[1]

—Arthur Briggs

ARTHUR BRIGGS SOLDIERED ON. In February 1935, he met the great saxophonist Coleman Hawkins, whom he had admired from afar since Hawk's early recordings with Fletcher Henderson in the 1920s. Now Hawkins was pushing the boundaries of swing music, defining the tenor saxophone as a star vehicle in jazz. Of all the superlatives attached to Hawkins's name, perhaps most important is the nickname given by his fellow musicians: Bean, short for Beano, short for B and O, short for Best and Only.

Hawkins was invited to Paris to perform for the Hot Club, which had just started the seminal jazz magazine *Jazz Hot* (today it is the oldest jazz magazine in the world and is still publishing on the Internet). With a few days to kill in Paris, he went to the Sweet and Hard Club to watch Briggs's band perform. One night, he joined the band onstage and played a version of "Sweet Sue" that lasted an hour and a half. "He must have blown about forty choruses on his own," Grappelli recalled.[2]

Briggs loved Hawkins from the start. "We got along so nicely together," he said. "He was such a wonderful person." Like Briggs, Hawkins was mild-mannered and good-natured. Like Briggs, Hawkins had a sharp sense of style. "He would think of his shoes, his socks," Briggs recalled. "I remember him paying $20, $30 for a pair of stockings, socks. He was crazy about beautiful shirts, not eccentric shirts, but beautiful quality cashmere, silk. That's where he would spend his money, and he would talk all day about his dress. He would dress like a prince, you know, he was always well dressed and thought the world of himself and he did have his mustache. . . . Yeah, he would always think of his mustache, cut 'em and trim 'em himself."[3]

On February 23, the Hot Club brought Hawkins and Briggs together at the Salle Pleyel, a vast, gorgeous concert hall in Paris. Panassié worried about staging the concert in such a large hall, both for the quality of the sound and for the Hot Club's ability to fill it, but he decided there was no other way to introduce the music and the magazine to the world. He was right to worry; the music was a near disaster. To Briggs's dismay, the Hot Club had foisted a handful of young players on him at the last minute. These kids were as arrogant as they were mediocre, and Briggs spent most of the first set nervously watching as they commandeered the show. "At one point we were there, Hawkins and I, with our instruments in our hands, watching them to find out what was going on," Briggs said. "The concert was no longer ours but theirs."[4]

At intermission, while Grappelli chewed out the young Turks, Hawkins threatened to quit. "That's enough," he told Briggs. "Let's go now!" Briggs calmed him down, and the second half went as planned, garnering a standing ovation. "The band was a bastard," Hawkins said later, "but . . . I played my ass off."[5]

Despite the difficulties, the music had its intended effect. Briggs brought the house down with "Grabbin' Blues," the off-the-cuff masterpiece he had recorded with Freddy Johnson in 1933. Hawkins was also brilliant. As Delaunay wrote,

> When [Hawkins] improvised, it was as though it liberated a formidable strength long contained, like energy let loose from a dam. His eyes closed, his eyelids heavy, an obstinate look on his face, his head down low, his shoulders hunched—it was as though he was embracing his saxophone with all his body. . . . He gave birth to sorrowful, sumptuous arabesques of swelling notes, each one carved out like a jewel, their harmonious combination creating the most priceless of necklaces.[6]

Unfortunately, the costs of mounting the production and printing the magazine, which wasn't ready in time for the concert, in addition to Django's absurd salary, left the Hot Club six thousand francs in debt. Briggs and Big Boy Goudie agreed to put on a private concert to make up the difference, but even this fell short. Desperate, Delaunay begged Briggs and Hawkins to make a recording with violinist Michel Warlop, featuring the pride of French jazz, including Django and Grappelli, along with several new Hot Club members.

It isn't clear why Briggs continued to help an organization that had treated him so poorly. Perhaps he just wanted to get on wax with Hawkins. Whatever his reasons, on March 2, 1935, Briggs and the band cut three sides: "What a Difference a Day Makes," "Blue Moon," and "Avalon." With Briggs, Hawkins, Reinhardt, and Grappelli together, these sessions should have been legendary. Instead, Hot Club machinations marred the performances. "The house had proposed arrangements without even knowing how many orchestral elements we would have," Briggs said. "The musicians of the H.C.F were not all at this time of very high level, and the large arrangements which were proposed risked exceeding them." Briggs and Hawkins rewrote the orchestration "taking into account the possibilities of each of the musicians of the Hot Club de France, since we knew each of them and their capacity," but when they told the artistic director, he sneered at the black jazz men who thought they knew how to arrange better than a European. "You aren't musicians," he said. Looking back on this moment, Briggs said sharply, "He would have done better to keep that to himself."[7]

Again Briggs showed mastery over his impulsive nature. Rather than teach this artistic director a lesson by stranding him without a trumpet player, Briggs let his work speak for itself. The band ran down the new arrangement, and "the art director agreed that there was nothing to do but play this way." Briggs and Hawkins played admirably on the cuts, and the band was serviceable behind them. Hawkins in particular was pleased with the results: "I think [the recordings] might turn out better than the ones I made in Holland," he said, referring to his album *The Hawk in Holland*.[8] However, jazz lovers can only wonder what heights the band might have reached had Delaunay dispensed with the mediocre backing musicians and allowed the core group to do as they pleased.

This is no idle wonder: three months later Briggs returned to the studio with the Quintette (minus Hawkins) and cut another version of

"Avalon." To compare the two recordings is to compare a lamp to the sun. The version with Hawkins isn't bad—in fact it has several great moments—but the version with the Quintette explodes from the speaker, beginning with a solo from Grappelli that is somehow lilting and beautiful while played at a breakneck speed. Django follows, sounding like a man with twenty fingers. All the while, Briggs punctuates the downbeats with muted trumpet, and then he introduces himself with a syncopated six-note blast, swinging into perhaps the best solo he ever recorded. This was a band with unlimited potential.

For Briggs, the potential was never realized. Other than a few unreleased recordings in September, he never recorded with the Quintette again. He also never forgot the bitterness of reading in *Jazz Hot* that it was Panassié who had formed and organized the Quintette, or the pain of watching the Quintette perform on television and hearing Charles Delaunay and Maurice Cullaz claim ownership of the band. It was the same arrogance that nearly ruined the concert with Hawkins—the French jazz lovers' need to own the music, even at the expense of the musicians who played it. "I'm sitting here listening to them," Briggs recalled. "Grappelli was supposed to be present. He didn't show up. I said to myself, 'Thanks.' Grappelli understood. I saw Grappelli afterwards, and he said, 'Someone told me about the television setup and I didn't intend to go because it wasn't true.'"[9]

The Quintette toured France, sowing seeds in every town and province where they performed. By the middle of 1935, wrote jazz historian William Shack, "No provincial city could afford *not to* have a Hot Club. Nice, Bordeaux, Marseille, and Nancy, among the earliest to form chapters, were joined by Amsterdam, Utrecht, Milan, and Barcelona."[10] The group became Europe's greatest contribution to jazz. For Briggs, it was a victory without spoils.

28

*"I've longed to go back . . . to walk along Broadway
and look at the lights."*[1]

—Josephine Baker

IN HIS MEMOIRS ARTHUR BRIGGS never mentioned Josephine Baker.
He and Baker had crossed paths many times, including the night Duke
Ellington visited Bricktop's, but if he had an opinion about her, he kept
it to himself. Briggs's family believes he and Baker might have had hard
feelings—he was likely scandalized by her overt sexuality—although this
remains a matter of conjecture. The omission is all the more glaring
because, in April 1935, near his thirty-fourth birthday, Briggs performed
two gala concerts with the Creole Goddess herself.

These were no ordinary concerts. Nearly 2,500 people packed into
the Salle Gaveau for what a news report called a "highbrow jazz recital,"
sponsored by the French literary, historical, political journal *Université
des Annales*. The *Chicago Defender*, which had sent reporter Edgar Wiggins to Paris as a foreign correspondent, ran an account of the event that
was picked up by African American newspapers throughout America.
Wiggins wrote a glowing review, heaping praise on the "celebrated trum-
petist" Briggs, who played another showstopping rendition of "Grabbin'
Blues," as well as Baker, "the idolized darling of the Parisian stage,"
who came onstage dancing to "The Blue Danube." With Briggs behind
her, she performed "Haiti," her recent hit song. At the end, the crowd
showered the stage with roses and orchids.[2]

The triumph brought Briggs's name once again to an American
audience. The *Baltimore Afro-American*, adding to Wiggins's account,

said, "Briggs is getting to the point where he is trying to make Europeans forget about Louis Armstrong."[3] The *Chicago Defender* ran a picture of Briggs gazing down at his trumpet, with the caption: "Sensational young trumpeter is already being hailed as another Louis Armstrong. Paris music lovers say he plays and sings just like Louis and almost as well."[4] Millions of black Americans all over the country read these accounts, vicariously following Briggs's exploits. For the first time in twenty-five years of toil, Briggs had a legitimate shot at fame in America as a solo star.

He wasn't interested.

Baker still hadn't given up on America, however. She yearned to be recognized in her home country. She had spent the past two years trying to shed her reputation as a sexy dancer and make her name as a true artist. She starred in *Paris Qui Remue*, a lavish revue at the Casino de Paris, where she replaced the previous year's star, Mistinguett. The plan was to milk the rivalry between Paris's two greatest female performers, and it worked. Thirty years older than Baker, Mistinguett saw the young star as a threat. One evening at a film premiere, she saw Baker in the crowd and said, "Well, pickaninny, why don't you come up and salute me?" Baker spat in her face. Mistinguett spat back. It made the papers.

In *Paris Qui Remue*'s most famous scene, Baker played a colonial girl in love with a French colonist and sang "J'ai Deux Amours,"* telling of her two loves: her country and Paris. The French were enchanted to hear her sing about Paris, rather than the exotic jazz for which she was known. Weeks later, she recorded the first of many versions of the song. It became an icon forever attached to her name, and it changed her persona. No longer was she the exotic naked dancer. Now she was an artist.

Always sensitive to the pressure of fame, Baker began living two lives. She purchased Le Beau-Chêne, a nineteenth-century chateau on the outskirts of Paris, and attempted to settle down with her husband Pepito and her ducks, chickens, geese, pheasants, turkeys, dogs, cats, rabbits, piglets, parrots, parakeets, macaws, cockatiels, monkeys, and tortoises. By day, she wore work clothes and dirtied her hands in her garden. By

---

* "Two Loves Have I."

night, she was still the glamorous performer. She sought peace in her idyllic new home but struggled to find it. A former servant attested, "She was always in a crisis. I never knew what started them. Sometimes there would be one per day; other times two per day or only one per week. Sometimes a crisis would last a week. They were like seizures that took hold of her."[5]

Perhaps it was the draining struggle to support her husband, and the constant crowd of hangers-on, and her menagerie, which now included a cheetah (she appeared with it onstage in *Paris Qui Remue*, and the producers gifted it to her; she named it Chiquita, bought it a diamond-studded collar, and paraded it down the Champs-Elysées). Or maybe it was Baker's misfortune that what she did easily with an audience she could not do in her personal life: connect. She was a woman of great passion and deep emotion, but in intimacy she remained aloof. Sex for Baker, as a former lover recalled, was physical, even political, but rarely romantic. Then again, in twenty-seven short years she had survived a race riot, been married twice by the age of sixteen (today we'd call it statutory rape), and achieved a level of fame no one could understand. Perhaps detachment was the price she paid for such a scarring, thrilling life.

After *Paris Qui Remue*, Baker set off on another long tour of Europe, with stops in Asia and Africa. She drove herself and her musicians mercilessly, playing two concerts each night and sometimes one in the afternoon. In Holland, she gave eleven concerts in six days. In England, she made her first appearance on an untested new format: television. In Greece, she performed for the entire Italian royal family at the Acropolis. Upon returning to Paris, she wrote a memoir and signed on to star in the film *Zouzou*, in which she played a woman in love with a white Frenchman. In the film, she is radiant, displaying near operatic vocal range and a natural talent for acting, deftly handling comedy and drama. Her reputation as a true artist was no longer in question, her star power never more certain. She had become the richest black woman in the world.

By the end of 1935, Baker and Pepito felt the time was ripe to conquer America. She signed with the 1936 Ziegfeld Follies and sailed with Pepito to New York in October. The Ziegfeld Follies were inspired by the *Folies Bergère*, the famously risqué Parisian review where Baker first wore her banana skirt. Americans were too prudish for nudity, but the show was similar in spirit. If Baker had a chance to reach American hearts, she would have to do it here, in a revue that showcased the strengths that made Paris fall in love with her.

The stage was set for conquest. Vincente Minnelli, the future Oscar-winning director who married Judy Garland and fathered Liza Minnelli, designed the sets and costumes. Ira Gershwin and Vernon Duke wrote the songs, and George Balanchine—the father of American ballet—choreographed the dances. The show also featured a talented cast of actors and comedians, including a young Bob Hope.

None of that was enough. Baker's trip to America was humiliating. Though she had lived through the worst of American racism, her years in Paris accustomed her to a different lifestyle. She wasn't ready to feel segregation's sting when she entered the St. Moritz Hotel and was told to use the servants' entrance to avoid offending the Southern guests. The emotional confusion continued when Baker visited her family in St. Louis, and her mother, despite feeling proud of her daughter's success, couldn't quite recognize the glamorous *Parisienne* as the girl she raised.

Like Briggs, Baker struggled to navigate a complex personal identity. For so long, she had been searching and fighting and working to find a place where she could exist, not as a black woman, but simply as a woman. Paris came close, but even there she would always be the exotic American. And by adopting Paris, with its foreign manners and customs, she unwittingly severed an elemental connection to her true home, a connection she might not have known existed if she had not returned to America to find it missing.

She tried to nurse her wounds in Harlem, singing incognito one night at the Apollo Theater's amateur night under the name Gracie Walker, but she spent so little time in Harlem, the black community felt snubbed. At a lavish dinner, where everyone spoke French, Baker asked the black maid for coffee in her adopted language. "You is full of shit," the maid shouted at her. "Talk the way yo' mouth was born."[6]

This treatment only made Baker more desperate to succeed. She put herself through punishing rehearsals. The dances were complicated, the costumes burdensome—during one routine she wore a gold-mesh dress that weighed one hundred pounds. The songs required every bit of skill she possessed. Vernon Duke said, "Ira Gershwin and I wrote two highly-spiced tropical arias . . . that would have scared [operatic soprano] Lily Pons out of her wits. Josephine mastered the acrobatic intervals and larynx-defying trills like a trouper."[7]

The show opened in New York and went on tour. Critics and crowds alike seemed to enjoy every bit of it, except one. As a biographer put it, "Josephine's performance . . . was slaughtered."[8] The *New York Times* wrote, "Josephine Baker has become a celebrity who offers her presence instead of her talent. . . . Her singing voice is only a squeak in the dark and her dancing is only the pain of an artist. Miss Baker has refined her talent until there is nothing left of it."[9] Cruelest of all was *Time* magazine, which called her a "Negro wench" and "a slightly buck-toothed young Negro woman whose figure might be matched in any nightclub show, and whose dancing and singing might be topped practically anywhere outside of Paris."[10] It was the worst professional failure of her career.

Baker possessed an iron will. One way or another, she was going to triumph in America. In February 1936, she opened a nightclub on East 54th Street in Manhattan. As the advertisements boasted, it was "Just as in Paree." The club allowed her the freedom she couldn't find in the Ziegfeld Follies. She hired a small band and sang with them as the mood struck her, maybe in English, maybe in French. She flouted segregation, choreographing a dance with three white male dancers. Sometimes she'd even stage a dance competition between her customers. She was in charge, and that suited her. The reviews were commensurate with her talent. "To miss hearing her and seeing her in her club," wrote the *New York Herald-Tribune*, "is to miss one of the most exciting and entertaining cabaret performers of our day."[11]

This soothed the sting of her failure at the Follies, but as Baker stared down seven more months in New York, she began to rue the contract she had signed. Luckily for her, one of the stars fell ill, forcing the show to temporarily close. Management offered cast members the option of leaving or staying on a retainer until the show reopened.

It was an easy choice for Baker. She bought a ticket to Paris, the only place she felt at peace.

Before she could leave, the American trip took one final, grim turn. This one was partly her fault. During the Ziegfeld Follies debacle, she had grown frustrated with Pepito, blaming him for the failure. She reconnected with an old flame and holed up with him in a Harlem apartment. Pepito was devastated. In January, he left Josephine and sailed back to Paris. Upon arrival, he saw a doctor and learned he had terminal cancer. As Baker prepared to leave America, she received word that Pepito, her husband and manager, the man who had done more for her career than anyone, was dead.

29

"A musician is a free man."

—Arthur Briggs

AFTER PERFORMING WITH JOSEPHINE BAKER, Arthur Briggs spent a year and more searching for the next phase in his career. He had earned the rare capacity to do whatever he wanted. He had his pick of musicians, cabarets, and countries—except Germany, where the rising Nazi party had effectively banned jazz—but he couldn't decide what to do. He flitted from gig to gig, sometimes joining other bands, sometimes reconfiguring his own group, always looking for the next groove to ride.

In September, Briggs took his band to The Hague, where he ran into Coleman Hawkins. It was a joyful reunion, especially for the homesick Hawkins. He was so happy to see Briggs he threw a party in his room at the Hotel Americain. Briggs then returned to Paris in November, where he began a monthlong engagement at Le Boeuf-Sur-le-Toit, a longtime haven for avant-garde artists such as Picasso, Erik Satie, Igor Stravinsky, Coco Chanel, and Jean Cocteau. French jazz musicians loved the club so much their term for a jam session was *"faire un boeuf."**

Briggs then spent another winter season in Cannes, where he performed at a charity gala alongside Mistinguett and Maurice Chevalier. Edgar Wiggins described the event in a dispatch for the *Chicago Defender*: "Many prominent figures of the social, political, and sporting life of this city attended, paid 300 francs ($20) to enjoy what was termed: 'A Night of Stars.' All of the participating stars—native and

---

* "Make the beef."

foreign—gave their services free."[1] Wiggins was clearly enamored with Briggs's playing. He had been comparing Briggs to Louis Armstrong for months, but in this dispatch, he tightened the comparison into a moniker that would follow Briggs for the next three years: the Louis Armstrong of France.

Though Briggs's reputation continued to grow, he hadn't yet found the spark of inspiration he felt with the Harlemites or the Hot Club. Part of this was the result of losing the Quintette, part of it was the natural exhaustion of an artist who had been working nonstop for a quarter of a century, and part of it was the creeping uneasiness suffusing Europe. By 1936, it was as if the entire Western world had been turned upside down and shaken by the ankles. America was desperate in the depths of Depression, Spain had entered a brutal civil war, Italy began officially promoting anti-Semitism, and Germany passed the "Law for the Protection of German Blood and German Honor," which stripped Jews of citizenship.

While Briggs entertained the few people who still had money enough to summer in Deauville, Adolf Hitler hosted the 1936 Olympics in Berlin. These were the first Olympics to be televised, and Hitler used the publicity to promote his theories of white supremacy, while also employing his propaganda machine to paint the Nazis in pleasant colors. It was a huge coup for Hitler, masking the depravity of his plans. There was a saying popular among party radicals and SA men: "Once the games are history, we'll beat the Jews into misery."[2]

Briggs still paid scant attention to world politics. He returned to Paris in the winter and made freelance recordings with chic French bandleader Ray Ventura. In November, he recorded a radio broadcast for Canetti, who offered Briggs a weekly radio slot, which Briggs declined. He already had an engagement in Vienna to last through December. More importantly, he was looking ahead to 1937 and the contract he'd just signed for six months in Egypt.

Briggs had found the next frontier.

In late December, Briggs took his American Cubano Boys to Cairo, where they were engaged simultaneously at four hotels—Shepheard's, the Continental-Savoy, the Semiramis, and the Heliopolis Palace. These hotels were playgrounds for the international aristocracy. The Heliopolis, with its gorgeous, iconic dome, its four hundred rooms, and its fifty-five luxury apartments, was the most lavish. It later became the presidential palace in Egypt. It was also used as a military hospital for British soldiers during WWI and would be used so again in WWII. The Semiramis was the first hotel built on the Nile. It boasted Cairo's first elevators, done in brass and mahogany, as well as its first European-style nightclub and "palatial red-carpeted staircases, exquisite chandeliers, life-size ebony statues and majestic reflections in Louis XVI style."[3] No less glamorous were the Continental-Savoy and Shepheard's, located within walking distance of each other. Both featured a shaded veranda from which the rich guests commanded a view of the street below. Of Shepheard's, one historian wrote, "It was a hotel from which explorers set off for Africa, where kings entertained mistresses, where movie stars rubbed shoulders with officers on leave from the desert and spies hovered in the hope of minds being softened by the congenial atmosphere. . . . Everybody stayed at Shepheard's from Mark Twain and Arabian adventurer Richard Burton to Noel Coward and Josephine Baker. Its parties and balls were legendary, its barmen the souls of discretion."[4]

For Briggs, it was routine work in a world he had never known. "There was a lot of culture difference between the Egyptians and the Europeans," he said. Briggs found the difference pleasing in at least one regard: "There was no segregation." He began work on December 29, 1936, playing tea parties in the afternoons—admission two shillings— and evenings at the Continental. Each hotel catered to a different clientele with different musical tastes, requiring Briggs and his band to be nimble. In his memoirs, recorded fifty years later, he described the work in great detail, showing that time had not dulled his sharp professional eye:

> At the Continental, we have the Anglo-Saxon clientele, the Anglo-Egyptian, the ambassadors, and the notables of all the countries. The music we did for them was based on Anglo-Saxon music—many Cole Porter compositions like "Night and Day," and "Begin the Beguine." Some Louis Armstrong pieces, like "Mack the Knife," or "Solitude" by Duke Ellington, and the huge Broadway musical comedy hit, "I'm Putting All My Eggs in One

Basket," which . . . was the favorite song in Cairo. At Shepherd's, we were forced to play in a totally different way: rhythmic music but very, very soft. There we had the Anglo-Caucasian clientele and the Egyptian elites. On Thursday afternoon, we had a tea dancing at the Semiramis, where the cream of the Egyptians was represented. This dancing tea was for everyone, but attended only by well chosen Egyptians and ambassadors. Normally, the place was completely booked. On Sunday afternoon, we played at the Heliopolis, a cosmopolitan rendezvous for the well-to-do people of Cairo and around. There, the customer's taste was quite different, rather Afro-Cuban, which was in vogue at home. Fortunately, I had planned for that . . . I prepared Cuban music very seriously and I had three excellent Cuban singers. . . . Every Sunday afternoon, it was full two hours before starting.[5]

But Cairo was not what it first appeared. The city strived to be another Paris, but its jazz scene was feeble. As a contemporary account in *Melody Maker* magazine noted,

The public will dance to anything, from a fourth-class amateur combination which would not dare play anywhere in England, to an imported colored swing band straight from New York. This is the reason why so many appalling combinations prosper in Egypt. . . . I have arrived at this conclusion not only by listening to and studying the bands in question, but also by questioning the so-called dance fans as to the merits of different orchestras to which they have danced. Some weeks ago I asked an excellent dancer what he thought of Arthur Briggs' Cubano American Boys, an excellent colored swing combination. . . . The dancer's reply as to my question concerning the band: "They are no good, they cannot play a tango and Viennese waltz!" This is the mentality of the dancing public in Egypt, and there is a sore need for education of those dancers, forming the majority, who do not know the difference between a swing band and a straight dance band, except that one is wrongly presumed to be colored and the other white.[6]

As he had done so many times, Briggs tried to satisfy this "sore need for education." One evening, he was called to the table of an imperious looking man with a spine like an iron rod. "I am Major Combes, Second Commander of the Eleventh Hussars, stationed in Egypt under the command of Colonel Yalbreys," the man said. He complimented Briggs's playing and said, "We have a military and dance band with pretty much the same composition, but we can see that there is a big difference between your orchestra and ours. It would be very nice of you to come and see if it is possible to do something."

Combes sent a car to drive Briggs and saxophonist Fletcher Allen to the army barracks, where they watched the hopelessly stiff military orchestra fumble through a jazz song. "That's nothing!" Allen said. Briggs was more diplomatic. He advised the major to choose three songs. "You play a song first, and then we'll play the same song," he said. In that way, Briggs hoped, the orchestra would hear what couldn't be put into words.

The first attempt did not go well. Before Briggs got through the first chorus, Combes stopped the music. "Are these the same notes?" he asked. The rigid military conductor said, "According to my ear, yes. But it isn't played the same way." Briggs tried to explain: "It's because we feel differently. It's rhythmic. We hear directly how to make people dance, how it should be played to inspire them, without the need to say a word."

"It doesn't seem very logical to me," the conductor said.

"If you want, we'll play another piece," Briggs replied. "Give us the most difficult piece you have in your repertoire."[7]

This too failed. Combes stopped Briggs midsong, saying, "Let's not go further." Instead he asked Briggs and Allen to join the military band, saying, "They are soldiers. They obey orders. They play as they have learned, but without inspiration." He hoped Briggs could inject the band with that inspiration. Briggs worked hard with the rhythm section, and as he recalled, "At the end of the second month it was really starting to get a little better. . . . The musicians began to communicate with each other. They had forgotten a little of their soldierly rigidity."[8]

Yet again, Briggs would do anything to spread his love of jazz. He had four jobs in Egypt, but he found the time to spend two months with a military band, patiently teaching them how to *feel* swing. He sought no reward. He did it simply because it was his passion. After recounting this story in his memoirs, Briggs was carried away with emotion, digressing into a heartfelt speech on what it meant to him to be a musician. "The name 'musician' is a magnificent name," he said. "We don't need to speak the same language; our music speaks all languages of all countries. When we play the music of the great masters we respect all the values of the notes and all the nuances that are written, which we do with pleasure. But when we play jazz—a word that I don't like—we are free. It's music that is cheerful and free, and it's played with heart, feeling and rhythm. . . . You must always have a big smile in your heart and it's that smile that you apply to your instrument."[9]

At the end of the engagement in Cairo, Briggs checked in on the military band and was pleased to hear "huge progress." Major Combes was more than pleased. He made Briggs a gift of nine silver cigarette cases—one for each member of the Cubano Boys—each one engraved with "Royal British Regiment, 11th Hussars, stationed at Cairo, 15 May 1937." And there was a tenth engraved cigarette case especially for Briggs. It was made of gold.

In June 1937, Briggs traveled to Alexandria for the summer season on the Mediterranean Sea. He performed at the Casino San Stefano, a few miles from the site where Caesar withstood a siege after the Battle of Pharsalus. It was a disaster. "The good clientele wasn't there," Briggs said. "If there were people interested in our music who wanted to dance, we'd continue to play, but it was quite rare." Most nights, the band was "doomed to do our job," playing to an empty house, waiting out the end of the contract. Morale sunk so low that they didn't even care to explore Alexandria. The moment the engagement ended, Briggs hastened home to Georgina, and to Montmartre, where he had recently bought an apartment at 7 Rue Félix Ziem. The small apartment would soon be his only haven.

Hanging on the horizon were the clouds of war.

30

"Haven't we all got a heart? Haven't we all got the same ideas about happiness? Please tell me . . . Isn't it love?"[1]

—Josephine Baker

WHILE BRIGGS FINISHED HIS WORK in Alexandria, the Nazis held a rally in Nuremberg. Hitler had duped many world leaders into thinking him respectable, but in Nuremberg he showed himself as he was: a shrieking madman, his heart corroded by duplicity and hatred. He gave an unhinged speech in which he called Jews "inferior through and through," and he began moving the Nazis into the most vicious phase of their existence.[2] Those who could have opposed him cravenly bowed to his authority, rescinded their moral obligations, and basked in the glow of his power.

Two months later, Josephine Baker married a Jewish man. Jean Lion was a dashing French industrialist who courted Baker in grand fashion and married her against his family's will. Baker could never resist the grand gesture. She made one of her own, renouncing her American citizenship and becoming a French citizen, but in this case, her romanticism clouded her vision. She and Lion lived opposite lives. He went to work before she woke up and came home after she had gone out for the night. She briefly thought of retiring, but, as a biographer remarked, "She could no more give up the stage and applause than she could stop breathing."[3]

At the chic Parisian restaurant Maxim's, Baker and Lion had a nasty fight and broke up. They reunited briefly when Josephine learned she was pregnant, but the one thing she wanted above all else—a child—was not to be. She had a miscarriage, her second. Then she learned that

Jean was having an affair. In a fit of revenge, she ran off with a wealthy Frenchman to Dordogne in southwest France.

Nestled between the Loire Valley and the Pyrenees Mountains, Dordogne is a region of panoramic, cinematic beauty. There, sitting on the crest of a low hill, surrounded by hundreds of acres of rolling land, Baker found Les Milandes. The house looked like a fairytale castle, with round towers and slated conical roofs protecting the dark corridors inside. The land was as luscious as the Garden of Eden, and for a romantic like Baker, Les Milandes was the delicious red apple. She bit. Baker rented the house, not knowing how much she would need it.

The winter of 1938 was bleak, and Les Milandes lacked heat, so for the moment, Baker stayed in Paris. After watching dire newsreel footage of poverty and malnutrition in Parisian slums, she hired a car, filled it with cheap food, coal, and toys, and had her chauffeur drive it slowly through the streets, while she sat in the back heaving out gifts to the poor.

In spring, the weather warmed but the chill spread: Hitler annexed Austria. He marched his troops into Vienna, where he was greeted as a conqueror, and commandeered the elegant Weinzinger Hotel, taking the owner's suite for himself. As it happened, during Baker's disastrous tour of Vienna a decade before, the owner had hung a picture of Baker above his bed. That night, while Hitler slept in a stolen bed in a stolen country, he looked up into the eyes of the Black Venus.

Despite these alarming events, life went on mostly as before. Baker decided to tour again and hired a man named Viggo to hire a group of artists to follow her through Sweden and Denmark. Included in the group were Arthur Briggs and his new band—now styled Arthur Briggs and His Boys. The tour started off with ten fine days at Stockholm's Tivoli Theatre, where Briggs said, "Everything was going very well on stage, the orchestra, the artists, the newspaper critics, and the public."[4]

Briggs had specified in his contract that he would only play closed theaters, as the weather in Sweden was still too cold for an outdoor concert, but in Norrköping, he was asked to play in a park. "We said it was impossible," Briggs said. The promoter insisted, saying Briggs was obliged by contract to perform. "Maybe you can," Briggs retorted, "but not us. We can't play music with gloves!"[5]

The tour got worse in Göteborg, Sweden's second-largest city, where the promoter failed to provide advance publicity. "The first night, there was almost no one," Briggs said. The band was paid half price. After eight days of performing, the promoter informed the troupe he only had enough money to drive them to Copenhagen, but nothing more. "We were given a meeting in a large room where there were already other artists from another company waiting," Briggs said. "It seemed to me that they were waiting for the same thing as us: to be paid." The promoter informed the troupe that they would have to sign on for a summer contract or they would not be paid for their last week. Briggs engaged a lawyer and returned to the promoter, saying, "Pay us first, and then we will sign the contract for the summer." The promoter was hard up; Briggs either had to take the deal or leave. Briggs had learned to control his impulses, but this was too much. He took his band and stormed back to Paris feeling "happy to be out of business."[6]

Baker, it seems, had more difficulty getting free. On May 2, 1938, she wrote Briggs a letter in broken French:

> Dear Mr. Briggs,
>
> I went to Copenhagen to find some money to settle all accounts with you, as well as the other artists. Unfortunately, it is taking longer than I thought. Besides, I don't have any money from the [next] Baker tour, which was supposed to have started already, because following our unfortunate tour in Sweden it has been delayed until October 9th. I am addressing you, dear Mr. Briggs, for you are the most serious of the group, begging you to help me so I can pay all the artists. I don't remember the exact amount. . . . So I am sending vouchers that [Viggo] will give you, which will be paid by me no later than eight days before your departure in June. It is very unpleasant for me to write you this letter, but as you know, I lost 10,000 francs without complaining. . . . If everyone accepts a voucher, it will be over and we will be able

to start again in peace and friendship. I thank you, personally, for your good and pleasant collaboration and I say to you, with great pleasure: goodbye. See you this summer!

Your Josephine

Briggs replied:

I received your letter, and I understand that you are unhappy. . . . Considering this situation, I can't do anything, because you owe us 500 Swedish kroner from our last contract with you. I'm sorry but I can't do anything.

Judging by the tone of the letters, Baker's feelings for Briggs were warm, but he did not feel the same way. If they had bad blood between them, it must have been here that it started to flow. It seems Baker's tour manager insulted Briggs several times—by insisting he perform outside in the freezing cold, by failing to publicize the tour, and by refusing to pay him what he was owed. It also seems Briggs knew of Baker's suspicious reputation with money. As a biographer noted, "She had a long history of weaseling such people as promoters, managers, and publicity agents out of their commissions, usually by retreating into a sort of fog of vagueness." It wasn't just vagueness; sometimes she used her star power as a sword. "When she put on the prima donna act," one business associate recalled, "she diminished the other person. You weren't aware that your legs had been cut from under you until you started to walk."[7]

Briggs always despised this sort of unprofessional behavior. He took great pride in treating his musicians fairly, especially with money. Add to that his discomfort with Baker's brazen sexuality, and he felt no responsibility to her, especially not while she owed him money. He had already found a way to make it right with his band: the director of the Namur Casino invited Arthur Briggs and His Boys to perform with Coleman Hawkins, and Briggs accepted. Briggs loved Bean, and he knew Namur was a safe bet. Just before leaving, however, he received a telegram from Copenhagen asking him to specify the members of his orchestra for the summer tour—apparently he hadn't officially refused to play, or his refusal was misunderstood. He didn't answer. As he signed the contract for Namur, his phone rang incessantly with calls from Copenhagen. He took the phone off the hook, "so as not to bother the neighbors."[8]

31

"I did not want to go back to the U.S.A."

—Arthur Briggs

ARTHUR BRIGGS AND HIS BOYS featuring Coleman Hawkins opened at the Namur Casino in September 1938. Briggs led most of the set, with Hawkins accompanying the band on a few songs. "Most of the time [Hawkins] was free in the baccarat room," Briggs said. "He didn't gamble, he'd just be at the bar . . . I couldn't believe that anyone could drink so much alcohol and that it would have so little effect on him. When we were working at the Casino he would drink a bottle of brandy a day . . . and when I sent someone to fetch him to play he'd come straight as ever."[1]

In Namur, Briggs ran into Robert Goffin. This time, Goffin had no stack of jazz records under his arm. Instead, he brought Briggs a warning: "Arthur, you better leave Europe because it will be in a bloody mess!"[2] Briggs ignored this advice. He had sworn off America, and he hadn't seen Grenada since he left at age sixteen. Europe was his home, and in Europe he would stay.

France had already begun preparing for a German invasion by constructing the Maginot Line—nearly one thousand miles of concrete fortifications, obstacles, and weapon installations spanning the borders of Italy, Germany, Switzerland, and Luxembourg. The French had thought of everything, from underground railways to air-conditioned living quarters for garrisoned troops. The line was impervious to most forms of attack and in some places was twenty-five miles thick. Many thought it impenetrable, including Briggs.

163

As war drew near, Briggs returned to a hushed, frightened Paris. Thousands had already fled. The winter cabaret season was postponed because, according to one manager, "there are no people in Paris."[3] Throughout the city, and indeed most of Europe, there was a queasy calm.

Then came Kristallnacht.

In late October, Hitler ordered the expulsion of more than twelve thousand Polish-born Jews from Germany. They were allowed a single suitcase for their belongings and were forced to leave in one night. Their neighbors looted their abandoned homes, and Nazi authorities confiscated whatever remained. The Jews were herded onto trains and taken to the Polish border, where Polish guards sent them back to Germany. Days passed with no food or shelter, as twelve thousand people marched back and forth between Poland and Germany, unwanted in either country. Finally, four thousand deportees were allowed into Poland. The others had no haven on earth.

Deportee Sendel Grynszpan sent a postcard describing the events to his seventeen-year-old son Herschel, who lived in Paris with an uncle. Four days later, Herschel bought a revolver and a box of bullets, entered the German embassy in Paris, and fired five shots at German secretary Ernst vom Rath, two of which ripped into vom Rath's stomach. The young man made no attempt to escape; he freely confessed to the shooting. In his pocket was a postcard, written to his parents but never sent. It read: "My dear parents, I could not do otherwise, may God forgive me, the heart bleeds when I hear of your tragedy and that of the 12,000 Jews. I must protest so that the whole world hears my protest, and that I will do. Forgive me."

Two days later, Rath died. Goebbels immediately began a campaign against the Jews on German National Radio. Author Milton Mayer recalled the campaign's vile messages: "Are Germans to be sitting ducks all over the world for Jew murderers? Are the German people to stand helpless while the Führer's representatives are shot down by Jew swine? . . . Is the wrath of the German people against the Israelite scum to be restrained any longer?" Rath's death gave Hitler an excuse to do what he already intended to do. Making it seem like a popular uprising, he quietly ordered a pogrom.

On the night of November 9, 1938, rioters smashed, burned, and desecrated hundreds of synagogues throughout Germany, many of which smoldered through the night in full view of local firefighters, who had received orders to intervene only to prevent flames from spreading to German buildings. Nazis desecrated Jewish cemeteries, while Hitler Youths shattered the shop windows of an estimated 7,500 Jewish-owned commercial establishments and looted their wares.

The pogrom was especially destructive in Berlin and Vienna, where Briggs had enjoyed his greatest successes in the 1920s. Mobs of SA men roamed the streets, attacking Jews and forcing them to perform acts of public humiliation. "University professors were made to scrub the streets with their bare hands, and pious old men with white beards were forced into temples and compelled to perform leg squats and yell 'Heil Hitler' in unison," recalled Viennese author Stefan Zweig. "Innocent people were herded together on the street like rabbits and taken to sweep the grounds of SA barracks. All the hateful, sick, dirty fantasies that had been conceived in nocturnal orgies of the imagination were rampantly visible on the streets in broad daylight."[4]

Some thirty thousand Jewish males were arrested and transferred to Dachau, Buchenwald, and other concentration camps. "The first days were the worst," wrote one prisoner at Buchenwald. "They deprived us of water. . . . Your mouth completely dried out, your throat burned and your tongue literally stuck to your gums. When they handed out bread on the third day, I could not choke it down because I did not have any saliva in my mouth. . . . It was as if all hell had broken loose."[5]

Kristallnacht—literally "Crystal Night," named for the shards of broken glass that littered the streets and glinted in the light of burning synagogues—was a turning point. Though the Nazis' Final Solution had not yet been outlined, Kristallnacht made it inevitable. Three days later, Hermann Göring called a meeting of top Nazi leadership, and said, "Gentlemen! Today's meeting is of a decisive nature. I have received a letter written on the Führer's orders requesting that the Jewish question be now, once and for all, coordinated and solved one way or another."[6] Joseph Goebbels, in his diary, was clearer. "It is now tabula rasa," he wrote. "The radical opinion has emerged victorious."[7]

32

"I decided to stay, but I paid for it."[1]

—Arthur Briggs

IN THE WAKE OF KRISTALLNACHT, Arthur Briggs struggled to keep a normal schedule. In December, he played in *La Grande Nuit du Jazz* at the Paris Coliseum, alongside the Hot Club Quintette, Garland Wilson, Valaida Snow, and others, and then he returned to Belgium for Christmas and the New Year. In early 1939, he was contracted to play the Moulin Rouge, but instead of signing on for an entire season, as was customary, Briggs took his contract month to month due to the instability of the moment. He had to disband his orchestra because so many musicians had been conscripted into the army, and he hired a new group of freelancers. "For a conductor, it was becoming unmanageable," he said.[2]

It wasn't just conductors. In March, the Nazis took Czechoslovakia. Now all of Europe began to tremble. From minute to minute the situation changed. War seemed inevitable; war seemed avoidable. War would start tomorrow, or it would never start. Hitler struck with one hand while soothing with the other, manipulating France and England into a policy of appeasement. By the time they realized their mistake it was too late.

Briggs opened at the Moulin Rouge in April. At thirty-eight years old, he was showing signs of aging but not slowing down. His landlady at 7 Rue Félix Ziem recalled, "When I brought his mail to him, around noon, he had just got up, you know, he was in a dressing gown. He had a net on his head to keep his hair like that, to keep it in place. He was very elegant, you know, always impeccable, very neat. And in the evening for his shows, in order to look thinner, he wore a corset. That way he was standing upright; he looked like a young man."[3]

Corset or not, Briggs played with the joy of his sixteen-year-old self. *Chicago Defender* columnist Edgar Wiggins, who was gutting it out in Europe, testified to Briggs's undimmed fire: "Paris jitterbugs have found a real haven at the Moulin Rouge dance hall, where Arthur Briggs and his swing orchestra supply that invigorating music that transforms humans to happy, carefree, jumping things."[4] The crowds needed the transformation. So did Briggs. The world offered fewer and fewer reasons to feel happy and carefree.

Europe was infected with the cancer of nationalism. Even Paris had become dangerous for immigrants and other marginalized groups. Two months before Edgar Wiggins reported on Briggs's performance at the Moulin Rouge, he wrote an ominous column for the *Chicago Defender*:

> Unfortunately our small group that's established here for the benefit of offering these people our unique creation, jazz, rhythm, or swing (as you like), are severely affected by laws that are aimed particularly at hundreds of thousands of political refugees from numerous Continental countries that have poured into France in the past two decades . . . in this democracy that boasts "equality" to all regardless of race, creed, or color, it has been frightfully demonstrated by the recent arrests, and expulsion of prominent Negro artists who, caught in France's general shake-up to clear the country of undesirables, were treated in the same manner as any one of the multitude of European refugees, that might represent nothing and probably entered this country poverty-stricken or diseased, to escape the horrors of a revolution or a dictator, just because they were a bit negligent about having their French identity papers in correct order. Albert Barnes, trumpetist, enjoys the distinction of being the only young Race musician conducting a swing band in Paris today. The others are old-timers, namely, Willie Lewis, Arthur Briggs, and Benny Peyton.[5]

After a few months at the Moulin Rouge, Briggs decided to forego the summer season in Paris and instead found lucrative freelance work on the outskirts of the city. He partnered with his friend, British jazz pianist Tom Waltham, and drove to the suburbs, sometimes traveling fifty or sixty miles to play private parties. During these voyages, Briggs and Waltham grew close. The friendship would save Briggs's life.

Meanwhile, Hitler prepared to invade Poland. He gave orders to "kill without pity or mercy all men, women, and children of Polish descent or language." In the black predawn of September 1, 1939, more than one million German troops thundered across the Polish border, while the Luftwaffe bombed Polish airfields, and German warships and U-boats attacked Polish naval forces in the Baltic Sea. Two weeks later, the Soviets, who had just signed a pact with Germany, aided in the invasion not knowing that Hitler's eastward push would soon envelop Russia in two of history's deadliest battles. By the beginning of October, Poland was divided in half between Germany and Russia. There was no longer any question of Hitler's intent. Appeasement had failed. France and England, having signed a treaty guaranteeing Poland's independence, were obliged to declare war on Germany.

World War II had begun.

For six months, nothing happened. These months became known as the Phony War. As journalist Alexander Werth described it, "In Paris you would hardly, on the face of it, have thought that there was a war on at all—except, of course, that nearly all the men you knew had been called up. . . . The *Chevaux de Marly* in the Place de la Concorde and the base of the Obelisk were sandbagged (it gave the Obelisk an even more phallic look than usual). . . . But apart from little things like that there was, on the face of it, little in Paris to remind you of the war."[6] For Briggs, the Phony War meant indefinite unemployment. France ordered nightly blackouts as a precaution against German bombers, putting an end to the Parisian nightlife. In a strange way, Briggs welcomed the rest. It was the first real vacation he had taken in twenty years. The only problem, Briggs recalled, was that "everything was closed—nothing else for us men of a certain age but to stay at home."[7]

While Briggs waited at home, the American consulate told all American citizens without urgent business in Paris to leave the city. For the last time, Briggs considered fleeing. He thought of his wife, a Belgian citizen. What if she wasn't allowed into America? What if they were separated? Scariest of all, what if they made it to America together as an interracial couple? Briggs well knew the danger he and Georgina would face in a country where interracial marriage was illegal in thirty of forty-eight states, and where the penalty for a black man caught breaking this law was often death by lynch mob. Even in Harlem, he had no guarantee of safety from racial violence. Most compelling of all, Georgina didn't want to leave. For the last time, Briggs decided to stay.

Many black expats in Paris were forced into a similar dilemma. Some, like Briggs, had married in Europe. Others started families there. Eugene Bullard was just one of many confronted with the heart-wrenching choice of braving the Nazi invasion or leaving his French wife and children. Always a fighter, Bullard not only stayed, he went looking for the war. First he tried to rejoin his old regiment from World War I, packing a knapsack and marching toward the front. On the way, he met fleeing refugees who told him the fight was already over. He went to Orléans and offered his services to the 51st Infantry, joining a machine gun company on the Loire River. Three days later, in the village of La Blanc, an exploding artillery shell blew him across the street and smashed him headfirst into the wall of a building. Eleven soldiers died around him; Bullard survived. Injured and alone, he fled the Nazi advance, catching rides where he could and walking the rest of the way in excruciating pain, using his rifle as a crutch. He staggered to a military hospital, where a doctor wrapped his injuries and told him to move on. Bullard took fresh water and a tin of sardines and continued walking, sleeping in fields and roadside ditches. He reached Bordeaux after two days and collapsed at the Traveler's Aid Society, where the American consul issued him a passport and gave him twenty dollars. Bullard then made his way to Biarritz, where he saw a woman carrying her dead child. He persuaded her to give the child up "to heaven," and borrowing a French soldier's trenching tool, he dug a grave and buried the child. Several days later, he escaped on a ship to America.

Not everyone who stayed in Paris was a war hero. Many black Americans simply did not want to leave the relative paradise they had found in the City of Light. Bricktop held out as long as she could, but eventually her friends persuaded her to leave. "The last night I saw the Paris of Bricktop," she said, "it was pouring down rain. The car drove through the dimly lit streets at a snail's pace, and I looked out at the city I loved and wondered when I would see it again."[8]

After weeks of blackouts, Paris returned to an approximation of normalcy. "A decree was issued," Briggs said. "The amusement establishments could open again, but only until midnight, provided that the curfew is respected, and that no light should be visible from the outside." Surprisingly, Briggs didn't consider going back to work—"I was very happy to be able to go to the movies," he said.[9] Then he was asked to form a group of freelancers for Le Club on the Champs-Elysees. This lasted until the end of the year, when the proprietor disappeared.

By the middle of January 1940, Paris sunk to minus 20 degrees Celsius. In February, Briggs braved the cold to record for Charles Delaunay's Swing label, putting together a makeshift band, including Django Reinhardt, and cutting four songs: "Melancholy Baby," "Sometimes I'm Happy," "Scatterbrain," and "Braggin' the Briggs." The latter was a jam that was too long for a 78, and too good to cut short, so the label released it in two parts. To hear these recordings is to understand why Briggs was called the Louis Armstrong of France. His style is more nuanced, more assured, more inventive than ever.

He wouldn't record again for five years.

On June 9, 1940, Germany attacked France. The Maginot Line only had one weak point, and that was where Hitler struck. His armies invaded and conquered Belgium and Luxembourg, which allowed them to skirt the Maginot Line and make a daring dash through the Ardennes Forest into France. Checkmated, the French government fled to Bordeaux, leaving Paris open for the taking. On June 14, 1940, German troops entered the city by the Porte de la Villette, sending more than one million people fleeing in their wake.

For Arthur Briggs, there was only one thing to do.

Hide.

33

"I wisely stayed at home."[1]

—Arthur Briggs

THERE WAS A BULLDOG IN PARIS named Poggy. The dog's owner was one of a million people who decided to flee after the German invasion. This man, a jazz musician, was not heartless; he loved Poggy, but he could not take the dog with him, so he begged mercy from a friend, a fellow musician who was staying in Paris, a man he knew he could trust. And so, Arthur Briggs adopted a dog. Many people would have felt burdened by such a responsibility in the face of mortal danger. Not Briggs. He called it "a wonderful gift."[2]

The consul had warned Briggs to stay inside unless absolutely necessary, so throughout the summer, he left the apartment only two or three times a day, depending on Poggy's needs. He walked around the neighborhood until the dog was done sniffing fence poles and greeting dog friends and pulling at the leash to chase squirrels, then he returned to hiding. Meanwhile, Hitler toured Paris to view his spoils. He ended his tour in Montmartre at the Sacré-Coeur, less than a mile from Briggs's apartment. Perhaps Briggs and Poggy were out for a walk as the Führer ascended the Butte.

Hitler was pleased with what he saw. With rigid efficiency, his soldiers had transformed Paris into a German city. White signposts sprung up on every Parisian street with German lettering to direct military traffic. Nazis commandeered empty houses and buildings and hung posters depicting a uniformed Aryan soldier gazing at a child in his arms, with the slogan: "You have been abandoned; put your trust in the German soldier."[3] Every day at the stroke of noon, more than two hundred German soldiers marched down the Champs-Elysees to the Place de la Concorde. Ahead of them a brass band played "Prussia's Glory." Nazis toppled nearly two hundred bronze statues and melted them down for shell casings. They ripped down the French flag everywhere it flew and hoisted the swastika, even planting one atop the Eiffel Tower.

With this work done, curfews were lifted, and the Germans invaded Paris's nightlife, drinking and carousing in the cabarets into the wee hours of the morning. It was like *le tumulte noir*, except the noir was missing. Hitler banned black performers from working in Paris, and many establishments prominently displayed signs in large letters reading: FOR ARYANS ONLY. Briggs had seen such signs in America's Jim Crow South. He never expected to see them in Paris.

Hunger was a new enemy, as food shortages became acute and rationing restricted daily supplies. Ration tickets were good for two eggs, 3.2 ounces of cooking oil, and two ounces of margarine. The meat ration was so small that, according to a popular joke, it could be wrapped in a subway ticket, unless the ticket had been used, in which case the meat might fall through the hole punched by the conductor's perforator. The staple of most Parisian diets was the rutabaga, a variety of turnip formerly fed to cattle.[4]

Briggs did his best to stay hidden, knowing every knock at his door could be the last. And one day it came. *Knock, knock.* He opened the door. It was Aimé Barelli, his trumpet student in Cannes.

"Arthur, I'm here," Barelli said.

"I'm glad you're here," Briggs replied.

Barelli looked like death in a tattered army uniform. He had just returned from the front, having barely survived the German onslaught. He limped to Paris, where he knew no one, and found a musician's cafe. There, he struck up a conversation with a stranger and asked if the man knew Arthur Briggs. The stranger happened to be Briggs's friend Maurice Mouflard, who said, "It's like you asked me if I know the water fountain on Place Pigalle! Of course we know each other! I see him very often; he lives nearby. I'll take you there."[5]

Briggs welcomed Barelli and Mouflard into his hiding place. He gave Barelli clean clothes, but the young man needed more than clothes. "I know no one," Barelli said. "I have nowhere to go." Briggs turned to Mouflard: "I don't go out, as you know, but I'd like you to drive my friend Aimé to rue Chaptal to the Hot Club de France. There you'll certainly find Delaunay and see together what it's possible to do."

"I don't have an instrument," Barelli sighed.

"Yes, you have an instrument," Briggs replied. "You see that one there." He pointed to his trumpet. "It's yours."

"Impossible," Barelli said.

"For me, I know it's finished," Briggs said. "You can start it up again. Go ahead, take it. It's yours. I heard you play; I'm sure you'd make it sing."[6]

Barelli left with Briggs's shirt on his back and Briggs's trumpet under his arm. It was the trumpet that thrilled nightclubs from Constantinople to Cairo; the trumpet that graced some of the best European jazz records in existence; the trumpet that joined in joyful noise with Armstrong, and Reinhardt, and Hawkins, and Baker; the trumpet that defined *Arthur Briggs*. Losing it was a kind of death, yet Briggs was eager to suffer that loss so that his friend might gain by it.

He was running out of time anyway.

Many black jazz musicians that stayed in Paris had already been arrested and taken God knew where. No one knows how it happened to Briggs. He never told the story, not even to his family. His daughter recalls hearing that he was out walking Poggy when the Nazis found him. The only fact that remains is this: on the morning of October 17, 1940, Arthur Briggs was arrested as an enemy of the Reich.

He likely underestimated the severity of the threat he faced. As the French artist Jean Weinfeld recalled of his own capture, "Everything was almost elegant, even graceful. There was a German officer who told my wife, 'Madam, this is only for a check. Don't lose hope; your husband will return in a day or two.'"[7]

Perhaps Briggs thought his detention would be short as he packed his valuables into a trunk, took it to the American Express for safe-keeping, bid Georgina and Poggy adieu, and delivered himself into the hands of his captors.

Part III

"And behold the tears of such as were oppressed, and they had no comforter; and on the side of their oppressors there was power."

—Ecclesiastes 4:1

34

October 1940

FIFTY MILES NORTHEAST OF PARIS lies the commune of Compiègne. It is a symbolic place, one that draws history the way a metal rod draws lightning. There, Charlemagne's son Louis the Debonair was deposed; there, Joan of Arc was captured; there, Germany surrendered World War I and France surrendered to Hitler. There, Arthur Briggs was sent as a prisoner of war.

The camp at Compiègne was wretched. "We found [the lavatories] in a disgusting state on our arrival," recalled Canadian war hero Frank Pickersgill. "There were eight seats for a thousand men. . . . We were most reluctant to go to this spot, and never went unless absolutely obliged. Even then, disgust, to which very soon was added the cold—not to speak of the inadequate food—provoked in many of us a sort of inhibition."[1]

This was Briggs's first experience of captivity. Had he stayed in Compiègne, especially after it became a main waystation for the death camps, he might not have survived the war. Luckily, his friend Tom Waltham was imprisoned at Stalag 220, also known as La Grand Caserne, in St. Denis, six miles north of Paris. With permission, Waltham had formed an orchestra of prisoners, and he asked the Nazis to send Briggs to lead the brass section. After a week in Compiègne, Briggs was shipped to his new home.

Housed in an old Swiss Guard barracks built in the mid-1700s, the camp at St. Denis was, Briggs noted, "organized like a little city."[2] Briggs entered through the main gate, beneath two machine-gun nests fitted with searchlights, and walked past a heavily guarded gateway into the camp. He was now surrounded by a twelve-foot high, electrified barbed wire fence. Briggs entered the Nazi offices, where he surrendered his personal documents and was issued his new identity—a number printed on an armband. He was led past the parade ground, its flagpole flying the swastika. In front of him loomed the brooding Caserne building. Condemned as unfit for human habitation, the Caserne housed nearly seventeen hundred men. The number would soon swell to some twenty-three hundred, living in a space meant for half that number. In the Caserne's grim shadow squatted huts, hastily built to hold the excess. The huts were cheaply made and feeble against the winter cold.[3] This is where Briggs lived.

Briggs was imprisoned with fellow British citizens and other civilian enemies of the Reich. Roughly half the prisoners spoke no English. Many were as dangerous as the sneering Nazi guards. Racketeers and bookies abounded. Pickersgill, who was also sent from Compiène to St. Denis, recalled these prisoners as "lousy swine." One such "loathsome type" ran the canteen, overcharging the men for toothbrushes and other amenities and pocketing the difference.[4] Other prisoners were nobler. William Joseph Webb, a British civilian, kept a daily diary of camp life from October 1940 to the end of 1942. The punishment for being caught with a diary was three days in solitary confinement in an unheated cell with nothing to eat but bread and water. During the lethal winters, Webb risked death to record his testimony, leaving history richer for his courage.

Briggs barely had time to get settled before Tom Waltham wrapped him in a warm embrace. "I asked that you be sent here!" Waltham said excitedly. "We need you to handle the brass section." Waltham introduced Briggs to the orchestra, twenty or so musicians of varying ability, including two trumpeters who were "very young, very amateur." Briggs immediately took the trumpeters under his care. Arnold Präger, an Australian, was "a very well-bred boy with a good musical background," Briggs said. Murphy, the other boy, spoke only Flemish. "This boy had a proud character that could not hide his lack of talent and training," Briggs said. "It was immediately obvious that he had learned on his own. He didn't master his instrument. He had no flexibility or sensitivity." Always the optimist, Briggs added, "I thought they had courage, and with help, they would manage to play their part."[5] Briggs had no trumpet but was allowed to send a letter to Maurice Selmer of the famous horn-making family, who sent three new horns to St. Denis, one for each trumpeter.

Music was a fixture of life in St. Denis, as it was in most Nazi camps. The Nazis allowed their prisoners to form orchestras, or *Lagerkapellen*, for many reasons. Music was used to accompany manual labor and to humiliate prisoners, who were nearly starved and worked to death and were still forced to summon the strength to sing. In death camps it was used to "drown out the screams of the dying."[6]

Here again Briggs was lucky. St. Denis was a prison camp, not a labor or extermination camp, meaning the orchestra didn't have to force men to work or mask the sounds of death. Instead, Briggs performed at the pleasure of his captors. He soon became the center of the camp's musical life, forming a small jazz combo with Waltham, and singing Negro spirituals in a vocal trio with two other black prisoners, including Gay Martins, an old friend from the Southern Syncopated Orchestra. In addition, the commander at St. Denis, a man Briggs called Mr. Gillis, made Briggs camp trumpeter. His duties were to blow the Reveille at seven in the morning for the wake-up call; at nine o'clock for first checkup, when the Nazis examined the rooms; at five or six in the evening, depending on the season, for second checkup; and at nine at night to signal lights out. The men stood for hours at these checkups, while the guards scoured their barracks, flipped their mattresses, and ransacked their few possessions for contraband. A roll call could come at any time, depending on the commander's whims, and between inspections, German spies known as "Mouton"* roamed the camp pretending to be prisoners.

Briggs's trumpet duties earned him special comforts, including food privileges. The daily ration at St. Denis was a *Komisbrod* (a roll of black bread), cabbage soup for lunch, and a similar soup for dinner, or a spoonful of ersatz jam with a small lump of margarine. Briggs recalled,

---

* Sheep.

"When I got to the camp and saw what they were dishing out for food, I said, 'I couldn't blow my instrument on that.'"[7] Gillis let Briggs eat with the kitchen staff, which was a mixed blessing. The food wasn't better; there was just more of it. Instead of living near starvation, Briggs had the luxury of desperate hunger.

The guards also granted Briggs one visit per week, instead of the usual one visit every three weeks. These visits were as nourishing as food. It became a sport for the prisoners to rush the fence on visiting day and watch the women walk by. If this sport didn't sate their sexual hunger, it at least blunted the pangs. After spending every day and night in the company of two thousand miserable men, Briggs must have rejoiced at seeing his wife, but intimacy of any sort, even the slightest touch, was impossible. Briggs and Georgina met across a table in a flimsy hut filled with chicken wire, while armed guards patrolled the room. Webb's son left a detailed description of the visiting process:

> Going to visit Father was a trying experience as it took all day . . . [there was the] train to St. Denis station, then there was a two kilometer walk, along a cobble-stone road, to reach the camp. . . . There was no guarantee that the visit could even take place. . . . When I first saw Father four months after being picked up in July, I found him to be terribly thin. He had aged incredibly and had a haggard hunted look about him, his clothes just hanging on him. All the internees were the same. They were being starved to death. . . . The parcels were deposited at a small hatch window in the outer barrack wall. A German guard, depending on the mood he was in, took the parcels without any further ado, or he could keep you waiting. Their favorite trick was to keep the visitors, mostly women and children, waiting as long as possible outside the hatch entrance gate. There was no shelter from the elements. When the hatch was opened the soldier insisted on examining the parcel contents and in addition insisted on viewing our documents. Articles were often rejected for no reason and there was no redress. It was a slow painful procedure and you could never be sure what to expect. . . . You entered a small fenced area on presentation of identity papers. Everyone

listened attentively for the loved one's name and number to
be called out. When this occurred, you entered through a side
gate into the barrack compound. . . . We moved forward into
the [visiting] hut which was divided by two parallel three feet
wide tables, which went the length of the hut. Below the tables
was a fine chicken wire stretching to the floor. Soldiers ordered
us to sit, and they patrolled at the back of us. The far door of
the hut was opened, and the internees rushed into the central
area. . . . The babble of voices made it hard to talk sensibly; it
was more in the nature of a shouting match as we shared our
news. Everyone had to remain seated. Eye contact with a guard
had to be avoided, for if that happened he would stay behind
you as he became suspicious.[8]

Visitors were allowed to bring parcels, but these were often held
for days or never delivered. The Nazis strictly forbade the visitors from
passing anything to the prisoners in the visiting hut, and the punishment for being caught was loss of visits and mail for two months and
confinement in an unheated cell, regardless of the time of year, on bread
and water, for ten days. Here again, Briggs earned a luxury with his
trumpet. When Georgina visited, Briggs recalled, "she brought me a hot
meal whenever she could."[9]

Georgina's first visit likely took place on the fifth of December 1940.
That day, the prisoners returned from the visiting hut wild with fear
after their wives were all arrested. The internees began demonstrating
outside Gillis's office. It snowed, but the men demonstrated anyway,
marching until their shoes and pant legs were filthy and sodden. Two
days later, Briggs tried to ease tensions, giving a concert of Negro spirituals, at which Webb noted the trio "sang low and sweetly, 'Sonny
Boy.'"[10] Still, passions remained high. The next day, Webb wrote, "Men
are all in the dumps and worrying about wives taken away." Then, on
the ninth: "Raining. Dreadful. Office has changed all visiting hours and
times, again. . . . So much thieving." And again on the eleventh: "All men
demonstrating outside office, wanting news of wives and whereabouts.
Would not leave. Germans angry. Soldiers came out with arms."[11]

While the men demonstrated, Briggs learned the true reason his transfer to St. Denis had been granted. Otto von Stülpnagel, commander of Nazi-occupied France, had ordered a classical concert. He wanted it ready in one month. "It seemed impossible!" Briggs said. "I thought we would never have the time to do it right."[12] Adversity is the truest test of character. In prison, tasked with entertaining the men who sent him there to suffer—and maybe die—Briggs's first concern was playing the music right. They could take everything from him but that.

Stülpnagel requested three pieces: Strauss's "Radetzky March," Smetana's "The Bartered Bride," and Beethoven's Fifth Symphony. This was no small order. Few jazz trumpeters would dare such a feat, let alone with a backing group of amateurs. But Briggs had something greater planned. His professional eye recognized that three selections did not make a concert. He wanted a wider emotional arc. He wanted control. After a discussion with Waltham, he added two more pieces: Johann Strauss II's, "The Blue Danube" and the popular German military march, "Die Alte Kameraden."

Now he had a concert.

Briggs and Waltham wrote arrangements to fit the makeshift orchestra, and they rehearsed twice a day, from 10:00 AM to noon, and again from three to five in the evening. This provided Briggs with a spiritual escape. For four hours a day, he forgot the festering latrines in the yard, forgot the gray barracks full of lice and men, forgot the Nazi guards nervously fingering their machine guns. For four hours, his stomach didn't grumble, and his teeth didn't chatter. For four hours, he wasn't a prisoner—he was a musician.

Briggs honed his brass section the way Will Marion Cook once honed him. He tested their reading abilities, which he found satisfactory, and drilled them until they knew every nuance of every piece. "Without boasting," he said, "our section became over time very, very solid."[13] His goal was nothing less than musical alchemy, taking the base metal of an amateur orchestra and turning it to gold.

"Radetsky March" and "Die Alte Kameraden" were easiest to arrange. Both had the proud, brassy bounce Briggs had mastered at the Fourth of July marching band competition in 1918. Harder was "The Bartered Bride," its violins fluttering like hummingbird wings, its cellos

punctuating like tugboat blasts. To perform this piece required virtuosic speed and dexterity, the kind Briggs showed with the "Carnival of
Venice" in Belgium in 1922. Harder still was "The Blue Danube," which
required precise control of emotion and dynamics. Here, Briggs evoked
his passionate performance of "Edmee" with the Savoy Syncopators in
1925. Hardest of all was Beethoven's Fifth Symphony. It required everything: dizzying speed, emotional control, and masterful execution. For
this piece, Briggs drew on his classical training as a teenager in London, the New Orleans fire he learned from Bechet, the nights he played
softly but with feel at Bricktop's, and the spontaneous jam sessions with
Freddy Johnson, Django Reinhardt, and Coleman Hawkins. He put his
entire life into the concert. It was his revenge.

35

"We live as those exiled to some dim star."[1]

—A. H. Pullen, St. Denis prisoner

WINTER HIT LIKE IT HAD a score to settle. "Freezing," Webb wrote on the third of December 1940. "Tripe stuff for dinner—awful. No more fresh stuff left."[2] Two days later, the hot water was gone. Each morning broke like a brittle bone. The men awoke and trudged to the washroom, where they splashed frigid water on their blue-cold bodies. Then the pipes froze, and there was no water at all.

Arthur Briggs played a concert on New Year's Eve, but it was only a bit of levity on the gallows. His guts were twisted with hunger. In four days he had to join his ragtag orchestra, mount a makeshift bandstand, and in the bitter cold play the hardest show of his life.

In his memoirs, Briggs recalled the concert's date as January 25, 1942. The year is certainly wrong—he was still trying to pass off the story of his American birth, so he claimed his arrest took place after Pearl Harbor. The day, however, is less certain. Here we must turn to Webb's diary. On January 25, 1941, Webb made the following entry: "We've been given more lights to eat and this time it was rotten and stank. We are not taking any more. Men up in arms and quite right too."[3] Compare this to his two entries on January 4, in which he wrote: "Camp all ready for a visit by a General. Will he come?" and "All camp cleaned up, as per orders, expecting visit by General. Will he turn up?"[4] It seems likely, if not incontrovertible, that Briggs performed for the Nazis on January 4, 1941.

Briggs performed in the St. Denis theater, which the prisoners built themselves using Red Cross boxes for the stage and cigarette tins for stage settings. Several artists among the men designed decoration and scenery. "It looked like a real theater," Briggs recalled, "with a big podium raised for concerts."[5] Here the internees put on shows for each other, including a rendition of *Cinderella*; here the commander of Nazi France waited to be entertained.

Stülpnagel was an old-school soldier with the grim visage of a man who had spent his life in the service of death. He looked like a cartoon villain, with a cadaverous face, black moustache, bulbous forehead, and high, receding hairline. He even wore a monocle clamped beneath a devilishly arched eyebrow. He was "arrogant, vain, somewhat of a caricature," as one German soldier recalled.[6] He had retired in 1939 as a decorated war hero, but when the Nazis took Paris, Hitler called him to duty again.

Stülpnagel believed in Germany's war but did not understand the Nazis' obsession with Jews, as it had no strategic importance. During the occupation of Paris, he objected when high-ranking Nazis confiscated priceless art collections from prominent French Jews. His protests eventually reached Hitler's desk, but to no avail. Despite these flashes of humanity, however, Stülpnagel followed orders like a true soldier. He fined the Jewish community in France one billion francs, sanctioned the shooting of nearly two hundred hostages, and announced that "a large number of criminal Judeo-Bolshevik elements will be deported for forced labor in the East."[7]

As Briggs watched Stülpnagel and his retinue take their seats, he felt conspicuous as "the only ink spot on the stand."[8] Gillis beckoned the band to begin, and they started on "Die Alte Kameraden," receiving "tremendous applause."[9] It is astounding that Briggs suggested one of the Nazis' favorite songs to open the concert, but even when performing for his captors he couldn't forget the lesson he learned in Scotland in 1920: play to the audience's tastes.

Next came "The Bartered Bride," which ended with "an intense silence." Then, Briggs recalled, "The applause started and didn't stop." After the audience regained its composure, the orchestra began Beethoven's Fifth, its iconic, ominous introduction seemingly made for winter in prison. As the last note rang out, the crowd erupted again, clapping and shouting for seven full minutes. "We thought that the theater was going to collapse, the applause was so strong," Briggs said.[10] Briggs, the masterful manipulator of emotion, had shown the audience the height of passion; now the orchestra eased into the sentimental "Blue Danube," a tender waltz full of lilting loveliness, its push-pull rhythm sometimes rushing into triumph, sometimes slowing into melancholy. "The ending was just as brilliant," Briggs said.[11] The concert finished with a sentimental turn, as the entire camp sang along to "Radetsky March." Gillis demanded an encore, and Briggs said, "The enthusiasm in the end was as great and even more."[12]

Stülpnagel applauded as heartily as anyone. He was especially impressed with the black trumpeter who had mastered Beethoven, and he asked for an audience. Before Briggs could bask in his triumph, he was face to face with the Nazi commander of France.

"I congratulate you," Stülpnagel said. "I never thought it was possible, but I've heard it myself."

Briggs understood: Stülpnagel never thought it was possible for a *black* man to show such culture and talent. "They believed that everything that was not Caucasian was a monkey," he later said.[13] Briggs felt the old impulsive fire rising in his heart. He was still the man who rode segregated subways in Harlem and listened to Marcus Garvey speak, still the man who studied under Will Marion Cook and performed with the Coterie of Friends, still the man who never wanted the baggage of race but carried it always. He knew Stülpnagel could kill him with a single command, but he had been pushed too far. Briggs looked Stülpnagel in the eye and said, "Es gibt viel Sachen die man nicht kennen." In German he said it. "There are many things you do not know."[14]

Stülpnagel ignored the insolence.

"You're quite right," he said. Then, taking his leave of Briggs, he said in English, "I shall never forget this evening."[15]

Arthur Briggs had achieved great feats in life. None was greater than this night. He honored his profession under the hardest of circumstances. But he did something more—he risked his life for dignity. He forced the commander of Nazi-occupied France, a soldier in the war for white supremacy, to see him as a man.

36

"War was injustice. But war could bring justice too."[1]

—Josephine Baker

IN THE SUMMER OF 1939, Josephine Baker became a spy. Jacques Atbey, head of military counterintelligence in Paris, visited her at Le Beau-Chêne and asked her to join the war. "The people of Paris have given me everything," Baker said. "I am ready, Captain, to give them my life."[2] Atbey's boss, secret service chief Paul Paillole, was nervous. "Our department mistrusted would-be Mata Haris," he said. "I was afraid that she was one of those shallow show business personalities who would shatter like glass if exposed to danger." Atbey knew better. "Josephine was made of steel," he said.[3]

Atbey believed Baker's status as a world famous artist offered the perfect cover for gathering intelligence. She was already a regular guest at government embassies throughout Europe. All she had to do was attend parties where high-ranking military officers mingled, their tongues loosened with champagne, their minds occupied with her beauty, and absorb information. When she heard something important, she would duck into the bathroom, write it on a scrap of paper, and pin the paper to her underwear. "It seemed the perfect way to fight my war," she said.[4] "My notes would have been highly compromising had they been discovered, but who would dare search Josephine Baker to the skin?"[5] Within a week, she produced what Atbey called "some extremely useful information."[6]

During the Nazi invasion of France, Baker also served with the Red Cross in Paris, caring for homeless refugees fleeing the countryside,

191

visiting wounded soldiers in the hospital and singing to them in the wards. "My heart sank at the sight of those exiles, broken body and soul by defeat," she said. "There were old people and innocent children to tend, physical and spiritual wounds to heal."[7] She even used her skill as a pilot to fly Red Cross supplies into Belgium.

After France surrendered, the country was split roughly in half. The top half went to Germany; the bottom half stayed with France under Philippe Pétain's puppet government in Vichy. Les Milandes was well below the demarcation line, and when Paris became unsafe, Baker crammed her Packard full of clothes and possessions, along with her maid, two Belgian refugees, and three dogs, and drove to her fairy tale castle. She had been filling empty champagne bottles with gasoline in case of emergency, and she took these too.

Baker never expected to use Les Milandes this way, but it fit her purposes perfectly. "The vast chateau with its secret nooks and crannies made an ideal hiding place," she said. "And hide we did."[8] That summer, she provided cover for several fighters on their way to join the nascent resistance, including a French naval officer and a Breton aviator. Baker and her guests stayed indoors huddled around a radio listening to Charles de Gaulle's crackling broadcasts as he tried to raise an army from his exile in England. "We were deeply moved by the General's voice uttering words we had despaired of hearing, phrases that touched our innermost beings," Baker said.[9]

Baker put herself in great danger hiding these men. Like Briggs, she lived in constant fear that each knock at the door would be the last. And one day it came. *Knock, knock.* A strange man with an American accent stood at her door. "Foxy, when are we going to join de Gaulle?" he said. Baker recognized Atbey beneath his disguise. He asked her to aid in his escape to England, where he intended to join the resistance.[10]

Before she could help Atbey, there came another knock. This was the one she dreaded: five Nazi soldiers stood at her door. "We are informed, madam, that you are hiding weapons in your chateau," one soldier said. "What have you to say to that?" Baker didn't miss a beat. "I think that *monsieur l'officier* cannot be serious," she replied. "It is true that I had Red Indian grandparents, but they hung up their tomahawks quite a while ago now, and the only dance I've never taken part in is the war dance."[11] Even Nazis weren't immune to Baker's charm. They left her alone.

It was a close call, though—too close. Paillole sent Baker to Lisbon, capital of neutral Portugal; Atbey went along disguised as Baker's manager. Using invisible ink, he wrote sensitive intelligence on her sheet music, intending to smuggle it to the British in Lisbon. Again, Baker provided the perfect cover. In case of capture, she and Atbey had only a handful of sheet music and a believable excuse: the great chanteuse could not perform without music.

When the Portuguese consulate delayed her passport, Baker called the ambassador of Brazil, a man she knew to be an admirer, and requested visas on the pretext that she and Atbey were heading for Rio de Janeiro. She gave instructions for Atbey's passport to read, "Accompanying Mme. Josephine Baker," giving his disguise extra credibility but also implicating herself if he got caught. In late November 1940, Baker drove south to the Pyrenees, carrying documents that could get her killed. She took a train to Spain and a plane from Madrid to Lisbon, a city that was "awash with double-dealing, rumor, malice and deceit at every level of government and society," according to one biographer.[12] There, Baker made front-page news. Her fame enabled her to attend the usual diplomatic parties, where she continued to gather information, pinning notes to her underwear or stuffing them in her bra. Meanwhile, at the British Embassy, Atbey delivered what looked like a handful of sheet music. Years later Captain Paillole said, "The destiny of our Allies . . . was written in part over the pages of 'J'ai Deux Amours.'"[13]

After Lisbon, Baker helped build a network of spies in Marseilles. For this mission, she booked herself into "the grandest hotel in [Marseilles]." But after months without a paying gig, and after refusing money for spying, she couldn't afford her old lifestyle. Soon the glamorous Black Venus was reduced to renting an unheated room in a cheap hotel "filled to the gills with whores."[14] She wore an overcoat to bed and developed walking pneumonia.

Sick, freezing, and poor, Baker decided to put on a show to raise money and cover her movements. As Briggs prepared his concert in captivity, Baker prepared one of her own. She assembled the score of *La Créole* (an operetta she performed six years prior), hired a cast, coached them in their parts, scrounged for costumes, and booked an opera house in Marseille. The opera house didn't believe she could pull off such an ambitious project, but her dancing partner told them, "You don't know Josephine. She can do anything."[15]

She was made of steel.

37

"We don't see the end of this."[1]

—William Joseph Webb

NINETEEN FORTY-ONE WAS A PIVOTAL YEAR, both for the war and for the prisoners at St. Denis. During this year, America and Russia were forced to join the fight against Germany, the Nazis began their so-called Final Solution, and food shortages at St. Denis brought the prisoners to the brink of starvation. For those who survived, as Arthur Briggs survived, some of the beauty went out of life forever.

The winter of 1940–'41 was the second of three consecutive record-breaking winters in Europe, all of which Briggs suffered in captivity. It was lethally cold—lethal it seemed to everything but the bugs. "Here there are always rooms being emptied and men going to hospital to be 'disinfected' from bugs," Webb wrote on January 8. "Place crawling with them."[2] The Nazis banned newspapers, leaving the prisoners in desperate ignorance of the world outside the barbed wire. The food repelled even starving men: horse heads, cat meat, lights (lungs), guts, teeth, rotten potatoes, and foul bread.[3] The cabbage soup often had worms floating in it. "If you had nothing else to eat, you had to just scoop the worms out and eat it," Briggs said.[4]

Crowded, hungry, and cold, many men began to lose control. To Briggs's dismay, one of these men was Murphy, the trumpeter he had taken under his wing. Briggs always liked Präger better, and Murphy knew it. This caused a rivalry between the young men. One night, Briggs asked Präger to replace him for the final call. "Moments before it started, we heard someone start playing, but making false notes and hiccups," Briggs recalled. It was Murphy. "His pride had been stung, and he wanted to show that he was capable of it."[5] Präger approached Murphy, who brandished his fist. A fight broke out, and the internees burst from their barracks. As the guards scrambled to stop the brawl, Briggs took his trumpet and played the call for lights out. Webb recorded the event in his journal: "Position complicated by some idiot playing 'games' at roll call. All punished . . . it's an anxious time."[6]

Not until March did winter relent. Then the weather became so beautiful it almost made life worse. In a normal year, Briggs would have been finishing his winter residency now, maybe at the Abbaye or the Moulin Rouge, and looking ahead to summer in Cannes or the Côte d'Azur. The mere memory was enough to drive a man mad.

Luckily, he had the orchestra.

Music saved more than just Briggs. One detainee recalled it as more important than the priests who said Mass at St. Denis. "In the church services of the camp, both Catholic and Protestant priests exhorted their flock to patience," he wrote. "But we were not all churchgoers. . . . However when Arthur Briggs's posters were put up, and we read of them or heard read: 'Arthur Briggs and his Boys,' 'Plantation Songs,' 'Hot Jazz,' 'Special Number' and the like, the sky regained a better hue. The 'kitchen hands,' the 'latrine cleaners' and other fatigues workers put more rhythm into their task while priests and teachers committee members and bureau officials rubbed their hands with satisfaction, all at the prospect of an agreeable evening."[7] Music was a universal religion. Briggs always believed in its power; now he wielded it on behalf of two thousand men as a weapon against despair.

By Briggs's fortieth birthday, he had become famous among the prisoners. Webb began referring to him by name, as he did on April 13: "Today we have the Briggs band coming to our service, it was lovely. . . . Eight men the band, Tom Waltham on piano, Briggs and pal on saxophone, 2 good ones on fiddles, another on viola. They played low and soft."[8]

Music was often the only nourishment at St. Denis. By the end of April, the prisoners received one good meal per week. The rest was inedible. "To-day am famished," Webb wrote. "Another experience, but now feel what hunger means to a man. . . . Some men in here are shadows of themselves. . . . Dinner was watery soup . . . managed to soak a few dog biscuits and put some jam on them, was able to suck at them."[9] On the eighth of May, Briggs and his fellow prisoners were inoculated in the left breast for typhoid. Many became sick and weak. "Lots of us are looking pale and worn out," Webb wrote. "All getting thinner."[10]

That summer was as brutally hot as the winter was bitterly cold. June opened with a fete day concert from Briggs and the orchestra. "They are some orchestra," Webb wrote. "Briggs and Waltham and supporters deserve our great and blessed thanks."[11] The concerts were now held outside in the open air. Residents of the apartment buildings surrounding the camp opened their windows and watched Briggs and the orchestra perform, as they did on the twenty-second, sweating buckets in the stifling air. "It's now a nudist camp in here," Webb wrote. "No relief to be got anywhere."[12]

The apartment residents did more than just watch the concerts; they became a covert source of vital information. Prisoner Jean Weinfeld recalled, "We found silent links with the [people in the apartments]. We invented a sign language that allowed us to know about things. For example, thumbs down, that means there was a German defeat."[13] Soon, a thriving gambling scene grew in the camp, with imprisoned bookies taking bets and apartment dwellers signing the results of horse races.

In June, the men were lifted by a piece of good news: Germany had invaded Russia in Operation Barbarossa, breaking the neutrality pact between the two nations. This pitted a powerful force against Hitler. But what seemed like good news quickly soured. "Russian news are bad, we hear," Webb wrote on July 18.[14] The news wasn't just bad; it was apocalyptic. In six months, Stalin lost more than seven million soldiers to death, injury, or capture. To look at a map of Europe at the end of 1941 was to see territories Hitler controlled either outright or through puppet governments.

As pressure mounted, Briggs continued performing to keep himself and the prisoners sane. On the fifth of June, after a dinner of two slices of raw ham, he played an open-air concert until 9:00 PM, and scarcely a window was left unattended in the surrounding buildings.

Three days later, a general of the Red Cross visited St. Denis and made several complaints about the state of the camp. The Red Cross also began distributing parcels of food, which surely saved Briggs from malnutrition and starvation. Had the Red Cross visited St. Denis two weeks later, they would have found a different camp. On the nineteenth, the old German guards were replaced with a batch of nasty young Nazis. Two days later, nearly five hundred internees were shipped from Drancy, with hundreds more to follow. Drancy needed the space. It had become a collection point for Jews on their way to the gas chambers in Poland.

After years of sending Jews to forced labor camps, Hitler now pursued a policy of extermination. Invading Russia was the first step: mobile killing units swept into Soviet territories and murdered nearly one and a half million Jews on the spot. On July 31, Hermann Göring set in motion the next phase of the plan—the Final Solution, during which more than six million Jews would be murdered in death camps.

Briggs knew nothing of death camps, not yet. His horizon was severed by barbed wire. All he knew was that nearly one thousand men were added to St. Denis by the end of July. They were double-bunked in hastily built barracks, twenty-four men to a room. "Just like an ant heap now," Webb wrote. "Gnats, infestation all over the camp.... Watched 450 (men from Drancy) arrive. Poor fellows, what a job they had to cart their belongings from the transport hut. After that they stood for hours as they waited to get their room or hut allocation.... The big double hut is to house 240 men! All uproar in camp.... Expecting another 550 men on Monday."[15]

Briggs felt uneasy. He especially feared for Georgina. Visits at St. Denis had been moved to a new hut, and the men were warned they'd only have twenty minutes with their loved ones. Briggs wanted to protect Georgina, but he could not even protect himself. Still, he found a way. On August 2, 1941, in a Nazi prison camp, he officially married the woman he had called his wife for eleven years. Two days later, his heart full, he played a concert.

On August 13, the prisoners were inspected for lice, sending a stream of dirty men holding dirty mattresses to the hospital for delousing. The weather was so hot the food rotted. Rats dragged away the rotten food, and cats dragged away the rats. That day, news came of a meeting between Winston Churchill and Franklin D. Roosevelt, which had taken place three days earlier. They had met onboard the U.S.S. *Augusta* off the coast of Newfoundland in hopes of solidifying British and American opposition to Hitler. It was the first of eleven wartime meetings between the two leaders, and it was full of emotion. Both men understood the danger they faced. When Churchill and Roosevelt first met, neither could find his voice. After a pregnant pause, Churchill said, "At long last, Mr. President," to which Roosevelt replied, "Glad to have you aboard, Mr. Churchill." Over two days of negotiations, they hashed out an agreement, called the Atlantic Charter, featuring eight "common principles," including the restoration of self-government in all Nazi-occupied countries. Both leaders left the meeting frustrated, however. Roosevelt hoped the charter would change American public opinion, which was adamantly opposed to war. It did not. Churchill had come with one purpose: "To get the Americans into the war."[16] He did not.

Then came December 7, 1941. That morning, Japan attacked the American naval base at Pearl Harbor, killing some 2,400 soldiers and civilians—roughly the entire population of the St. Denis prison camp. Roosevelt made his famous speech about the infamous day, and America was at war with Japan. Surprisingly, Webb made no reference to Pearl Harbor in his diary. The guards at St. Denis still banned newspapers, so it is possible the prisoners didn't know what happened until much later. Whatever they knew, the course of history had changed. As a Japanese ally, Germany declared war on America, leaving Hitler with another formidable foe.

On Briggs's second Christmas in prison, the priests staged a show in blackface. To the crowd's delight, one pranced around "as a 'Nigger' dragging a cardboard box," Webb wrote.[17] Briggs made no mention of the event, but as a veteran of bands led by Noble Sissle and Will Marion Cook—men who despised blackface—he must have taken offense. If these priests, charged with spreading Christ's message of brotherhood, could be so blind—if they could hate Nazism and not recognize the same evil infecting their own hearts—what chance was there for the rest of the world? As America and Russia joined the fight for freedom, Arthur Briggs had good reason to wonder if anyone was fighting for him.

38

"We've got to show that blacks and whites are treated equally in the American army . . . or else what's the point of waging war on Hitler?"

—Josephine Baker

JOSEPHINE BAKER KNEW WORLD WAR II was bigger than Hitler. From the start, she equated Nazis with the American racists who terrorized her as a child in St. Louis. Perhaps this is what gave her the courage to risk her life in the fight.

La Créole had hardly begun before the French Resistance ordered her to North Africa. She went to a doctor, hoping to manufacture an excuse to leave the opera, and X-rays showed shadows on both of her lungs. This was the price of ignoring her walking pneumonia. At least she had a good excuse to leave. Baker went with Atbey to Algiers, home of the Kasbah, and then to Casablanca, the dangerous, romantic port of Morocco soon to be immortalized on film. They settled finally in Marrakech, hoping the dry desert air would clear her lungs.

Instead of resting, she worked. In the spring, she embarked on a short tour of Spain, once again using her performances as a cover for intelligence gathering, and then returned to Marrakech. She lived for a time in the lavish palace of Si Thami El Glaoui, Pasha of Marrakech. Thirty years Baker's senior, Glaoui was a virile, powerful man. He kept 365 concubines in as many bedrooms in his palace, and for pure sexual charisma, he was Baker's equal. Soon after bedding down in his palace, Baker learned she was pregnant. It isn't clear if Glaoui was the father—Baker also shared an intense attraction with Atbey, and they likely had a love affair while working for the Resistance—but Glaoui took a keen interest in what followed.

In June, Baker and Atbey were out for a walk when she doubled over in pain. As she staggered home, her temperature spiked. She collapsed into bed, trembling with fever, twisting in anguish. Atbey brought ice and stuffed it into bed with her, but still she burned. After three days, when it was clear she was near death, Atbey risked blowing his cover and dashed outside to hunt for an ambulance, but none could be found. He laid Baker in the back seat of a car and drove two hundred and fifty miles to a hospital in Casablanca. There she had her third miscarriage.

After an emergency hysterectomy, she developed peritonitis and septicemia, which before the advent of antibiotics was usually a death sentence. Infections scarred her abdominal linings, which in turn caused intestinal blockages. She needed further surgery but was too weak to undergo it. She lost weight, not from starvation as Briggs did, but from sickness, until she looked like a skeleton. "She was doubled up with her legs up to her head and bust," Atbey recalled. "Her face was tight. Her skin was waxy, as if she were dead."[1]

Baker had once told Atbey she was prepared to give her life for France. Now she was so sick, rumors of her death began spreading around the world. When Langston Hughes began writing for the *Chicago Defender* that year, he was assigned Baker's obituary. But even at death's door, barely able to move her limbs, she proved useful to the cause. The American vice consul in Casablanca visited her hospital room often, where he had the perfect cover to exchange information with Atbey.

Not until the middle of 1942 did Baker regain the strength to undergo surgery. Her agony continued through summer and into winter as her body was cut again and again, but the operations were successful. By November, she had recovered enough to take interest in the Battle of Casablanca raging outside her hospital room.

The battle was of enormous strategic importance. With puppet governments in Norway and Denmark, a neutral Sweden, control of France, and an alliance with Italy, Hitler was protected from the north, west, and south. He continued pushing into Russia, hoping to conquer and seal the east. If the Allies could wrest control of North Africa, they would have a base to weaken Hitler from the south.

On November 8, American warships sliced through the Strait of Gibraltar and patrolled the Mediterranean Sea to provide cover for the invasion. Vichy French ships met them to defend Morocco's neutrality, which France had guaranteed in the Compiègne Armistice. The U.S.S. *Massachusetts*, with nine sixteen-inch guns, gave America an artillery advantage. When the terrible noise of the cannonade reached Baker's hospital room, she recalled, "I pulled an old sweater over my pajamas and rushed barefoot onto my balcony." Atbey begged her to return to bed. The wounds from her surgery were still fresh and might reopen. As the air crackled with explosions, she said, "No, Jacques. This is no time to be in bed."[2] The warships thundered for four days, and then Casablanca surrendered to the Allies.

After nineteen months in the hospital, Baker was released. Still weak, she traveled to Marrakech to finish her recovery. She immediately caught paratyphoid, a bacterial infection caused by salmonella, and was thrown back on her deathbed. "Her legs were now like sticks," wrote a biographer, "her cheeky little bum melted to nothing."[3] Wracked again with deadly fever, Baker wondered if she'd ever be well again. When she finally recovered, she confronted another terrifying thought: she was almost forty and hadn't performed in France for nearly three years. The few performances she did elsewhere were cover for her work as a spy. What if she came back from death's door to find she had lost her genius? Or worse, what if she still had it and no one cared?

She got the chance to find out when the Red Cross opened a club for American soldiers in Casablanca and asked her to perform. The wound from her last operation still hadn't healed, and she had stitches in her stomach, but she agreed on one condition: the club had to be integrated. "We've got to show that blacks and whites are treated equally in the American army," she said, "or else what's the point of waging war on Hitler?"

For her first performance in two years, Baker was so weak she could barely stand. Harnessing her last reserve of strength, she steadied her legs and descended a one-story staircase, singing "J'ai Deux Amours." Sidney Williams, Director of Red Cross Activities, recalled that she "turned the song into a prayer, ending on her knees with her hands clasped and moving many to tears."[4]

Baker was too weak to continue her work with Atbey, but she was not finished fighting. For the rest of the war, she staged U.S.O. style tours, trekking three thousand miles back and forth from Marrakech to Cairo, to entertain Allied troops. She also toured in the Mediterranean and Italy. On these tours, Baker raised more than three million francs for the Free French. At each stop, she sang for the wounded soldiers. One friend recalled in a letter, "One of my most treasured memories is the night when we dragged a little piano into the ward of that Canadian hospital and you sang 'I'll Be Seeing You' until you nearly dropped. How even the nurses stood with tears in their eyes and those poor helpless men—many of whom would never recover—lying on their backs unable to move, only their eyes showing the relief and comfort you gave them."[5]

Baker was now something bigger than an artist. She was a hero. One indelible image survives of her tremendous courage. During a performance for the troops in 1943, Morton Eustis, First Lieutenant of the 2nd Armored Division, recalled:

> Josephine had just finished "Darling Je Vous Aime Beaucoup" when a stream of racers began shooting up the sky a few miles away . . . the air raid siren wailed . . . the footlights went out . . . a voice over the loudspeaker shouted . . . Air raid . . . Air raid. . . . We all dispersed into a nearby field and lay down. . . . The ack-ack was spitting from all directions. . . . As suddenly as it started the raid stopped. . . . Josephine Baker was back onstage in her low-cut evening gown. . . . She took up where she left off. . . . A few more songs. . . . Then "God Save the King," "The Marseillaise," "The Star Spangled Banner." And the show was over.[6]

39

"All men are discouraged and have been for some time."[1]

—William Joseph Webb, St. Denis prisoner

IN 1942, THE MEN AT ST. DENIS began to break. Some succumbed to pneumonia. Others braved death to escape. One hanged himself in his cell. "Oh, it looks very bad," Webb wrote. "For supper on Sunday night, we got nothing, besides the little square piece of margarine handed out. . . . For our dinner we had barley soup, fit for feeding to pigs."[2]

One freezing morning in February, a guard burst into Briggs's barracks and ordered him to play the Reveille. It was 3:00 AM.

"Now?" Briggs asked.

"Schnell!"

"That was the only answer," Briggs recalled. "So I took my instrument, blew it a bit to warm it up, went to the window and played the alarm twice so that everyone in the barracks and the courtyard was sure to have heard it. When I turned around, I saw that there was already a soldier for inspection and counting of internees. It lasted two hours, and then they brought dogs and inspected the cellars and attics to see if anyone was hiding."[3] More men had escaped.

At noon, two soldiers arrived and posted a message from Carl-Heinrich von Stülpnagel, who had replaced his cousin Otto as the commander of occupied France: "Wanting to escape is normal for someone who is deprived of their freedom. But those who try to escape must know that they risk death in this attempt."[4] The prisoners had now suffered two winters on starvation rations. Snow covered the camp again, and dinner was thin vegetable soup with a dollop of grease. For many, death was a risk worth taking.

In January, the prisoners founded a newspaper. It was mostly used for reporting sports activities in camp, which now included hockey and boxing. Also included were artistically designed flyers for Briggs's concerts. One flyer survives for a "Super Variety Concert" in January, featuring eight attractions, beginning with "Arthur Briggs and His Orchestra," playing "Swing music." In the middle, Briggs came back for "more swing music." Then he played a "community medley." The paper printed lyrics for seven songs, including "Three Blind Mice," "Roll Out the Barrel," and "Let's All Go Down the Strand." Briggs dutifully performed this light fare for his fellow prisoners. He closed the concert with "still more swing music."

Briggs often said the Nazis forbade jazz in St. Denis, so the swing at this concert was likely not fit for the name. History bears out this recollection: Hitler always hated jazz. He promulgated many decrees seeking to kill the music, but it was too popular to kill even for a mass murderer. In one of the war's most bizarre experiments, Goebbels tried to use jazz's popularity as a weapon, hiring several of Berlin's best musicians to form a Nazi jazz band. The band, Charlie and His Orchestra, recorded standards laced with propaganda, which Goebbels broadcast on shortwave radio, hoping to undermine British morale. Typical was the band's version of the classic "You're Driving Me Crazy," recorded after Churchill met Roosevelt. The song begins with a normal verse and chorus to lull the listener, and then singer Karl Schwedler interjects, "Here is Winston Churchill's latest tearjerker." He speaks the next verses:

> Yes the Germans are driving me crazy,
> I thought I had brains, but they shattered my planes.
> They've built up a front against me, it's quite amazing,
> Clouding the skies with their planes.
> The Jews are the friends who are near me to cheer me,
> believe me they do,
> But Jews are the kind that will hurt me, desert me and laugh
> at me too.
> Yes, the Germans are driving me crazy,
> My last chance, I'll pray, to get in this muddle the USA.

Goebbels distributed these records among prisoner-of-war camps, making it possible that Briggs heard them. Briggs would have recognized songs like "Miss Annabelle Lee," which he recorded with the Savoy Syncopators in 1927, and which Charlie and His Orchestra contorted into "Little Miss BBC." Men in the camps often listened to the records until they figured out what was on them; then they smashed them to pieces.

If these records dented British morale, the Royal Air Force didn't hear about it. At the beginning of March 1942, R.A.F. jets screamed over St. Denis on their way west, bellies full with bombs. The men heard explosions in the distance, and like children on Christmas morning they rushed out of their barracks into the yard, where the guards shot at them. Later there appeared a notice in the camp: during an enemy raid, all internees were ordered inside the moment the alarm sounded. Any man seen in the yard, no matter what his reason, would be shot.

For the hope-starved men of St. Denis this was a victory, if only a psychological one. The Nazis were scared. On April 2, Briggs was torn from sleep by the terrible rumble of an Allied bombardment, along with the piercing tattoo of Nazi anti-aircraft guns. Four days later, it happened again. "By Jove what fireworks," Webb wrote. "I stood at [my] window and watched flares of different colours sent up to lighten the sky. Lots of search lights and firing went on for well past 5 AM."[5] The new guards at St. Denis punished the prisoners for the Allied advance, instituting new penalties for being caught without a prison armband, for smoking in their presence, for failing to salute, and more.

Meanwhile, Briggs continued to salve the men's souls with music. In mid-April, he and Waltham prepared a concert of scenes from Mozart's *Don Giovanni*, along with Beethoven's *Egmont* "Overture," and after intermission, a set of swing tunes. For *Don Giovanni*, two actors were chosen from among the men: Joseph Blumberg as the licentious cad Don Giovanni and Jimmy Hale as the young peasant girl Zerlina, who is drawn to Giovanni's sexual charisma. The orchestra performed five excerpts from the opera, including the sensuous overture, as well as Giovanni's plaintive plea, "I Am Under Your Window." Then came the brooding, tragic *Egmont* "Overture," which Beethoven composed for a play by the great Goethe. These were extraordinary pieces to attempt in a prison camp, but Briggs and Waltham had too much pride to do anything less than astound their audience.

Still, Briggs could only do so much. By summer, morale cratered again. The sex-starved men began avoiding the fence on visiting day. Seeing the line of women only added to their agony. As Weinfeld recalled, "I can truly testify . . . we were no longer interested in women. There was the rise of homosexuality, and it brought about conflicts that we wouldn't have had if the women were with us: ferocious jealousies, loves of three or four prisoners for the same object, for the same subject. So there were open and hysterical fights. Fighting for purely emotional, sexual, or other reasons. So this aspect became worse and worse because of the confinement." He noted that behavior in the camp, sexual and otherwise, changed incrementally, so that "a man who came back after the first year, if he should see himself, would not recognize himself."[6]

In August, a shipment of hopeless French Jews crowded into the camp. "So down and out, children separated from parents etc.," Webb wrote. "Hear one of them jumped out of a window. . . . God only knows what's in store for all of us, poor British's in here, especially when one sees what is happening to the Jews!" Three days later, he wrote again, "Our Internees Jews have had some squealing and gnashing of teeth this past week. I saw a case of mother and son, about 6 yr. old, come in Thursday morning instead of 2 pm visit-time. She had to give herself up at 2 pm to be taken away and the kiddy separated from parents. Allowed to see hubby, but boy not allowed to see his father, boy ran back to say goodbye, crying 'Daddy!' But not permitted in, although kid got near to gate and mother. Separate and taken away, but where to?"[7]

The worst horrors of the Holocaust had just begun. The mobile killing squads in Russia were inefficient and required German soldiers to shoot their victims in cold blood. This took an emotional toll on even the most rabid Nazi soldier. Himmler preferred death camps, which were more organized and impersonal, and by 1942, the Polish death camps of Auschwitz-Birkenau, Treblinka, Belzec, Sobibór, Lublin, and Chelmno were running with cruel efficiency. At Auschwitz, gold was pulled from the teeth of Jewish corpses and melted to enrich the Nazis. At Treblinka, prisoners were forced to cut wood to fuel the cremation pits where they were soon to die. At Belzec, only seven Jewish prisoners out of half a million survived the war. At Sobibór, many female prisoners were raped before being killed. At Lublin, more than 18,000 Jews were killed on a single day. At Chelmno, prisoners were made to think they were about to take baths for disinfection as they were herded into the gas chamber.

Hitler had gone too far, figuratively and literally. In August 1942, he penetrated deep into Russia, reaching Stalingrad, where his troops would suffer an apocalyptic winter. At roughly the same time, the Allies scored their first decisive victory in the Pacific Theater at the Battle of Guadalcanal. In November came the Battle of Casablanca, which Josephine Baker watched from her hospital balcony. "There began to be a lot of gossip circulating in the camp as there was an Allied landing in North Africa," Briggs recalled. "Our German guards were not very happy to know that the Allies had taken a step forward."[8] The Allies had not only taken a step forward, they had pushed the Axis back thirteen hundred miles from Egypt to Tunisia, pinning them between newly arrived American and British troops in Morocco and Algeria. The tide was turning.

Briggs was emboldened. At the end of every concert, before leaving the bandstand, he performed an old Negro work song called "Better Days Will Come Again." Published circa 1876 by George Cooper, the American poet who famously wrote lyrics to many of Stephen Foster's songs, "Better Days Will Come Again" was likely born much further back in time. During slavery, work songs were the secular counterpart to Negro spirituals, sung in the fields to ease the backbreaking labor with rhythm. As Frederick Douglass recalled, "Slaves are generally expected to sing as well as to work. A silent slave is not liked by masters or overseers. . . . Slaves sing most when they are most unhappy. The songs of the slaves represent the sorrows of his life; and he is relieved by them only as an aching heart is relieved by its tears."[9]

It isn't clear how Briggs came to know "Better Days Will Come Again," but he would have heard it in America any time he rode a Pullman car. In the 1920s, the Pullman Railroad Company boasted itself as the largest employer of black Americans, although working conditions for these employees were dreadful. To earn a full month's salary a Pullman porter had to work four hundred hours or log eleven thousand miles—either way required more than ten hours of work, seven days a week.

When the workers threatened to unionize, the Pullman Company sought to distract them. Porters were organized into vocal quartets and taught to play musical instruments. This, the company hoped, would both ease tensions with the workers and improve the experience of the customers. Nearly one-quarter of the porters—some two thousand men—performed music on the trains. They incorporated old work songs, using them in the same way their forbears did, as a relief from sorrow. They latched onto one song in particular, singing it so often it became known as "The Pullman Porters Song." That song was "Better Days Will Come Again."

Briggs drew from this deep well of history to deliver a coded message of hope to his fellow prisoners. He passed courage to them through the blast of his trumpet. The effect was electric. "As soon as I hit the first note, all the internees would come to attention," Briggs recalled. There he stood, facing two thousand hope-starved men, wobbling on hunger-weakened legs, but standing nonetheless, standing in defiance of their captivity, and thanking him with their eyes for his strength, because it was now theirs too. One can only imagine the punishment Briggs would have faced for such insubordination, but he risked it anyway. With emotion, with passion, with *fire*, he breathed the melody into his horn, while the lyrics sounded silently in his head:

> *Don't be sighing, little darling,*
> *Better days will come again.*
> *Dry your teardrops, lovely roses*
> *Soon forget the passing rain.*
>
> *Don't be sighing, little darling,*
> *Brighter skies will shine above.*
> *Life is gladness, hope is round us,*
> *While our hearts are full of love.*
>
> *Oh, your smiles can make it summer,*
> *Though the wintry days might blight,*
> *We will fondly cling together,*
> *As we've done in days so bright.*

Don't be sighing, little darling,
Sunshine follows after rain;
Though the shadows now are falling,
Better days will come again.

Seeing the men standing, the Nazi guards demanded to know what Briggs was playing. "It's our signature tune," he lied. "It's the end of the concert. That's all there is. They're getting up because they're thanking us for the concert we just played." Later, he slyly added, "You know it wasn't that."[10] One internee recalled the Nazis' reaction: "When at the end of a performance the master trumpeter in clear tones would blow us into 'Better Days Will Come Again' the Germans would look with envy at their caged victims."[11] The German guards could not understand the strange power that straightened the spines of their prisoners any more than the American slave driver could understand the power that gave succor to his slaves. The power was the song, the song of the unconquerable human spirit, the song that gave birth to jazz. Briggs spent his entire adult life trying to teach Europeans this song. He wanted them not just to hear it or play it but also to *feel* it.

Finally, he succeeded.

40

"Our life runs swiftly to its destined doom,
Swifter than life was ever meant to run.
We have no future in the coming world;
Whate'er befalls, our day, at least, is done."[1]

—Neville J. N. Foreman, St. Denis prisoner

IF THERE EVER WAS HELL ON EARTH, it was the Battle of Stalingrad. For six and a half brutal months, Germany laid siege to the Russian city. Incendiary bombs reduced the buildings to ash, while Panzer tanks pounded the streets to rubble. By the winter of 1943, Stalingrad looked like the surface of the moon. At the brink of oblivion, the Soviets mounted a counterattack, encircling the stunned German army. Hitler's high command counseled retreat. He refused, ordering his men to stand and fight. As winter worsened, the Volga River froze. Supplies dwindled. The German army began to starve, but Hitler's mind did not change. He ordered a fight to the death. By the end of January, his men had abandoned hope. Frostbitten and starving, the Nazi commander in Stalingrad defied Hitler's orders and surrendered. Ninety-one thousand Nazis were marched to Soviet prison camps; fewer than 6,000 survived. In all, the Battle of Stalingrad left some two million soldiers wounded, missing, captured, or dead.

Arthur Briggs was not supposed to know about Stalingrad. He was still forbidden news of the outside world, except from German propaganda. Naturally, the prisoners of St. Denis found a way around this ban by smuggling wireless radios into the camp. They'd dismantle them and store the pieces separately in several rooms in case of a snap inspection. Each night, they assembled their radios, listened to the BBC news broadcast, and then dismantled them again. In one room, a radio was hidden in the chimney. One internee recalled, "The Germans practically tore the barracks apart, herding the prisoners out in their night clothes more than once, while the barracks were searched. But never did they look up the chimney."[2] The smuggled radios only gave the prisoners snapshots of the war; they could not see its whole shape. Briggs no more knew Stalingrad was the war's turning point than did the stray cats of St. Denis. "All we knew was that the German armies seemed to be having great difficulty," he said.[3]

Joseph Goebbels grasped the significance of Stalingrad immediately. Two weeks after the surrender, in an attempt to reignite his war-weary nation, he gave a speech calling for "total war." It was perhaps his most famous speech. It was also the first time the Nazis publicly admitted defeat. Goebbels tried to inject his words with strength, but lurking behind each one was desperation. "My task is to give you an unvarnished picture of the situation, and to draw the hard conclusions that will guide the actions of the German government, but also of the German people," he said.

> We face a serious military challenge in the East. . . . Now, we must accept things as they are and discover and apply the ways and means to turn things again in our favor. There is no point in disputing the seriousness of the situation. I do not want to give you a false impression of the situation that could lead to false conclusions, perhaps giving the German people a false sense of security that is altogether inappropriate in the present situation. . . . Total war is the demand of the hour. . . . We must use our full resources, as quickly and thoroughly as it is organizationally and practically possible. . . . The question is not whether the methods are good or bad, but whether they are successful. The National Socialist government is ready to use every means. We do not care if anyone objects. . . . The people and leadership are determined to take the most radical measures. The broad working masses of our people are not unhappy because the government is too ruthless. If anything, they are unhappy because it is too considerate. Ask anyone in Germany, and he will say:

The most radical is just radical enough, and the most total is
just total enough to gain victory. . . . Now, people rise up and
let the storm break loose![4]

After three years of war, the German people were in no mood for
a new storm. Their desperation increased when the Allies used their
stronghold in North Africa to mount attacks on Italy. In July 1943, Mus-
solini was deposed. Two months later, Italy surrendered. At the same
time, Germany teetered on the edge of defeat to Russia at the Battle of
Kursk. Meanwhile, America was building an atomic bomb.

With each German setback, the guards at St. Denis became meaner.
Arthur Chouinard, whose son played clarinet in the camp orchestra,
recalled spending seventeen days in a dark cell for giving chocolate to a
French child. Weinfeld recalled a day in winter when commander Gillis, a man he described as "perfectly crazy," kept the prisoners standing
outside in the cold for hours for no apparent reason. Weinfeld worked
up the nerve to say, "Punishment doesn't work if we don't know why
we're being punished."[5]

Briggs blamed the problems on "some youngsters that I'll never
forget. Kids, fifteen years old. They tried to boot you. We avoided them.
They were tough, what they would call 'the Hitler youth,' you see."[6]
Briggs despised being kicked and insulted by these children. The indig-
nity was almost unbearable. But he knew these young guards were the
most dangerous, lusting to prove their manhood by putting a bullet in
a prisoner's back.

More than ever, the prisoners leaned on art as a spiritual crutch.
They privately published a book of poems in the camp and practiced
painting on postcards. Several of these postcards survive; two are signed
by Briggs and the orchestra. Tom Waltham wrote a satiric song that
became a camp anthem, which he sung at every concert. Called "The
Brave Room Corporal," it was a bit of doggerel to make the men smile,
with lyrics such as:

> Who gets your cigarettes all right
> And tucks you up at ten each night?
> *C'est le chef de chambre*, the brave room corporal.

His rights are posted on the door,
And it's as clear as water,
You must respect him more and more,
And if you don't you oughter.[7]

The orchestra had become vital to camp life, even for the Nazi guards. Camp commander Gillis attended rehearsals as well as concerts, and one day, he offered Briggs a plum opportunity to leave the dreaded campgrounds and entertain German officers in Paris. Granted a chance to connect with the life he once knew, the life he had pined for during two brutal winters, Briggs refused. His music was not for sale, not to the Nazis, not at any price. "Briggs was only too pleased to avail himself of an occasion to repay a stigma thrown at what was disdainfully referred to as 'Negro music,'" wrote fellow prisoner Holman Jameson in 1948. "When the German commander of the camp in exchange for a whole day's leave to Paris asked him to form a musical group to entertain some German officers in Paris . . . Briggs replied in terms of a two-fold ground refusal: 1. As a man of color whose race has been publicly treated with contempt and their musical contribution despised by a German regime and philosophy. 2. As a British subject whose nation was at war with that regime."[8]

That winter, the Red Cross visited St. Denis and left a detailed description of the camp, which was printed in their journal *The Prisoner of War*. It evinces a common misconception about St. Denis. The Red Cross inspector wrote:

The internees are living in large barrack buildings and some huts; all these buildings are well arranged and heated. Each internee has at least three blankets and two sheets, a pillow-case and a sleeping bag. . . . The internees can take hot shower baths three times a week. The accommodation is at present overcrowded, but will soon be easier, as 200 elderly internees will shortly be sent to buildings attached to the municipal hospital at St. Denis, where they will be very comfortable. Around the barrack buildings are gardens with flower-beds and trees, with spaces for playing games such as football and clock-golf. Indoor games are also organized and there is a library, theatre, orchestra, art class and a school, which was started in 1941 and at present has two hundred pupils who study under the direction of an English schoolmaster. A camp committee of British internees directs all branches of the work and studies. The health of the internees is good and they are well cared for. There is good medical and dental attention. A very up-to-date dental laboratory has been installed, where there are six British dentists and four dental mechanics. The internees receive the same rations as German civilians. They also receive Red Cross food parcels every week. In 1942 a restaurant was opened in one of the huts and there is a very fine kitchen attached to it. The religious needs of the internees are attended to by a Protestant chaplain and two Roman Catholic chaplains; of the latter, one is English speaking and the other a French Canadian. Visits to the internees are allowed once a fortnight, but to those who work, once a week. The internees may write four letters and three cards a month, business letters not being included in these numbers. There is no limit to the number of letters internees may receive. . . . This is considered to be a very good camp."[9]

Because of such testimony, the modern view of St. Denis holds it as a benign prison camp. True, it was not Auschwitz, where more than one million prisoners were starved or worked to death, or murdered with Zyklon B in gas chambers, or cruelly experimented upon by Dr. Josef Mengele, the "Angel of Death," who performed experiments on prisoners, many of them children, including unnecessary amputations, chloroform injections to the heart, and in one instance, attempting to create conjoined twins by sewing two Romanis together back to back. But Briggs's suffering surely was not relieved because others suffered worse. The Red Cross article is factually correct in most respects—St. Denis had a library and a theater; there were sporting events and church services—but from firsthand accounts, it seems the inspectors saw what the Nazis wanted them to see. Briggs in particular recalled the Red Cross with disdain. "Something I want to tell you that I hope the world will understand one day is that the International Corps for Red Cross doesn't mean a thing," he said. "When they visited our camp, we were closed in our rooms, so what kind of inspection—how could they inform anyone of what's happening? They saw no internees at all. We were confined to our rooms, enclosed. When they visited, the Gestapo came also to visit with them."[10]

Weinfeld's recollections on the Red Cross give further credence to Briggs's distaste. "We did not see them," he said of Red Cross inspectors. "To tell the truth, they were content to see the officers; they did not even visit the barracks." Weinfeld felt the inspectors were little more than dupes in the German propaganda machine. "The Nazis claimed the camp of Saint Denis was like the other camps," he recalled. "As if to say, 'Look at it and you'll see everything else—you'll see Treblinka, Auschwitz, etc. Here's the same thing.' In fact, these gentlemen from the Red Cross wanted to be convinced, so they wouldn't have to go check in Germany, in Poland, or in Czechoslovakia."[11]

Webb also mentioned the futility of Red Cross inspections in his journal, writing in February 1942: "International Red Cross reps supposed to have visited the camp yesterday, if they did, we saw nothing of them. It's the same every time."[12] Webb's journal ceased with his release at the end of 1942, making it possible that conditions improved in 1943, but this seems unlikely. As the Nazis began to lose the war, they had little reason to improve conditions in their prison camps—especially not in November, when the Allies began bombing Berlin.

The truth is that the prisoners of St. Denis suffered greatly. They starved and nearly froze to death; they despaired and burned with unquenchable desires; they were beset with lice and diseases. "Four years of hell was not an easy thing to bear," Weinfeld said.[13] And yet, they also thrived like stunted plants on hardscrabble tundra. They created art and music. They started a café in an empty barrack (when asked the name of the café, Weinfeld wryly said, "It was just called 'The café.' We could not make a mistake—there was only one.") A baker among the prisoners cadged flour from the kitchen staff and baked pastries, which he sold to the men. One prisoner convinced a soldier outside the gates to plant seeds on a small stretch of land abutting the camp, giving the prisoners access to radishes and other small vegetables. After years of captivity, they had adapted and created a life—not because of the Nazis' kindness, but in spite of their cruelty. "There was everything in there," Weinfeld said. "Jealousy, joy, sadness, fights."[14]

As 1943 drew to a close, the smuggled radios in St. Denis continued bringing news of Allied advances. Roosevelt, Churchill, and Stalin met in Tehran and agreed to open a new front against Germany. Dwight Eisenhower was named Supreme Allied Commander in Europe. The bombing of Berlin continued apace. The prisoners still suffered greatly, but each time Briggs and the orchestra performed, a new note could be heard in the symphony: hope.

41

"If we lose, we will be able to count our friends on the fingers of one hand."

—Joseph Goebbels

FOR HITLER, 1944 BEGAN WITH a stunning defeat and then grew worse. In January, after nearly nine hundred days of siege, the Nazis were expelled from Leningrad. The siege exceeded Stalingrad as perhaps the longest and cruelest in human history. More than one million civilians died. Many of the living were so starved they resorted to cannibalism. In the end, Russia lost more people in Leningrad than America and Britain lost during the entire war. For Russia, the victory was devastating. For Germany, the defeat was fatal.

As the Soviets pushed the Nazis west, America and Britain moved north through Italy. Germany was now trapped on two sides by Allied armies and on one side by the Baltic Sea. On June 6, 1944, the Allies closed the trap in history's greatest seaborne invasion: D-Day. It began after midnight, when some two hundred thousand men were dropped behind enemy lines. They jumped from planes and rode ships to the beaches of Normandy. That morning, under heavy fire, they stormed the beaches. A hail of bullets mowed down twenty five hundred American men in a matter of hours. It was the bloodiest day in American history since the Battle of Antietam during the Civil War, but the invasion ultimately succeeded. Hitler was now surrounded by his enemies.

Briggs heard about D-Day at St. Denis, but the camp was so rife with lies and rumors, he did not believe it until one of the young Nazi guards shouted at the prisoners through the barbed wire, vowing that

Germany would kill the Allies in the water. "He was furious and ready to shoot anyone," Briggs recalled. "That's how we found out that the news was true." The relief was immense; salvation was on the way. "We were pumped up, but we couldn't show too much because the guards, even the old ones, were unhappy," Briggs said.[1]

That evening, the guards at St. Denis were replaced again with a fresh batch of young Nazis. "They took [their] places around nine in the evening with threats and with a lot of brutality," Briggs said. After Briggs played the Reveille for lights out, the young guards taunted the prisoners, trying to get them to reignite their fires. "They would've taken the opportunity to shoot," Briggs said. "They were waiting for that."[2]

The next morning, Gillis advised Briggs to avoid the yard. Tensions were too high. "It was a very difficult thing because going to the yard and walking in circles was the only way to get some fresh air and move," Briggs recalled. "We stayed in our rooms so as not to excite those young men, who were between fifteen and seventeen, and all crazy!"[3] His life became a paradox: the closer he got to freedom, the more he was confined. He passed the days playing cards and dominoes, organizing a singalong of spirituals and popular songs, and watching an ever-growing column of defeated Nazis stream by St. Denis as they fled the front.

By mid-July, Briggs recalled, "We began to see very clear signs of the Allies' dominance." Allied planes flew overhead night and day, and Nazi soldiers began stopping at St. Denis for water or fuel as they fled, often driving wrecked vehicles. Briggs didn't need a radio anymore; he could read the news on the Nazis' faces. "We saw that they were bitter, that they had lost their units, and above all they no longer had that pride they had before," he said.[4]

Still, Briggs and the inmates had to remain cautious. The guards looked for any reason to vent their frustration. "We were at the mercy of the guard's mood," Briggs said. "The days were sad and anxious, because everything could become very unpleasant at any time." Waltham suggested a concert to calm the camp, and soon Briggs was performing every day from 4:00 to 5:00 PM in the yard. "It distracted everyone, including the guards," he said. "It was wise."[5] The orchestra pushed its limits, introducing songs that the Nazis would have never allowed before, including Cole Porter's "Begin the Beguine" and "Night and

Day." Back at Bricktop's, Briggs was the first to perform "Night and Day" in a cabaret. Now he was perhaps the first to perform it in a Nazi prison camp.

Gillis disappeared at the beginning of August, leaving St. Denis without a commander. The prisoners listened to the radio in the open now, receiving updates every quarter hour. The guards didn't care. "We could see by the way they were acting that they only thought of returning home alive," Briggs said.[6]

Meanwhile, Hitler's general corps was rotting from inside with despair, defeat, and disloyalty. In July, several of his top men, including Carl-Heinrich von Stülpnagel, tried to assassinate him. After the attempt on his life, Hitler retreated to his *Wolfsschanze**, where he hid in a reinforced bunker under a dense tangle of fir trees. "Hitler had become an old man," wrote one historian. "His face was worn and drawn. His shoulders sagged. He cupped his left hand in his right to hide the faint trembling in his left arm. Some of Hitler's doctors were convinced he suffered from Parkinson's disease ... [the] hard raucous voice ... had faded now to the weak whisper of a senile man."[7]

After ordering Stülpnagel's death, Hitler summoned Dietrich von Choltitz, the new commander of Nazi-occupied Paris, to the Wolf's Lair and issued a shocking decree: "Paris must not fall into the hands of the enemy, or if it does, he must find there nothing but a field of ruins."[8] Choltitz was shaken. It seemed his commander in chief, the soul of Nazi Germany, had gone mad.

Choltitz faced an impossible decision: wantonly destroy the City of Light for no strategic purpose or disobey Hitler's orders and face the firing squad. He knew history would never forgive him for destroying Paris, but after the attempt on Hitler's life, Germany reinstated the medieval law of *Sippenhaft*, or kin liability. If Choltitz disobeyed, his entire family would pay the price.

Bravely, he refused to destroy Paris. Instead, he tried to broker a truce with the French Resistance. It failed. Desperate, he approached a foreign diplomat and discussed Hitler's orders. His only chance to save Paris, he said, was for the Allies to occupy the city. Unfortunately, the

---

* Wolf's Lair

Allies had no such plans, thinking it a waste of fuel and men. Choltitz begged the diplomat to reconsider. "You must realize that my behavior in telling you this could be interpreted as treason," he said. "Because what I am really doing is asking the Allies to help me."[9]

Meanwhile, Vichy's ministers fled as the French Resistance battled to liberate Paris. Freedom fighters moved against public buildings throughout the city, armed with whatever weapons they could find. Marie Curie's son-in-law snatched bottles from the laboratory where she discovered radium, and he turned them into Molotov cocktails.[10] The Hot Club of France offered its headquarters to the Resistance, storing guns and ammunition beneath the floorboards. The fighting spread into Montmartre and Montparnasse, and even into the suburbs. Briggs saw the fighters outside the camp at St. Denis.

As German soldiers fought the guerilla uprising, Choltitz secretly made arrangements with the Allies. He hinted to a liaison that, if the Resistance stormed his headquarters, he'd surrender. To the stunned men under his command, he said, "Gentlemen, I can tell you something that's escaped you here in your nice life in Paris. Germany's lost this war, and we have lost it with her."[11]

Choltitz was as good as his word. After a brief fight on August 25, 1944, he surrendered. Above the bullet-ridden buildings of Paris, the French flag, outlawed for more than four years, burst forth in triumphant color. The streets filled with a delirious mob. "La Marsellaise" came over the radio, and thousands of Parisians threw open their shutters, cranked the volume, and began to sing. The fourteen-ton bells of Notre Dame clanged. Not to be outdone, the nineteen-ton bell of the Sacré-Coeur thundered back. In Saint-Germain-des-Prés, someone turned on a record player and blared Louis Armstrong's "Basin Street Blues."[12] By noon, some brave soul had climbed atop the Eiffel Tower, ripped down the swastika, and planted a makeshift flag made from three old military bed sheets stitched together. One was dyed pink, one a washed-out blue, and the third a tattered gray, but it was the French tricolor nonetheless, and it flew over Paris once again.

At St. Denis, only a dozen unarmed German watchmen remained. Terrified, they approached the barbed wire and spoke to the prisoners in

good French: "We are alone! We are unarmed!" Briggs joined a delegation to discuss the situation and make sure it wasn't a trap. With a few
other men, he left the camp for the first time in nearly four years and
ran across the street to City Hall seeking help. "We especially feared
the arrival of the [Resistance]," he said. Briggs's fear evinced the depth
of his kindness. He wasn't afraid for himself; he was afraid of what the
Resistance would do to these old Nazi soldiers. Just days ago, these men
were his captors. Now he risked his life to save theirs. Said Briggs, "The
Resistance indeed arrived in less than an hour. Fortunately, the police
had time to arrive before them, to take these unarmed soldiers prisoner.
These soldiers wept in gratitude."[13]

With no guards at the gates, many prisoners fled. Briggs, always
measured, always cautious, deemed it unwise to go into the streets too
soon. He watched as several men ventured beyond the gates and were
immediately shot dead by two teenaged Nazi guards hiding just outside
the camp. Resistance fighters wanted to stone the young men, and if not
for Briggs they might have. Again he joined a group of prisoners, this
time to negotiate for the teenagers' lives. "Common sense won," Briggs
said. "The two kids were incarcerated under the guard of ten armed
men with orders to shoot anyone who would try to get them out to
stone them."[14] Briggs didn't have to save the lives of these murderous
teenagers, but he never let others define his moral compass. The Nazis
were cruel; Arthur Briggs was not.

That night, camp leaders went into the commander's office, took the
passports and papers, and gave them back to the internees. They also
confiscated machine guns and grenades and turned them over to the
French Resistance. The Swiss consul arrived and told the men they were
free but must wait until the next day for transportation. The orchestra
went into the yard, where Briggs played as he had never played before.
He blasted "La Marseillaise," its triumphant strains harmonizing with
thousands of singing voices in Paris. France was free. Briggs was free.

So he thought.

42

*"Dear heart, how little shall I count the cost
If I regain the beauty I have lost."*[1]

—James E. Thomas, St. Denis prisoner

SOMETIME IN THE THIRD CENTURY AD, so the story goes, the bishop of Paris stood atop the hill of Montmartre preaching a sermon on repentance when his head was cut off. Holding his severed head in his hands, he walked six miles north into the countryside, preaching all the way. On the spot where he fell and died, a basilica was erected in his honor. Completed in the year 1144, the basilica is widely considered the first structure to use all elements of Gothic style. As for the bishop, he was made a cephalophor—a saint who died by decapitation—and he became the patron saint of France and Paris. The town around the basilica was named after him: Saint Denis.

Eight hundred years later, Arthur Briggs gazed at Saint Denis's basilica, its Gothic spires looming over Stalag 220. It was his last day in captivity. At five o'clock the kitchen staff prepared breakfast. At seven, Briggs and Präger blew the Reveille for the final time. "Neighbors shouted at the windows," Briggs recalled. "It looked like a village feast."[2]

Then came the trouble. As a line of fleeing Panzer tanks passed the camp, one stopped outside the barbed wire gates. Its gun rotated toward the men inside. Thunder clapped like the voice of God. Shells that could pierce steel armor screamed into the camp. Terror choked the prisoners. Were they to die on the day of their freedom?

Briggs was done waiting for liberation. In front of the barracks the Swiss had placed a line of small pushcarts, which the prisoners could rent to carry their few possessions. Tank shells exploding around him, Briggs commandeered a cart, threw his posessions inside, and freed himself. He walked with a fellow prisoner toward Montmartre, tracing Saint Denis's path in reverse, his head still attached despite the Nazis' best efforts. He walked on weak legs down roads littered with wrecked German tanks and trucks. Just outside the city was a mile-long column of annihilated Panzer tanks, packed bumper to bumper, their twisted black hulking metal frames planted in the earth like tombstones. He felt free. "I can tell you that it was really good to be able to walk other than in circles!" he said.[3]

Briggs and his friend walked all the way to Paris through open warfare, shells exploding around them. Still they walked, two haggard, tattered, dirty, hungry, gaunt men pushing a cart filled with beggar's belongings, sharing only one thought: home.

At last they arrived in Montmartre. Briggs walked his friend home first. This was no small courtesy, as he surely was desperate to see Georgina and Poggy. Then it was his turn. He walked past the Cimetière de Montmartre and turned onto Rue Félix Ziem. As he neared his apartment building, he saw "almost the whole neighborhood waiting for me."[4] Maurice Mouflard, who brought Aimé Barelli to Briggs's apartment in 1940, somehow caught word of Briggs's release and announced it to all the musicians in Montmartre. After four years of desolation, Briggs returned home to be enfolded in the love of friends and reunited with the brotherhood of musicians.

The joy was mitigated by shock: a stranger had stolen his apartment. It isn't clear what happened to Georgina. Multiple contemporary news accounts mention a happy reunion between Briggs and his wife, but she must have deserted the apartment at some point during the war. Briggs settled into another, smaller apartment he owned in the building and waited for the police to sort it out. Meanwhile, he went to retrieve his trunks from the American Express and learned they had been stolen. His most precious possessions collected during twenty-five years of traveling the world in the service of jazz were gone forever. After several days, the intruder left Briggs's apartment with a small suitcase and walked toward Rue Lamarck, where he was apprehended. "In the discussion, the suitcase opened and a tiny little object fell," Briggs recalled. "The inspector put this object in his pocket and arrested the gentleman. . . . I did not learn any more, but since there were at least twenty people in plainclothes posted around the neighborhood down to Damremont Street, it is likely that the case was important."[5]

Finally, Briggs went home. Ever the stoic, he left no record of his feelings on returning to normal life after four years in prison. We can only glimpse Briggs's inner heart obliquely, through the poignant memory of Jean Weinfeld, the artist who suffered alongside Briggs at St. Denis for three years: "I was depressed at least two, three weeks, where everything seemed useless, superfluous," he said. "I wondered why I wanted to be free so much, to come home to a world in disorder. . . . Everything had to be reworked, everything had to be redone, everything had to be rebuilt."[6]

43

"Life was back to normal."[1]

—Arthur Briggs

ARTHUR BRIGGS REBUILT QUICKLY. As ever, his first thought was music. He visited the Hot Club headquarters "to see how it was." There he ran into several American officers, one of whom said, "You're Arthur Briggs—very happy to know you in person. I have all your records, and I really like what you do."[2] Briggs next walked to Place Pigalle "to see what was left of the musicians or if, by chance, I could find some friends." He went to the coffee house where he used to *faire un boeuf* with the Harlemites and met several musicians he had known before the war. "I'm trying to have an orchestra of eight musicians," Briggs told them. "Three saxophones, four rhythms, and me."[3]

He already had plans.

Soon all the musicians in Paris came to welcome him. "The news of my return had snowballed," he said.[4] Briggs asked after several old friends, including Ellie Glasner, the emcee at the Barberina who arranged his first recordings in Berlin. He listened with a heavy heart as her story was recounted: during the war, she became a leader in the German resistance. Three days before the Russians attacked Berlin, she was arrested, sent to Spandau Prison, and hanged in her cell.

Briggs also heard about Freddy Johnson, who spent two years in a Nazi internment camp in Bavaria. Years later, Briggs ran into Johnson, who was working with a young prodigy named Quincy Jones. The two old friends warily circled their shared past, until Johnson unburdened himself. He knew he had made a mistake with the Harlemites. "Arthur, if

I could start my life again I would not do it the same way," he said. For Briggs, there was nothing to do but reminisce about the days when the Harlemites "had the glory at hand," and bid his friend a fond farewell.[5]

Within weeks of his release, Briggs put a new band together and received from a friend "a little notebook with the new pieces that were played in America and in England." After four years of Beethoven and Nazi jazz, he had some catching up to do. The pieces were all from Glenn Miller, who had just died in service—he was flying to Paris to entertain the troops when his plane disappeared. Briggs threw himself into arranging the songs. "I started making very simple arrangements to have a homogeneity," he said. "I worked well and in a few weeks, I had twenty pieces ready, which wasn't bad. It was very simple, but I was very happy with myself."[6] Meanwhile, he spoke with a reporter for the *Chicago Defender* in September, telling of his time in captivity and his joy at being free. After hearing erroneous reports of his death, Briggs's American audience rejoiced at his miraculous survival.

In November, the Hot Club staged a jam session in Briggs's honor. "The concert drew a huge crowd and was immensely popular," wrote *Melody Maker*, which also noted, "The trumpeter has lost no time getting back to work. Today he is again prominent in Parisian jazz circles."[7] Briggs was back doing the only thing he ever wanted to do.

One day in late 1944, Briggs received a knock on his door. It was Maurice Mouflard and Aimé Barelli. Much had changed since these men visited four years prior. Briggs was no longer in hiding. Barelli no longer wore a tattered, bloody army uniform. His desperation had turned to joy, with a burgeoning career and a new child. Briggs's trumpet had brought him so much luck he didn't want to give it back. Instead, he offered to pay for it.

"It's not worth it," Briggs said. "I have three others: the ones that Mr. Selmer sent me in St. Denis, plus another one I had at home that you didn't see."

Mouflard chimed in: "But Arthur, I don't have an instrument!"

"Well, if you don't have an instrument, take one of those," Briggs said pointing to his three trumpets.

There the men stood, each holding one of Briggs's trumpets.

"I'll give it back to you as soon as I can buy one," Mouflard said, but Briggs would have none of it.

"Listen," he said. "We are three friends and three trumpeters who love each other like brothers. If we can walk hand in hand and help each other, this is the only thing that counts, especially in our profession."

"You know, nobody talks like you," Barelli said. "But I understood the lesson when you gave me your trumpet so that I could make a living. I realized that there is a great truth in life. It is generosity."

The men went to the coffee shop downstairs, where Briggs recalled, "The discussion took a deep philosophical turn, a little pompous." The owner of the cafe came to the table and interrupted: "Gentlemen, you are talking about things that are really useful in life. But let's move on. Have a bottle of champagne with me now. We'll drink to the health of France and all our allies by trying not to talk about this nightmare we have lived."[8] Briggs took a drink but could not forget the nightmare.

The Axis powers continued fighting for one year after Briggs's release. On April 22, 1945, Hitler learned the Soviets had reached Berlin. Eight days later, he killed himself in his bunker. As Allied soldiers liberated the death camps, the true horror of the Holocaust was exposed. Hitler, Himmler, Goebbels, and the rest of the Nazi command were responsible for more than six million murders. But it went further. Their war wiped out 3 percent of the entire world—between fifty and eighty million people, including seven million Russian civilians, three million Russian prisoners of war, and nearly two million non-Jewish Polish civilians.[9] The carnage continued through August; on the sixth, America dropped an atomic bomb on Hiroshima, Japan. Three days later, another one vaporized the city of Nagasaki. It was a merciless end to a monstrous war.

44

"It is no longer like before the war."[1]

—Arthur Briggs

AT THE END OF 1945, Arthur Briggs began a residency at Chez Florence. His return to cabaret life started slowly. "After a month, we didn't have very many people in the place," Briggs said. "The managing director said to me, 'You have another month.' I said, 'No, I'll have two more months. Otherwise I finish this evening.'" Briggs was again fighting for his musicians, making sure they had a steady gig, rather than month-to-month work. It paid off. "Within fifteen days, you could hardly move in the place," he said. The manager asked him to sign for a year, but Briggs refused. He'd only stay as long as people wanted to hear him. "The contract is the public," he said.[2] In the end, he stayed four years.

Briggs was playing again for the rich and famous, but it wasn't like before. Jazz had moved past him. While he played Glenn Miller, the cutting edge of jazz explored the bounds of bebop. Young players such as Miles Davis, Dizzy Gillespie, and Charlie Parker were creating a musical language Briggs could not speak, though he understood its spirit. That spirit was summed up by Thelonious Monk's famous remark, "We wanted a music that they couldn't play." *They* were white bandleaders who had been reaping the benefits of jazz since Briggs was a teenager. Unfortunately, in creating music *they* couldn't play, the new artists also edged out a veteran like Briggs, who had missed his chance to evolve with the music.

In April, Briggs turned fifty. He loved playing as much as ever, but he struggled to find musicians he wanted to play with. He began to search elsewhere for the spiritual connection and brotherhood he had always felt with music. In 1955, he joined the Freemasons. On the day of his induction, he recalled, "I really felt that I was living my last secular moments and that I was going to enter a new, more enlightened life." Sadly, it was not to be.

In 1956, Briggs was reading the American Masonic magazine and noticed a curious statistic: there were 307,000 white Masons in America. The magazine made no mention of black Masons. This Briggs could not abide. He did something extraordinarily out of character: he stood before his entire Mason lodge and delivered a passionate oration on racism. He began: "Venerable Master and all of you my brothers, it is with a heavy but sincere heart that I find myself obliged to give you some memories lived in the United States of America." He described arriving at Ellis Island and being struck by the "immense monument, the Statue of Liberty." He spoke of the North, where "in spite of [America's] fine principles, only Caucasian people enjoy all these rights." He called the evil by name: "White supremacy remains present in the heads as much as in the facts." He traced white supremacy back to George Washington, saying, "I want to recall the humiliating remarks that General Washington made as a reward after he crossed the Delaware River, thanks to the brilliant idea of poor slave Crispus Attucks: 'Keep the nigger down.'"

He explained to his French audience the significance of the word *nigger*, saying, "Being treated as a nigger is like receiving a sword stroke, for a person of color." He compared the etymology and definitions of the words *Negro* and *niggardly*. He spoke of his American tours with the SSO in 1919 and with Noble Sissle in 1931, telling of segregated restaurants and public parks with signs barring his entry. He told the story of Emmett Till, the teenager who had just been murdered in Mississippi for whistling at a white woman. He vented the fury in his heart, saying, "The Southerner is not a human being, he is . . . a monster who enjoys the blood of blacks. The poor boy, awakened in the middle of the night, was dragged by a car, hammered suddenly, disfigured, had his eyes torn out while he was still alive, and then was drowned in the river. This is the favorite sport of the Southerners. The crime of the kid: to have looked at a pretty white woman."

He said this as a black man who had married a white woman. He discussed the American Constitution, the recent ruling of *Brown v. the Board of Education*, and the nuanced hierarchy of color within the black American community. He told the story of Edmund Jenkins's father, who married a "nearly white mulatto girl," and was lynched.

Then, he came to his point: "Venerable Master and all my brothers, I ask your indulgence, knowing that a young Mason of my age should neither criticize nor give his opinion without being invited, but as a young Mason, I seek the light of improvement.... Perhaps it is involuntary, but I wonder if segregation really exists in this enlightened society."[3]

It was a powerful performance, as poignant as his rendition of Beethoven's Fifth Symphony in St. Denis, but it did not work. Segregation plagued the Masons throughout Briggs's fifteen years in the organization, and he quit in rage after one of his "brothers" made racist remarks. It was another bitter disappointment. Remarkably, after everything he had experienced, Briggs still believed in honesty, in charity, in humility, in fraternity; it still surprised and hurt him when others abused these ideals.

As the decade wore on, Briggs struggled to stay vital. He recorded an album of Calypso music called *Surprise Partie avec Lord Calypso and the Callboys* (Briggs was Lord Calypso; the album cover features him wearing a top hat and a monocle). It was the only record he ever regretted. He also recorded with his Briggs High Society Band, sometimes styled Briggs and His Society Orchestra, but it was mostly light fare, as evidenced by the band's name. With advances in technology, his trumpet sounded better than ever, his tone full and sharp, his phrasing inventive and evocative, but the music had nothing to do with jazz in the 1950s, a decade that saw Miles Davis's *Kind of Blue*, Sonny Rollins's *Saxophone Colossus*, and John Coltrane's *Giant Steps*.

The life Briggs knew and the music he loved were dying. His friends began dying too. Django passed in 1953; Briggs attended the funeral and paid homage to his friend with a radio broadcast in his honor. Six years later, Sidney Bechet wasted away from lung cancer. Near the end, Briggs visited Bechet often in Garches, near Paris. "I remember once, when he hadn't eaten for a few days, he called me on the phone—he suddenly wanted to eat a big pear," Briggs said. "He wanted to know if I could bring him one."[4] Briggs scoured the city for a pear but could not find one.

Days later, Bechet could barely speak, but he asked Briggs to help him sign his will. It was under his pillow. "Tomorrow, you'll hold my hand," Bechet said. "I'll sign." Briggs visited the next day, but Bechet did not recognize him. "I stayed a long time, waiting," Briggs said. "I looked under the pillow, but there was nothing. The entourage [Bechet's family] looked at me with hostile eyes."[5]

Bechet died the next day, May 14, his sixty-second birthday. Even after Bechet's death, Briggs still looked out for the man he used to babysit in the SSO. Along with Will Marion Cook's son, Mercer, he arranged a public funeral. "The two of us would lead the procession," Briggs said. "No one could dispute it." The funeral was chaotic, much to Briggs's dismay. "Everyone wanted to be placed next to the coffin," he said. He never understood this sort of pettiness, especially at a funeral. When it was finally over, he felt unfulfilled. Exiting the cemetery, Briggs and Cook ran into American trumpeter Jacques Butler, who noticed their long faces and said, "Let's go back!" The three men stood around Bechet's grave, alone except for the undertakers, and sang, "Swing Low, Sweet Chariot."[6]

45

*"I have always wanted to share my experience whenever
I had the opportunity."*[1]

—Arthur Briggs

A NEW DECADE DAWNED. The children born in the shadow of war grew
into the light of peace. They made love; they did drugs; they reinvented
music; they rebelled against everything old, not knowing or caring that
the generation they rebelled against had done the same thing forty years
before. In many ways, it was the same as the youth revolt in London and
Berlin after World War I, only this time Arthur Briggs was not young.

He was still young at heart. In 1955, he had met nineteen-year-old
Jacqueline Mulot and fallen in love. Long since separated from Georgina,
Briggs threw himself into his new relationship. It was the greatest love
he would ever know, outside of his trumpet. In August 1960, Jacqueline
gave birth to a daughter, Barbara. Briggs's life took on new meaning.
Jacqueline worked during the day, while Arthur stayed at home and
took care of his baby girl. Performing in a cabaret was no longer his
goal. After playing the season of 1962, he was offered another contract,
but he declined. "It had become too difficult and, despite the efforts I
had made it did not really work," he said.[2] His career as a professional
musician, his main concern for nearly fifty years, was finished.

For Briggs, it was a monumental split. He officially divorced Georgina and married Jacqueline. He rarely spoke of his career, rarely reminisced about his days as the greatest trumpeter in Europe. It was as if
the past no longer existed. All his energy went into his family. The love
between Briggs and his new wife was intense and all encompassing,

matched only by the love Briggs showed his daughter. He spoiled her with candy and cakes after school; he insisted she have proper musical tuition; he knew her dolls by name and often joined in playing with them. "We were very close, the three of us," Barbara said. "He was everything to me. He took me to school; he fetched me after. He helped me with my homework. We had a very special relationship together."[3]

He still loved music, but now he stayed home and played quietly to himself. "He'd put a mute in his trumpet and play for himself in the bathroom," Barbara recalled. "Once he got stuck. He couldn't open the door, and he started screaming. 'Try to open the door!' But I was too young."[4] In 1964, Briggs was asked to teach saxophone, trumpet, and drums at a school in Saint-Gratien. "This idea pleased me right away," he said. "At first I only had one trumpet student. But I loved it." A local newspaper reported on the great trumpeter giving lessons, and soon Briggs had as many students as he could handle. He also began directing a youth orchestra, which he called the Saint-Gratien Harlemites.

In August 1974, Briggs returned to America to celebrate his sister Inez's eightieth birthday. He hadn't seen America, or his family, in forty-three years. His visit turned into an impromptu family reunion, where he met his sister Inez's daughter, June Hall Murray, who was one year old when he left Grenada in 1917. He also reunited with Inez's grandson, James Briggs Murray, who scheduled two radio interviews for his great-uncle. When James offered to invite another jazz musician to appear with him, Briggs said, "Get me Doc Cheatham." James led the interview as Briggs and Cheatham appeared on *The Arlene Francis Show*, a daytime fixture on WOR in New York, and then the three men joined the broadcast on WRVR of Felipe Luciano, an original member of the Last Poets, one of the earliest influences on hip-hop music. It was a joyful reunion for the old friends and a chance for Briggs to reintroduce himself to the American audience he had forsaken in 1939.

America had changed in many ways since Briggs last saw it. Segregation was no longer the law of the land. The Civil Rights Act and the Voting Rights Act codified the long fight for racial justice. These victories were inconceivable when Briggs toured the country with Noble Sissle in 1931. And yet America remained bitterly divided by race. A mere six years had passed since Martin Luther King and Robert F. Kennedy were murdered. Richard Nixon represented white America's backlash to the civil rights movement. He campaigned on the Southern Strategy, speaking to white voters in coded racist language, and was elected twice (Briggs arrived just in time to see Nixon resign). Surely, Briggs had spent many painful nights in St. Denis rehashing his decision to stay in Paris, but would he have fared better in America?

If the experiences of Eugene Bullard and Josephine Baker are any guide, perhaps not. After returning from France in 1940, Bullard went home to Georgia to look for his family. His brother was dead, lynched for trying to assume ownership of his grandmother's farm. A few years later in New York, Bullard was severely beaten by the police at a concert. Soon after, he boarded a bus and was ordered to sit in the back. He refused, and in the ensuing fight he lost sight in his left eye. By 1959, this hero of two wars toiled in Midtown Manhattan as an elevator operator.

In April 1960, Charles de Gaulle, now president of France, visited America. Bullard attended the welcoming ceremony, where he relived his glory days in Paris and where a newspaper photographer snapped a picture of him kissing an elegant woman's hand. The hand belonged to Josephine Baker. She had finally conquered America with a successful run on Broadway and a massive tour that took her through the South. At every venue she visited, she insisted the band be integrated and that ticket sales not discriminate by race. The venue in her hometown of St. Louis refused her demands, so she refused to perform there, sacrificing $12,000 a week.

The more Baker experienced of American segregation, the more firmly she associated it with the views of the Nazi party. She began working with the NAACP, fighting American racism with the same vigor she brought to the French Resistance. In the South, as one friend recalled, "She used the drinking fountains, the lunch counters, and the ladies' rooms. They threw her ass out in the street and she walked right back in."[5] The Ku Klux Klan threatened her, so she called a press conference and declared, "I am not afraid of the Ku Klux Klan or any other group of hooded mobsters. I'll meet them in the South or anywhere else they like." In 1963, she attended the March on Washington and stood onstage while Martin Luther King delivered his "I have a dream" speech. She later told her brother, "[King] wasn't strong enough. He should have put his foot down and demanded rights for black people. I could have done it better."[6]

Baker spent the last decades of her life hounded by creditors. She was kicked out of Les Milandes due to unpaid debts and had to perform constantly to stay alive, but neither debt nor age could erase her spark. In 1970, a writer stood backstage with Baker before a performance, noticing "the aging jowls, the slight dowager's hump, the small, rather dumpy figure [that] looked ridiculous in the chorus-girl costume." Then, Baker was called onstage, "and before my unbelieving eyes, the superstar emerged from the frump and folds of age."[7] On April 8, 1975, Baker performed a retrospective revue in Paris, celebrating her fifty years in show business. Four days later, she suffered a cerebral hemorrhage. She was found in bed surrounded by newspapers full of glowing reviews of her final performance.

Briggs continued teaching until the end of 1984. "The director wanted me to stay forever, but I was tired," he said.[8] That same year, a young jazz trumpeter named Wynton Marsalis performed with the Boston Pops Orchestra. Marsalis had made it his mission to bring jazz to a new generation, but the song he chose to perform was Briggs's old workhorse, "The Carnival of Venice." After a lifetime of toil in the service of jazz, Briggs could rest easy; the music he loved was still alive.

Due to a congenital eye defect, Briggs slowly lost his sight. Even while blind, he insisted on independence. "He memorized the map of the apartment," his daughter recalled. "He never wanted any help."[9] Free from all commitments, he began recording his memoirs. When James Briggs Murray saw Briggs repeat the false story of his birth in South Carolina, he called his great-uncle in Paris and said, "Uncle Arthur, I see you're still telling that story." Briggs replied, "Well, son, do you think it's okay to tell the truth now?" After nearly seventy years, Briggs was still scared someone was going to punish him for the lie. Judging from his life experience, he had good reason to be cautious, but sadly his early life was left forever enshrouded in mystery. As for the rest of his life, he lived it all again in stunning detail: from the Harlem Renaissance to World War I; from the Jazz Age in Paris to the Hot Club de France; from recording jazz in Berlin to performing Beethoven in the prison camp at St. Denis.

As Briggs neared his ninetieth birthday, he developed lung cancer and slowly slipped away. "One day we were sitting at the table next to each other," his son-in-law Denis recalled. "Arthur said to me: 'I had a dream last night. There was a big garden with trees, four big trees in the corners. It was a big square. They were like the four towers of a castle, or a city. It was very beautiful and very calm.' He raised his blind eyes to the ceiling, and I think we both understood."[10] Briggs was envisioning the next world. He died on July 15, 1991, a decade shy of one hundred.

James Arthur Briggs was buried in the Cimetière de Montmartre. He rests a short walk from the Place Pigalle, where the old clubs are all gone, and *le tumulte noir* has faded from memory, but sometimes at night, with the right ears, you can still hear the ghostly echo of Bricktop singing a torch song, and Cole Porter exclaiming "What legs!," and Josephine Baker dancing the Charleston with her eyes crossed, and Scott Fitzgerald getting drunk on champagne, and Ernest Hemingway scribbling a short line in his notebook, and vibrating through the din, as clear as a bell, Arthur Briggs's trumpet making that jumping, happy noise.

A Note from the Author

"I will not mind if, after reading the book, you forget all the adventures and incidents that I recount; but I would be pleased if you did not forget the underlying moral."

—Sebastian Haffner, Germany 1933.

In August 2017, I traveled to Paris to meet Arthur Briggs's daughter. While there, I watched French news reports of a neo-Nazi rally in Charlottesville, Virginia. I watched my countrymen proudly wave swastikas and chant, "Jews will not replace us." Aghast, I watched the president of the United States fail to denounce these men or to condemn neo-Nazism, anti-Semitism, and white nationalism. I understood author Milton Mayer's words, written in his book on the Holocaust, *They Thought They Were Free*, in 1955: "I came back home a little afraid for my country, afraid of what it might want, and get, and like."

Over the course of the next year, far-right nationalist parties won significant gains in European and South American elections, while in America, eleven Jewish worshippers were slain in a Pittsburgh synagogue by a man who said he wanted all Jews to die. One of his victims was a ninety-seven-year-old Holocaust survivor. These are just some of the frightening echoes rumbling through our time, echoes of a painful past that we ignore, misunderstand, and forget at our own peril.

The evils that threatened Arthur Briggs's life are as present and powerful as ever. Perhaps they will always remain so. It is my hope that this book will, in some small way, serve as a reminder of how hard we once fought to defeat those evils, how hideous they are, and what it means to have courage in spite of them.

Epilogue

by James Briggs Murray

Your heartbeat is your drum; your voice is your sound. And, music is the sacred art—it's the language that we cannot see; we cannot touch. But it's the language of the universe—the language of the planet—that everybody can understand. So, to make me better understand Dizzy and Duke and Louie, and how they could go all over the world and be understood. And, to speak a language that the people of Norway can understand—that the people of Congo can understand—the people in Jamaica can understand—it's a very high, high language!

RANDY WESTON, VIRTUOSO PIANIST and educator, spoke those words during an oral history interview I produced in June 1996. I've heard similar sentiments from Wynton Marsalis, virtuoso trumpeter and educator in European classical and American classical (jazz) traditions. In his tireless efforts to raise awareness and preserve the legacies of the true jazz originators, Marsalis has emphasized that each has a unique sound, a unique voice—whether instrumentalist or vocalist. Many of us believe that when an artist has found his or her voice, it is symbiotically and inextricably connected to the very soul at its source. It has been the mission of folks such as Wynton Marsalis, prolific jazz pianist and educator Dr. Billy Taylor, and many others, to promulgate and preserve the voice and the legacy of the founders of jazz for the benefit of new generations. But how can this be achieved when so many listeners, indeed even many devoted music lovers, have no idea of who and what came before?

When my great-uncle, virtuoso trumpeter and educator Arthur Briggs, transitioned from this physical world in 1991 at age ninety, I was immediately reminded of one of my own transitions, and my first encounter with his music and the dilemma of jazz preservation. Early on a summer morning in 1961, I awakened with deep thoughts of navigating through the transition between elementary and high school. My thoughts continually cross faded with music emanating from my dad's— George J. A. Murray Sr.—high-fidelity sound system in our family living room. Permeating the air that particular morning were the sounds of Maurice Ravel, Duke Ellington, Louis Armstrong, Count Basie, Ella Fitzgerald, Miles Davis, Lord Kitchener, and Arthur Briggs. I was infinitely more familiar with the rhythm and blues and doo-wop offerings of my own young generation, but as an avid lover of myriad musical genres, I recall grilling my dad that morning about all of that music with which he loved to start his (and, by extension, my) Saturday mornings.

We talked about Ravel's *Bolero* and the centuries of great composers of European classical music with its prescribed notes and stylings for practitioners to follow. Then we shifted gears and Dad explained that, although jazz is partially scripted, it's so much more about improvisation and spontaneity. He explained that jazz was somewhat like pianist Mary Lou Williams had explained it to my mother, June Hall Murray, years before: "Jazz is like a conversation among friends. Sometimes your attention is drawn to a soloist; at other times, everyone is expressive simultaneously—mostly harmoniously. It may take a while, but eventually you'll understand what everyone is saying." I liked that! And I especially liked that my dad was playing some of the greatest pioneers, including my uncle Arthur.

Arthur Briggs has been among the least known of the early jazz pioneers because, after extensive travel in the late teens and 1920s, he'd remained exclusively in Europe after 1931. So, on that summer Saturday morning in 1961, I became determined to find Uncle Arthur someday— just as did the author of this book more than a half century later—to ask him about his music, and to ask what he thought of mine. I first met Uncle Arthur a decade later as I was en route from Istanbul to New York via Paris in the United States Air Force. Sitting in his Paris flat, along with his wife, Jacqueline, and daughter, Barbara Inez, I learned that the music my friends and I naturally loved and understood as our own had actually grown out of the music of jazzmen like Louis Jordan and others, whose up-tempo dance music had in turn grown out of several genres that emerged before their time—work songs, spirituals, blues, gospel, and jazz in its many forms. I was made to understand that what we thought was totally original, as master percussionist Max Roach later said to me in an interview, was actually "an addendum"—based on foundations laid down by those who'd come before.

So, as my friends and I moved on from R&B and doo-wop at our dance-hall parties and concert halls to emerging genres such as rock 'n' roll, salsa, soul, rock, funk, disco, and hip-hop, I always kept one eye in my musical rearview mirror, both to remain mindful of and also to help continue present-day acknowledgement and celebration of our pioneering forebears. I knew I could collect music and talk about it with friends for as long as I lived, but I wondered how my friends and I might continue to celebrate the old and the new for the multitudes who hadn't a retrospective connective clue. What a challenge! Unfortunately, I quickly discovered that my friends were mostly interested in the latest top hits in the genres of their own contemporary comfort zone. As for me, though, inspired by Uncle Arthur, I also started collecting "oldies" from other eras and genres; but I noticed that I was virtually alone in that pursuit. There had to be another way to preserve these legacies!

During my four-decade professional career at the Schomburg Research Center, as audiovisual curator and theatre director, in addition to collecting the music retrospectively and conducting oral histories, I tried to find that other way. Among other efforts, my theatre crew videotaped quarterly repertory concerts by bassist and educator Larry Ridley and his Jazz Legacy Ensemble, always including an extra microphone for Larry, not only to introduce the music and the artists, but also to give the history and context of the jazz legend whose music was being celebrated that day. Larry delivered personal and musical biographical data, followed by musical performances by his ensemble, for Wes Montgomery, Sarah Vaughan, Bud Powell, Thelonious Monk, Dizzy Gillespie, Kenny Durham, Philly Joe Jones, Cedar Walton, Art

Blakey and the Jazz Messengers, Oscar Pettiford, Paul Chambers, Charlie Parker, Oscar Brown Jr., Dexter Gordon, and numerous others. But our theatre had only 340 seats, and although we documented the programs via videotape, I was again frustrated by the limited numbers who might visit our library to learn from all that Larry Ridley and the Jazz Legacy Ensemble had shared.

But there was yet another extraordinary opportunity for jazz legacy preservation. As hip-hop culture and rap music took over the world, a key element of rap music became borrowing a few bars of music from successful recordings of earlier artists and genres—it was called sampling. I was excited about the prospects of collecting rap recordings that contained jazz samples, and excited that these new records might bring classic jazz back for a contemporary mainstream audience. During the middle decades of the twentieth century, Blue Note Records alone had produced albums capturing the sounds and voices of Sidney Bechet, James P. Johnson, Miles Davis, John Coltrane, Thelonious Monk, Horace Silver, Milt Jackson, Herbie Hancock, the Modern Jazz Quartet, Cannonball Adderley, Art Blakey, Lee Morgan, Eric Dolphy, Ornette Coleman, Wynton Marsalis, Terence Blanchard, and other jazz luminaries. What a treasure trove from which rappers could sample! But the very first platinum record awarded to Blue Note Records came in 1993, when an English jazz-rap group called Us3 released an album called *Hand on the Torch* which included the single, "Cantaloop (Flip Fantasia)." That single sampled Herbie Hancock's 1964 "Cantaloupe Island" and reached the top ten on Billboard's Hot 100. It was a rarity because, after forty years of rap releases, the most sampled artist is Soul Brother Number One, James Brown. While I love the music of James Brown, Herbie Hancock, Us3, and the music of other rappers who sampled R&B and jazz, I was frustrated one more time because classic jazz was taking a back seat.

I couldn't have known it in 1961, but it turns out that a few months after that very summer when I'd asked my dad about the music he'd been playing on Saturday mornings, an infant voice that was destined to resolve the jazz legacy dilemma, perhaps better than anyone else, was heard crying out its first sounds, emanating from the very birthplace of jazz—New Orleans. That infant voice belonged to Wynton Marsalis, the future virtuoso trumpeter, educator, and spokesperson for jazz pioneers, who in just three decades would become managing and artistic director of jazz at Lincoln Center, the premier venue for the preservation and celebration of the music of the masters of America's classical music, which we call jazz. Throughout his storied career, Marsalis's trumpet playing, perfected in both European classical and American classical jazz styles, has been much like the Pied Piper of Hamelin, luring older and younger generations—hardcore jazz enthusiasts and curious tourists alike—into the spectacular facilities and programs at New York's Lincoln Center and around the world. He educates, enlightens, and entertains global audiences about the pioneering founding fathers and founding mothers of jazz.

Marsalis also recently paid tribute to Buddy Bolden in a feature film dedicated to the life of the man considered by many to be the first true jazz innovator, and this gets at the heart of his importance, and the importance of the book you have just read. One hundred years is not as long as it seems. The era that produced jazz—the era that produced my uncle Arthur—is still current, still important, still *vital*.

James Briggs Murray is the great-nephew of James Arthur Briggs. Murray served for nearly four decades as founding curator of the Moving Image and Recorded Sound Division of the Schomburg Center for Research in Black Culture of the New York Public Library and for nearly two decades as evening producer and production manager for WOR-AM Radio in New York. He is currently a balladeer and a SAG-AFTRA voice artist.

Acknowledgments

THIS BOOK WOULD NOT HAVE BEEN POSSIBLE without the help of many people. I am most grateful to Barbara Briggs for trusting me with her father's story and to Denis Pierrat for his loving transcription of his father-in-law's memoir. James Briggs Murray, Arthur Briggs's great-nephew, was vital to the project in more ways than I have space to enumerate, and it was my singular pleasure to get to know him during the creation of this book. I thank him for his expertise and tireless dedication.

I would like to thank Yuval Taylor, Michelle Williams, and everyone at Chicago Review Press for believing in this book and helping see it to fruition through a long and sometimes tortuous process. I am lucky to have great agents, Thomas Flannery and David Vigliano, and I thank them for their support and professional acumen.

Special thanks go to Ashley Belanger, a trusted friend and editor whose sharp eye made these pages stronger; my cousin, Amanda Di Sciascio, who helped me contact Barbara Briggs, aided me with my research in Paris, and took a lovely walk with me to the Tuileries Garden; and Christophe Petitclerc, who traveled with me to St. Denis and helped me scour their archives (and who went back on his own and found a crucial document for me). I'd also like to thank Melissa Hebin and SpanTech Translations for helping translate Briggs's memoir, Dan Fitzpatrick for on-the-ground research in Grenada, and Julien Dourgnon for helping me when I came down with a fever in his Montmartre Airbnb.

Many jazz scholars came to my aid during the writing of this book, making it possible to pinpoint Briggs's movements with astonishing accuracy nearly a century after the fact. Dr. Rainer E. Lotz provided crucial information and perspective. I am also indebted to Dan

Morgenstern and the Institute of Jazz Studies at Rutgers University, Phil Schaap, Jeffrey H. Jackson, Anne LeGrand, Dan Vernhettes, Stephanie Birch, Robert Darden, Norman Goda, and the Imperial War Museum in London.

Finally, I owe the deepest debt to my family for their love and support, which carried me through many rough spots: Kyle Donnelly; Kathy Atria; Eric Atria; Collin Whitlock; Tina Turner; and my father, Drew Atria, who also provided valuable edits to the manuscript.

Notes

Chapter 1

1. Cecilia Karch Brathwaite, "London Bourne of Barbados (1793–1869)," *Slavery and Abolition* 28, no. 1 (May 21, 2007)

2. Sidney Bechet, *Treat It Gentle* (Twain, 1960), 4, 46, 48, 212.

3. Bechet, *Treat It Gentle*, 48.

4. LeRoi Jones, *Blues People: Negro Music in White America* (Quill, 1999), 79.

Chapter 2

1. Jones, *Blues People*, 48.

2. Arthur Briggs, *Arthur Briggs Memoir*.

3. Briggs, *Memoir*.

4. James Weldon Johnson, *Autobiography of an Ex-Colored Man* (W. W. Norton, 2015), 15.

5. Osofsky, *Harlem: The Making of a Ghetto*, 106.

6. Briggs, *Memoir*.

7. James Collier, Interview with Arthur Briggs.

8. Briggs, *Memoir*.

9. Chris Goddard, *Jazz Away from Home* (Paddington Press, 1979).

10. Briggs, *Memoir*.

11. Briggs, *Memoir*.

Chapter 3

1. William Bolcom, *Reminiscing with Noble Sissle and Eubie Blake* (Viking Press, 1973).
2. Goddard, *Jazz Away from Home*, 15.
3. Briggs, *Memoir*.
4. Briggs, *Memoir*.
5. Briggs, *Memoir*.
6. Collier, Interview with Arthur Briggs.
7. Collier, Interview with Arthur Briggs.
8. Marva Griffin Carter, *Swing Along: The Musical Life of Will Marion Cook* (Oxford University Press, 2008).
9. Collier, Interview with Arthur Briggs.

Chapter 4

1. Collier, Interview with Arthur Briggs.
2. Briggs, *Memoir*.
3. Briggs, *Memoir*.
4. Briggs, *Memoir*.
5. Collier, Interview with Arthur Briggs.
6. Carter, *Swing Along*.
7. Briggs, *Memoir*.
8. Goddard, *Jazz Away from Home*.

Chapter 5

1. Briggs, *Memoir*.
2. Briggs, *Memoir*.
3. Goddard, *Jazz Away from Home*.
4. Briggs, *Memoir*.
5. Terry Teachout, *Pops: A Life of Louis Armstrong* (Houghton Mifflin Harcourt, 2009), 59.

6. Collier, Interview with Arthur Briggs.

7. Darryl Bullock, *David Bowie Made Me Gay: 100 Years of LGBT Music* (Harry N. Abrams, 2017).

8. Goddard, *Jazz Away from Home*, 69.

9. Briggs, *Memoir*.

10. Briggs, *Memoir*.

11. Goddard, *Jazz Away from Home*.

12. Briggs, *Memoir*.

13. Briggs, *Memoir*.

14. Jones, *Blues People*, 100.

15. Jones, *Blues People*, 21–24.

16. Briggs, *Memoir*.

17. Goddard, *Jazz Away from Home*, 60.

Chapter 6

1. Collier, Interview with Arthur Briggs.

2. Briggs, *Memoir*.

3. Briggs, *Memoir*.

4. Briggs, *Memoir*.

5. Rainer Lotz and Horst P. J. Bergmeier, "James Arthur Briggs," *Black Music Research Journal* (Spring 2010).

6. Briggs, *Memoir*.

7. Lotz and Bergmeier, "James Arthur Briggs," 99.

8. Briggs, *Memoir*.

9. John Chilton, *Sidney Bechet: The Wizard of Jazz* (Oxford University Press, 1987), 38.

10. Briggs, *Memoir*.

11. Collier, Interview with Arthur Briggs.

Chapter 7

1. Goddard, *Jazz Away from Home*, 31.

2. Chilton, *Sidney Bechet*, 46.

3. Goddard, *Jazz Away from Home*, 31.

4. Chilton, *Sidney Bechet*, 37–38.

5. Chilton, *Sidney Bechet*, 38.

6. Briggs, *Memoir*.

7. Briggs, *Memoir*.

8. Briggs, *Memoir*.

Chapter 8

1. Collier, Interview with Arthur Briggs.

2. Bechet, *Treat It Gentle*, 128.

3. Briggs, *Memoir*.

4. Briggs, *Memoir*.

5. Collier, Interview with Arthur Briggs.

6. Jeffrey P. Green, *Edmund Thornton Jenkins: The Life and Times of an American Black Composer, 1894-1926.* (Greenwood Press, 1982).

7. Briggs, *Memoir*.

8. Collier, Interview with Arthur Briggs.

9. Interview with author.

Chapter 9

1. Briggs, *Memoir*.

2. Demeusy and Rye, "The Bertin Depestre Salnave Musical Story."

3. Briggs, *Memoir*.

4. Briggs, *Memoir*.

5. Briggs, *Memoir*.

6. Collier, Interview with Arthur Briggs.

Chapter 10

1. Mark Miller, *Some Hustling This: Taking Jazz to the World, 1914-1929.* (Mercury Press, 2005).

2. Briggs, *Memoir.*

3. Collier, Interview with Arthur Briggs.

4. Briggs, *Memoir.*

5. Briggs, *Memoir.*

6. Briggs, *Memoir.*

7. Briggs, *Memoir.*

8. Howard Rye and Jeffrey Green, "Black Musical Internationalism in England in the 1920s," *Black Music Research Journal* 15, no. 1 (Spring 1995): 98.

9. Briggs, *Memoir.*

10. Briggs, *Memoir.*

Chapter 11

1. Lotz and Bergmeier, "James Arthur Briggs," 103.

2. Goddard, *Jazz Away from Home.*

3. Briggs, *Memoir.*

4. Briggs, *Memoir.*

5. Collier, Interview with Arthur Briggs.

6. Briggs, *Memoir.*

7. Briggs, *Memoir.*

8. Briggs, *Memoir.*

9. Collier, Interview with Arthur Briggs.

10. Briggs, *Memoir.*

11. Briggs, *Memoir.*

Chapter 12

1. Collier, Interview with Arthur Briggs.

2. James Weldon Johnson, *Black Manhattan* (A. A. Knopf, 1930), 779.

3. Goddard, *Jazz Away from Home*, 295.

4. Briggs, *Memoir*.

5. Collier, Interview with Arthur Briggs.

6. Briggs, *Memoir*.

7. Briggs, *Memoir*.

8. Briggs, *Memoir*.

9. Briggs, *Memoir*.

10. Briggs, *Memoir*.

11. Briggs, *Memoir*.

12. Briggs, *Memoir*.

13. Briggs, *Memoir*.

14. Goffin, *Aux Frontieres Du Jazz*.

15. Briggs, *Memoir*.

16. Briggs, *Memoir*.

17. Goddard, *Jazz Away from Home*.

Chapter 13

1. F. Scott Fitzgerald, *The Jazz Age* (New Directions, 1996), 4.

2. Lotz and Bergmeier, "James Arthur Briggs," 105.

3. Briggs, *Memoir*.

4. Briggs, *Memoir*.

5. Ralph Nevill, *Days and Nights in Montmartre and the Latin Quarter* (Herbert Jenkins Limited, 1927).

6. Goddard, *Jazz Away from Home*.

7. Nevill, *Days and Nights*.

8. T. Denean Sharpley-Whiting, *Bricktop's Paris: African American Women in Paris between the Two World Wars* (SUNY Press, 2015), 65.

9. Smith, "Ada 'Bricktop' Smith Papers: 1926-1983," February 11, 2016.

10. William A. Shack, *Harlem in Montmartre: A Paris Jazz Story between the Great Wars* (University of California Press, 2001), 32.

11. Sharpley-Whiting, 30.

12. Briggs, *Memoir*.

13. Craig Lloyd, *Eugene Bullard: Black Expatriate in Jazz-Age Paris* (University of Georgia Press, 2000).

14. Bechet, *Treat It Gentle*, 153.

15. Goddard, *Jazz Away from Home*.

16. Shack, *Harlem in Montmartre*, 54.

17. Ernest Hemingway, *A Moveable Feast* (Charles Scribner's Sons, 1964), 155.

18. Ada "Bricktop" Smith, "Ada 'Bricktop' Smith Papers: 1926–1983."

19. McBrien, *Cole Porter: A Biography*, 96–97.

20. McBrien, *Cole Porter*, 108.

21. McBrien, *Cole Porter*, 108.

22. Eells, *The Life That Late He Led: A Biography of Cole Porter*, 81.

23. Smith, "Ada 'Bricktop' Smith Papers: 1926-1983."

24. Sharpley-Whiting, *Bricktop's Paris: African American Women in Paris Between the Two World Wars*, 48.

Chapter 14

1. Collier, Interview with Arthur Briggs.

2. Goffin, *Aux Frontieres Du Jazz*.

3. Briggs, *Memoir*.

4. Lotz and Bergmeier, "James Arthur Briggs," 104.

5. Briggs, *Memoir*.

6. Briggs, *Memoir*.

7. Briggs, *Memoir*.

8. Briggs, *Memoir*.

Chapter 15

1. Lotz and Bergmeier, "James Arthur Briggs," 115.

2. Lotz and Bergmeier, "James Arthur Briggs," 112.

3. Lotz and Bergmeier, "James Arthur Briggs," 111.

4. Briggs, *Memoir*.

5. Briggs, *Memoir*.

6. Briggs, *Memoir*.

7. Briggs, *Memoir*.

8. Briggs, *Memoir*.

9. Collier, Interview with Arthur Briggs.

10. Briggs, *Memoir*.

11. Briggs, *Memoir*.

12. Collier, Interview with Arthur Briggs.

13. Briggs, *Memoir*.

14. Briggs, *Memoir*.

Chapter 16

1. Josephine Baker and Jo Bouillon, *Josephine* (Harper and Row, 1977), 29.

2. Sharpley-Whiting, *Bricktop's Paris*, 43.

3. Ean Wood, *The Josephine Baker Story* (Sanctuary, 2000), 165.

4. Wood, *Josephine Baker Story*.

5. Wood, *Josephine Baker Story*.

Chapter 17

1. Collier, Interview with Arthur Briggs.

2. Kay Boyle and Robert McAlmon, *Being Geniuses Together: 1920–1930* (North Point Press, 1984), 95–96.

3. Sharpley-Whiting, *Bricktop's Paris*, 68.

4. Briggs, *Memoir*.

5. Collier, Interview with Arthur Briggs.

6. Briggs, *Memoir*.

7. Briggs, *Memoir*.

8. Briggs, *Memoir*.

9. Collier, Interview with Arthur Briggs.

10. Briggs, *Memoir*.

11. Briggs, *Memoir*.

12. Briggs, *Memoir*.

13. Briggs, *Memoir*.

Chapter 18

1. Briggs, *Memoir*.

2. Teachout, *Pops*, 13.

3. Collier, Interview with Arthur Briggs.

4. Lotz and Bergmeier, "James Arthur Briggs," 119–120.

5. Goddard, *Jazz Away from Home*, 28.

Chapter 19

1. Alan Schroeder and Heather Lehr Wagner, *Josephine Baker: Entertainer* (Chelsea House, 2006).

2. Wood, *Josephine Baker Story*.

3. Wood, *Josephine Baker Story*.

4. Lotz and Bergmeier, "James Arthur Briggs," 121.

Chapter 20

1. Fitzgerald, *The Jazz Age*, 13.

2. Briggs, *Memoir*.

3. Bolcom, *Reminiscing*.

4. Briggs, *Memoir*.

5. Briggs, *Memoir*.

6. Briggs, *Memoir*.

7. Briggs, *Memoir*.

8. Briggs, *Memoir*.

9. Fitzgerald, *The Jazz Age*, 14.

Chapter 21

1. Chilton, *Sidney Bechet: The Wizard of Jazz*, 81.

2. Collier, Interview with Arthur Briggs.

3. Briggs, *Memoir*.

4. J. A. Rogers, "Sissle Orchestra Won Job on Merit," *Baltimore Afro-American*, July 19, 1930.

5. Briggs, *Memoir*.

6. Briggs, *Memoir*.

7. Michael Dregni, *Django: The Life and Music of a Gypsy Legend* (Oxford University Press, 2004), 75.

8. Goddard, *Jazz Away from Home*, 139.

9. Goffin, *Aux Frontieres Du Jazz*.

10. Sudhalter, "'Doc Cheatham: Good for What Ails You' Liner Notes," 1977.

Chapter 22

1. Goddard, *Jazz Away from Home*.

2. Briggs, *Memoir*.

3. Osofsky, *Harlem: The Making of a Ghetto*, 187.

4. Briggs, *Memoir*.

5. Briggs, *Memoir*.

6. Goddard, *Jazz Away from Home*.

7. Collier, Interview with Arthur Briggs.

8. Briggs, *Memoir*.

9. Briggs, *Memoir*.

10. Goddard, *Jazz Away from Home*, 285.

11. Briggs, *Memoir*.

12. Goddard, *Jazz Away from Home*, 285.

13. Briggs, *Memoir*.

14. Collier, Interview with Arthur Briggs.

15. Briggs, *Memoir*.

16. Briggs, *Memoir*.

17. Briggs, *Memoir*.

Chapter 23

1. Collier, interview with Arthur Briggs.

2. James Haskins and Bricktop, *Bricktop* (Welcome Rain, 2000), 145.

3. Briggs, *Memoir*.

4. Briggs, *Memoir*.

5. Haskins and Bricktop, *Bricktop*, 158.

6. Haskins and Bricktop, *Bricktop*, 32.

7. Haskins and Bricktop, *Bricktop*, 153.

8. Goddard, *Jazz Away from Home*.

9. F. Scott Fitzgerald, *Babylon Revisited and Other Stories* (Scribner, 2003), 210–214.

10. Goddard, *Jazz Away From Home*, 220.

11. Briggs, *Memoir*.

12. Goddard, *Jazz Away from Home*, 137.

Chapter 24

1. Shack, *Harlem in Montmartre*.

2. Dregni, *Django*, 77.

3. Briggs, *Memoir*.

4. Briggs, *Memoir*.

5. Briggs, *Memoir*.

6. Briggs, *Memoir*.

7. Collier, Interview with Arthur Briggs.

8. Briggs, *Memoir*.

9. Collier, Interview with Arthur Briggs.

10. The Street Wolf of Paris, "Montmartre: Yours and Mine," *Philadelphia Tribune*, November 16, 1933.

11. Collier, Interview with Arthur Briggs.

12. Collier, Interview with Arthur Briggs.

13. Briggs, *Memoir*.

14. Haskins and Bricktop, *Bricktop*, 189–190.

Chapter 25

1. N. J. Canetti, "Our Paris Letter," *Melody Maker*, June 9, 1934.

2. Lotz and Bergmeier, "James Arthur Briggs," 136.

3. Briggs, *Memoir*.

4. Briggs, *Memoir*.

5. Briggs, *Memoir*.

6. Briggs, *Memoir*.

7. Goddard, *Jazz Away from Home*.

8. Collier, Interview with Arthur Briggs.

9. Hugues Panassié, "Arthur Briggs," *Jazz Tango*, July 1934.

10. Laurence Bergreen, *Louis Armstrong: An Extravagant Life* (Broadway Books, 1997).

11. Briggs, *Memoir*.

12. Briggs, *Memoir*.

Chapter 26

1. Collier, Interview with Arthur Briggs.

2. Briggs, *Memoir*.

3. Charles Delaunay, *Django Reinhardt* (Cassell and Company, 1961), 74.

4. Delaunay, *Django Reinhardt*, 61.

5. Delaunay, *Django Reinhardt*, 107.

6. Stephane Grappelly, "Stephane Grappelly Tells—for the First Time—the True Story of Django Reinhardt," *Melody Maker*, February 20, 1954.

7. Collier, Interview with Arthur Briggs.

8. Delaunay, *Django Reinhardt*, 74.

9. Briggs, *Memoir*.

10. Collier, Interview with Arthur Briggs.

11. Briggs, *Memoir*.

12. Briggs, *Memoir*.

13. Briggs, *Memoir*.

14. Briggs, *Memoir*.

15. Edgar Wiggins, "Louis Armstrong O.K. on Air," *Chicago Defender*, December 22, 1934.

Chapter 27

1. Goddard, *Jazz Away from Home*.

2. Grappelly, "True Story of Django Reinhardt."

3. Goddard, *Jazz Away from Home*.

4. Briggs, *Memoir*.

5. John Chilton, *The Song of the Hawk: The Life and Recordings of Coleman Hawkins*, 116.

6. Briggs, *Memoir*.

7. Briggs, *Memoir*.

8. Chilton, *The Song of the Hawk*, 118.

9. Collier, Interview with Arthur Briggs.

10. Shack, *Harlem in Montmartre*, 94.

Chapter 28

1. Wood, *Josephine Baker Story*.

2. Edgar Wiggins, "Jo Baker Refuses Offers to Come to U.S.: Fears Home Folks Would Criticize Her Dancing," *Chicago Defender*, April 13, 1935.

3. Charles Isaac Bowen, "On the Air," *Baltimore Afro-American*, April 13, 1935.

4. *Chicago Defender*, "Louis the Second," March 16, 1935.

5. Wood, *Josephine Baker Story.*

6. Wood, *Josephine Baker Story.*

7. Wood, *Josephine Baker Story.*

8. Wood, *Josephine Baker Story.*

9. Wood, *Josephine Baker Story.*

10. Schroeder and Wagner, *Josephine Baker: Entertainer*, 50–51.

11. Wood, *Josephine Baker Story.*

Chapter 29

1. *Chicago Defender*, "Race Stage Stars Work at Benefit For Paris' Poor," January 4, 1936.

2. Volker Ullrich, *Hitler Ascent: 1889–1939* (Alfred A. Knopf, 2016), 566.

3. Semiramis InterContinental, "Semiramis History," Blog, http://designcoordinators.com/projects/semiramis_cd/content/history.html (accessed November 24, 2018).

4. Andrew Humphreys, "The Hotels." *Egypt in the Golden Age of Travel* (blog), http://grandhotelsegypt.com/?page_id=10 (accessed May 28, 2019).

5. Briggs, *Memoir.*

6. Ray Shohet, "A Swing Band Is No Good Unless It Plays Viennese Waltzes!" *Melody Maker*, September 4, 1937.

7. Briggs, *Memoir.*

8. Briggs, *Memoir.*

9. Briggs, *Memoir.*

Chapter 30

1. Schroeder and Wagner, *Josephine Baker: Entertainer.*

2. Ullrich, *Hitler Ascent*, 658.

3. Wood, *Josephine Baker Story.*

4. Briggs, *Memoir.*

5. Briggs, *Memoir.*

6. Briggs, *Memoir*.

7. Wood, *Josephine Baker Story*.

8. Briggs, *Memoir*.

Chapter 31

1. Chilton, *The Song of the Hawk*, 148.

2. Briggs, *Memoir*.

3. Edgar Wiggins, "War Scare Blamed for Poor Business," *Chicago Defender*, October 22, 1938.

4. Ullrich, *Hitler Ascent*, 661.

5. Ullrich, *Hitler Ascent*, 673.

6. US Holocaust Memorial Museum, "Kristallnacht," Blog, https://www.ushmm .org/wlc/en/article.php?ModuleId=10005201 (accessed May 28, 2019).

7. Ullrich, *Hitler Ascent*, 678.

Chapter 32

1. Collier, Interview with Arthur Briggs.

2. Briggs, *Memoir*.

3. Briggs, *Memoir*.

4. Wiggins, "Across the Pond," *Chicago Defender*, May 8, 1937.

5. Wiggins, "Across the Pond," *Chicago Defender*, February 18, 1939.

6. Shack, *Harlem in Montmartre*, 109.

7. Briggs, *Memoir*.

8. Sharpley-Whiting, *Bricktop's Paris*, 17.

9. Briggs, *Memoir*.

Chapter 33

1. Briggs, *Memoir*.

2. Briggs, *Memoir*.

3. David Pryce-Jones, *Paris in the Third Reich* (Holt, Rinehart and Winston, 1981).

4. Shack, *Harlem in Montmartre*, 104.

5. Briggs, *Memoir*.

6. Briggs, *Memoir*.

7. Michel Dreano, "Interview with Jean Weinfeld" (St. Denis Municipal Archive, n.d.), 2.

Chapter 34

1. Frank Pickersgill, *The Making of a Secret Agent: Letters of 1934–1943* (Ryerson Press, 1948), 49.

2. Collier, Interview with Arthur Briggs.

3. William Joseph Webb, *William Joseph Webb: Internment Camp Journals. Period 26th July 1940 to 31st December 1942. At Laharie Camp in the Landes and St. Denis Military Barracks* (British Imperial War Museum, London, n.d.).

4. Pickersgill, *The Making of a Secret Agent*, 177–178.

5. Briggs, *Memoir*.

6. Guido Fackler, "Music in Concentration Camps 1933–1945," *Music and Politics* (blog), http://quod.lib.umich.edu/m/mp/9460447.0001.102/--music-in-concentration-camps-1933-1945?rgn=main;view=fulltext (accessed May 28, 2019).

7. Collier, Interview with Arthur Briggs.

8. Webb, *Internment Camp Journals*, 169–176.

9. Collier, Interview with Arthur Briggs.

10. Webb, *Internment Camp Journals*, 1:12.

11. Webb, *Internment Camp Journals*, 1:15–16.

12. Briggs, *Memoir*.

13. Briggs, *Memoir*.

Chapter 35

1. A. H. Pullen, in "Saint Denis."

2. Webb, *Internment Camp Journals*, 1:14.

3. Webb, *Internment Camp Journals*, 2:5.

4. Webb, *Internment Camp Journals*, 2:1.

5. Briggs, *Memoir*.

6. Pryce-Jones, *Paris in the Third Reich*.

7. Pryce-Jones, *Paris*.

8. Collier, Interview with Arthur Briggs.

9. Briggs, *Memoir*.

10. Briggs, *Memoir*.

11. Briggs, *Memoir*.

12. Briggs, *Memoir*.

13. Collier, Interview with Arthur Briggs.

14. Lotz and Bergmeier, "James Arthur Briggs," 144.

15. Goddard, *Jazz Away from Home*.

Chapter 36

1. Baker and Bouillon, *Josephine*, 117.

2. Wood, *Josephine Baker Story*.

3. Baker and Bouillon, *Josephine*, 120.

4. Baker and Bouillon, *Josephine*, 118.

5. Baker and Bouillon, *Josephine*.

6. Wood, *Josephine Baker Story*.

7. Baker and Bouillon, *Josephine*, 118–119.

8. Baker and Bouillon, *Josephine*, 119.

9. Baker and Bouillon, *Josephine*, 119.

10. Baker and Bouillon, *Josephine*, 120.

11. Wood, *Josephine Baker Story*, 222–223.

12. Lynn Haney, *Naked at the Feast: A Biography of Josephine Baker* (Dodd, Mead and Company, 1981).

13. Baker and Bouillon, *Josephine*, 120.

14. Haney, *Naked at the Feast*.

15. Baker and Bouillon, *Josephine*, 122.

Chapter 37

1. Webb, *Internment Camp Journals*, 2:12.

2. Webb, *Internment Camp Journals*, 2:3.

3. Webb, *William Joseph Webb: Internment Camp Journals*, 2:4.

4. Collier, Interview with Arthur Briggs.

5. Briggs, *Memoir*.

6. Webb, *Internment Camp Journals*, 2:6.

7. Holman Jameson, "Parisian Arena of Le 'Hot Jazz' Inspired by Former U.S. Musician," *Baltimore Afro-American*, February 14, 1948.

8. Webb, *Internment Camp Journals*, 3:2.

9. Webb, *Internment Camp Journals*, 3:6.

10. Webb, *Internment Camp Journals*, 2:19.

11. Webb, *Internment Camp Journals*, 2:20.

12. Webb, *Internment Camp Journals*, 2:26.

13. Dreano, "Interview with Jean Weinfeld," 7.

14. Webb, *Internment Camp Journals*, 3:7.

15. Webb, *Internment Camp Journals*, 3:9.

16. Unknown, "The Atlantic Conference and Charter, 1941," https://history.state.gov/milestones/1937-1945/atlantic-conf (accessed October 30, 2018).

17. Webb, *Internment Camp Journals*, 4:47.

Chapter 38

1. Wood, *Josephine Baker Story*, 230–233.

2. Baker and Bouillon, *Josephine*, 129.

3. Wood, *Josephine Baker Story*.

4. Wood, *Josephine Baker Story*.

5. Wood, *Josephine Baker Story*, 239.

6. Smith, "Ada 'Bricktop' Smith Papers: 1926–1983."

Chapter 39

1. Webb, *Internment Camp Journals*, 4:24.

2. Webb, *Internment Camp Journals*, 4:18.

3. Briggs, *Memoir*.

4. Briggs, *Memoir*.

5. Webb, *Internment Camp Journals*, 6:3.

6. Dreano, "Interview with Jean Weinfeld," 6, 12.

7. Webb, *Internment Camp Journals*, 7:17.

8. Briggs, *Memoir*.

9. Sandy Pekar and Judy Whittaker, "African American Work Songs and Hollers," *Voices across Time: American History through Music* (blog), http://voices.pitt.edu/come-all-ye/ti/2006/Song%20Activities/0405PekarWhittaker WorkSongs.html (accessed November 18, 2018).

10. Collier, Interview with Arthur Briggs.

11. Jameson, "Parisian Arena."

Chapter 40

1. Neville J. N. Foreman, in "Saint Denis."

2. Unknown, "Nazis Didn't Look up Chimney: Well-Hidden Radio Kept British Internees up-to-Date on the War," *Winnipeg Tribune*, September 29, 1944

3. Briggs, *Memoir*.

4. Goebbels, "Nation, Rise Up, and Let the Storm Break Loose," *German Propaganda Archive* (blog), http://research.calvin.edu/german-propaganda -archive/goeb36.htm (accessed November 3, 2018).

5. Dreano, "Interview with Jean Weinfeld," 11.

6. Collier, Interview with Arthur Briggs.

7. Unknown, "Saint Denis."

8. Jameson, "Parisian Arena."

9. Unknown, "Saint Denis," *The Prisoner of War: The Official Journal of the Prisoners of War Department of the Red Cross and St. John War Organisation*, April 1944.

10. Collier, Interview with Arthur Briggs.

11. Dreano, "Interview with Jean Weinfeld," 2.

12. Webb, *Internment Camp Journals*, 4:22.

13. Dreano, "Interview with Jean Weinfeld," 2.

14. Dreano, "Interview with Jean Weinfeld," 22.

Chapter 41

1. Briggs, *Memoir*.

2. Briggs, *Memoir*.

3. Briggs, *Memoir*.

4. Briggs, *Memoir*.

5. Briggs, *Memoir*.

6. Briggs, *Memoir*.

7. Larry Collins and Dominique Lapierre, *Is Paris Burning?* (Warner Books, 1965), 35.

8. Collins and Lapierre, *Is Paris Burning?*, 209.

9. Collins and Lapierre, *Is Paris Burning?*, 188.

10. Collins and Lapierre, *Is Paris Burning?*, 109.

11. Collins and Lapierre, *Is Paris Burning?*, 259.

12. Collins and Lapierre, *Is Paris Burning?*, 257.

13. Briggs, *Memoir*.

14. Briggs, *Memoir*.

Chapter 42

1. James E. Thomas, in "Saint Denis."

2. Briggs, *Memoir*.

3. Briggs, *Memoir.*

4. Briggs, *Memoir.*

5. Briggs, *Memoir.*

6. Dreano, "Interview with Jean Weinfeld," 22.

Chapter 43

1. Briggs, *Memoir.*

2. Briggs, *Memoir.*

3. Briggs, *Memoir.*

4. Briggs, *Memoir.*

5. Briggs, *Memoir.*

6. Briggs, *Memoir.*

7. Lotz and Bergmeier, "James Arthur Briggs," 144.

8. Briggs, *Memoir.*

9. US Holocaust Memorial Museum, "Documenting Numbers of Victims of the Holocaust and Nazi Persecution," Blog, https://encyclopedia.ushmm .org/content/en/article/documenting-numbers-of-victims-of-the-holocaust -and-nazi-persecution (accessed November 6, 2018).

Chapter 44

1. Briggs, *Memoir.*

2. Briggs, *Memoir.*

3. Briggs, *Memoir.*

4. Briggs, *Memoir.*

5. Briggs, *Memoir.*

6. Briggs, *Memoir.*

Chapter 45

1. Briggs, *Memoir.*

2. Briggs, *Memoir.*

3. Interview with author.

4. Interview with author.

5. Wood, *Josephine Baker Story.*

6. Wood, *Josephine Baker Story.*

7. Wood, *Josephine Baker Story.*

8. Briggs, *Memoir.*

9. Interview with author.

10. Interview with author.

Bibliography

Allen, Ralph. "British Aplomb Got Nazis: Major Strolled Unhindered in Paris." *Winnipeg Tribune*, September 13, 1944.

Age. "Britishers in Paris: Herded in Prison Camps." December 7, 1940.

Age. "Britons in France Interned." October 22, 1940.

Baker, Josephine, and Jo Bouillon. *Josephine.* New York: Harper and Row, 1977.

Bechet, Sidney. *Treat It Gentle.* New York: Hill and Wang, 1960.

Berendt, Joachim-Ernst, and Gunther Huesmann. *The Jazz Book: From Ragtime to the 21st Century.* Chicago: Lawrence Hill Books, 2009.

Bergreen, Laurence. *Louis Armstrong: An Extravagant Life.* New York: Broadway Books, 1997.

Bolcom, William. *Reminiscing with Noble Sissle and Eubie Blake.* New York: Viking Press, 1973.

Bottomley, Maurice. "Harry Gold at the Cafe de Paris." *Cocktails With Elvira* (blog). Accessed October 18, 2016. https://elvirabarney.wordpress.com/2011/12/06/harry-gold-at-the-cafe-de-paris/.

Bowen, Charles Isaac. "On the Air." *Baltimore Afro-American*, April 13, 1935.

Boyle, Kay, and Robert McAlmon. *Being Geniuses Together: 1920–1930.* Berkeley, CA: North Point Press, 1984.

Brathwaite, Cecilia Karch. "London Bourne of Barbados (1793–1869)." *Slavery and Abolition* 28, no. 1 (May 21, 2007): 23–40.

Briggs, Arthur. *Arthur Briggs Memoir,* n.d.

Bullock, Darryl. *David Bowie Made Me Gay: 100 Years of LGBT Music.* New York: Harry N. Abrams, 2017.

Byers, Ann. *The Holocaust Camps.* Berkeley Heights, NJ: Enslow, 1998.

Canetti, N. J. "From the Boulevards." *Melody Maker*, July 14, 1934.

Canetti, N. J. "Our Paris Letter." *Melody Maker*, June 9, 1934.

Carter, Marva Griffin. *Swing Along: The Musical Life of Will Marion Cook.* Oxford: Oxford University Press, 2008.

Caskie, Donald. *The Tartan Pimpernel.* London: Oldbourne Book, 1957.

Chicago Defender. "Broadway Gets 1st All-Nations Band of 'Name' Musicians: 'Not an Experiment' Famed Bookie Claims." August 29, 1942.

Chicago Defender. "Lights Are on Again Along Paris, France's, Famous 'Broadway.'" September 21, 1946.

Chicago Defender. "Louis the Second." March 16, 1935.

Chicago Defender. "New Orleans to Paris Pals Mourn Death of Jazz Star Sidney Bechet." May 23, 1959.

Chicago Defender. "Noble Sissle and His Band Soar to Top." September 21, 1929.

Chicago Defender. "Race Stage Stars Work at Benefit for Paris' Poor." January 4, 1936.

Chilton, John. *A Jazz Nursery: The Story of the Jenkins' Orphanage Bands of Charleston, South Carolina.* London: Bloomsbury Book Shop, 1980.

Chilton, John. *Sidney Bechet: The Wizard of Jazz.* Oxford: Oxford University Press, 1987.

Chilton, John. *The Song of the Hawk: The Life and Recordings of Coleman Hawkins.* Ann Arbor: University of Michigan Press, 1990.

Clutton-Brock, Oliver. *Footprints on the Sands of Time: RAF Bomber Command Prisoners of War in Germany 1939–45.* London: Grub Street, 2003.

Collier, James. Interview with Arthur Briggs, n.d.

Collier, James.*Louis Armstrong: An American Genius.* Oxford: Oxford University Press , 1983.

Collins, Larry, and Dominique Lapierre. *Is Paris Burning?* New York: Warner Books, 1965.

Danzi, Michael, as told to Rainer E. Lotz. *American Musician In Germany 1924–1939.* Norbert Ruecker, 1986.

Davis, John, and Gary Clarke. "Recordania: Jazz in Germany." *Accordion Times and Musical Express*, January 9, 1948.

Delaunay, Charles. *Django Reinhardt.* London: Cassell, 1961.

Demeusy, Bertrand, and Howard Rye (Trans.). "The Bertin Depestre Salnave Musical Story." *Storyville*, September 1978.

Desjardins, Maurice. "Canadians Tell of Four Years in Filthy Hun Camp Near Paris." *Ottawa Journal*, August 29, 1944.

Dreano, Michel. "Interview with Jean Weinfeld," St. Denis Municipal Archive, n.d.

Dregni, Michael. *Django: The Life and Music of a Gypsy Legend.* Oxford: Oxford University Press, 2004.

Dunbar, Rudolph. "Famous Musician Freed from Nazi Prison." *Kansas City Plain Dealer*, September 22, 1944.

Dunbar, Rudolph. "Paris Blossoms Again with Negro Music as the Theme." *Chicago Defender*, November 11, 1944.

Dunbar, Rudolph. "Trumpet Player Briggs Freed After Four Years in Nazi Camp Near Paris." *Chicago Defender*, September 23, 1944.

Ecker, Margaret. "Moose Jaw Youth Tells of Four Years in Nazi Prison Camp." *Lethbridge Herald*, November 8, 1944.

Eells, George. *The Life That Late He Led: A Biography of Cole Porter*. New York: G. P. Putnam's Sons, 1967.

Fackler, Guido. "Music in Concentration Camps 1933–1945." *Music and Politics* (blog), 2007. Accessed May 28, 2019. http://quod.lib.umich.edu/m/mp/9460447.0001.102/--music-in-concentration-camps-1933-1945?rgn=main;view=fulltext.

Feather, Leonard G. "Vive Le Hot!: Snapshots of Paris and Its Dance Music." *Melody Maker*, November 17, 1934.

Fitzgerald, F. Scott. *Babylon Revisited and Other Stories*. New York: Scribner, 2003.

Fitzgerald, F. Scott. *The Jazz Age*. New York: New Directions, 1996.

Foy, David A. *For You The War Is Over: American Prisoners of War in Nazi Germany*. New York: Stein and Day, 1984.

Friedlander, Saul. *Nazi Germany and the Jews, 1939–1945: The Years of Extermination*. New York: Harper Collins, 2007.

Goddard, Chris. *Jazz Away from Home*. New York: Paddington Press, 1979.

Goebbels, Joseph. "Nation, Rise Up, and Let the Storm Break Loose." *German Propaganda Archive* (blog). Accessed November 3, 2018. http://research.calvin.edu/german-propaganda-archive/goeb36.htm.

Goffin, Robert. *Aux Frontières du Jazz*. Paris: Sagittarius, 1932.

Goring, Hermann. "Letter from Hermann Goring to Head of Security Police and SD." Accessed October 30, 2018. http://www.ghwk.de/fileadmin/user_upload/pdf-wannsee/engl/goering.pdf.

Grappelly, Stephane. "Stephane Grappelly Tells—for the First Time—the True Story of Django Reinhardt." *Melody Maker*, February 20, 1954.

Green, Jeffrey P. *Edmund Thornton Jenkins: The Life and Times of an American Black Composer, 1894–1926*. Santa Barbara, CA: Greenwood Press, 1982.

Guardian. "Arthur Briggs: An American in Paris." July 19, 1991.

Haffner, Sebastian. *Defying Hitler: A Memoir*. New York: Farrar, Straus and Giroux, 2002.

Haney, Lynn. *Naked at the Feast: A Biography of Josephine Baker*. New York: Dodd, Mead, 1981.

Haskins, James, and Bricktop. *Bricktop*. New York: Welcome Rain, 2000.

Hemingway, Ernest. *A Moveable Feast*. New York: Charles Scribner's Sons, 1964.

Hubler, Richard G. *The Cole Porter Story: As Told to Richard G. Hubler*. Cleveland, OH: World Publishing, 1965.

Humphreys, Andrew. "The Hotels." *Egypt in the Golden Age of Travel* (blog). Accessed May 28, 2019. http://grandhotelsegypt.com/?page_id=10.

"Interview with Arthur Briggs of June 28th, 53." Radiodiffusion-Television Francaise. French Broadcasting System, n.d.

Jameson, Holman. "Parisian Arena of Le 'Hot Jazz' Inspired by Former U.S. Musician." *Baltimore Afro-American*, February 14, 1948.

Johnson, James Weldon. *Autobiography of an Ex-Colored Man*. New York: W. W. Norton, 2015.

Johnson, James Weldon. *Black Manhattan*. New York: A. A. Knopf, 1930.

Jones, LeRoi. *Blues People: Negro Music in White America*. New York: Quill, 1999.

Laqueur, Walter. *The Holocaust Encyclopedia*. New Haven, CT: Yale University Press, 2001.

Leininger-Miller, Theresa. *New Negro Artists in Paris: African American Painters and Sculptors in the City of Light, 1922–1934*. New Brunswick, NJ: Rutgers University Press, 2001.

Lest We Forget. "Orchestras." Blog. Accessed December 5, 2016. http://www.holocaust-lestweforget.com/orchestra.html.

Lloyd, Craig. *Eugene Bullard: Black Expatriate in Jazz-Age Paris*. Athens: University of Georgia Press, 2000.

Lotz, Rainer, and Horst P. J. Bergmeier. "James Arthur Briggs." *Black Music Research Journal*, Spring 2010.

Lusane, Clarence. *Hitler's Black Victims: The Historical Experiences of Afro-Germans, European Blacks, Africans, and African Americans in the Nazi Era*. Oxfordshire, UK: Routledge, 2003.

Melody Maker. "Famous Negro Trumpet-Player's Adventures under Nazis in France." December 30, 1944.

McBrien, William. *Cole Porter: A Biography*. New York: Alfred A. Knopf, 1998.

McCardell, Lee. "McCardell Describes Capture of 35 Prisoners." *Baltimore Sun*, August 2, 1944.

Miller, Mark. *Some Hustling This: Taking Jazz to the World, 1914–1929*. Toronto: Mercury Press, 2005.

Nevill, Ralph. *Days and Nights in Montmartre and the Latin Quarter*. London: Herbert Jenkins Limited, 1927.

Ottawa Journal. "Frank Pickersgill Evades Hun Jailers." December 7, 1942.

Osofsky, Gilbert. *Harlem: The Making of a Ghetto*. Chicago: Ivan R. Dee, 1996.

Panassie, Hugues. "Arthur Briggs." *Jazz Tango*, July 1934.

Panassie, Hugues. "Le Saxophoniste Coleman Hawkins et Le Quintette Du Hot-Club de France." *Comoedia*, March 11, 1935.

Pekar, Sandy, and Judy Whittaker. "African American Work Songs and Hollers." *Voices across Time: American History through Music* (blog). Accessed November 18, 2018. http://voices.pitt.edu/come-all-ye/ti/2006/Song%20Act ivities/0405PekarWhittakerWorkSongs.html.

People's Voice. "Arthur Briggs Freed in Paris Liberation." September 23, 1944.

Philadelphia Tribune. "American Colony in Paris Fetes War Mothers, Widows." July 27, 1933.

Pickersgill, Frank. *The Making of a Secret Agent: Letters of 1934–1943 Written by Frank Pickersgill and Edited with a Memoir by George H. Ford*. Ontario: Ryerson Press, 1948.

Pick, Margaret Moos. "A Night at Bricktop's: Jazz in 1930s' Montmartre." *The Jim Cullum Riverwalk Jazz Collection* (blog). Accessed December 1, 2016. http:// riverwalkjazz.stanford.edu/program/night-bricktops-jazz-1930s-montmartre.

Pryce-Jones, David. *Paris in the Third Reich*. Holt, Rinehart and Winston, 1981.

Red Cross and St. John War Organisation. "Saint Denis." *The Prisoner of War: The Official Journal of the Prisoners of War Department of the Red Cross and St. John War Organisation*, April 1944.

Rogers, J. A. "Sissle Orchestra Won Job on Merit." *Baltimore Afro-American*, July 19, 1930.

Rye, Howard, and Jeffrey Green. "Black Musical Internationalism in England in the 1920s." *Black Music Research Journal* 15, no. 1 (Spring 1995): 93–107.

Schaap, Jeremy. *Triumph: The Untold Story of Jesse Owens at Hitler's Olympics*. Boston: Houghton Mifflin Harcourt, 2007.

Schroeder, Alan, and Heather Lehr Wagner. *Josephine Baker: Entertainer*. New York: Chelsea House, 2006.

Semiramis InterContinental. "Semiramis History." Blog. Accessed November 24, 2018. http://designcoordinators.com/projects/semiramis_cd/content /history.html.

Settel, Arthur. "Cairo, Paris of the Near East, Boasts around 100 Niteries and Dance Halls." *Variety*, March 31, 1937.

Shack, William A. *Harlem in Montmartre: A Paris Jazz Story between the Great Wars*. Oakland: University of California Press, 2001.

Sharpley-Whiting, T. Denean. *Bricktop's Paris: African American Women in Paris between the Two World Wars*. Albany: SUNY Press, 2015.

Shohet, Ray. "A Swing Band Is No Good Unless It Plays Viennese Waltzes!" *Melody Maker*, September 4, 1937.

Simmen, Johnny. "Storyville 115 0004." *National Jazz Archive: The Story of British Jazz* (blog). Accessed December 5, 2016. http://archive.nationaljazzarchive.co.uk/archive/journals/storyville/storyville-115/46011.

Smith, Ada "Bricktop." "Ada 'Bricktop' Smith Papers: 1926–1983." Schomburg Center for Research in Black Culture, New York Public Library. Accessed February 11, 2016.

Street Wolf of Paris. "Montmartre: Yours and Mine." *Philadelphia Tribune*, November 16, 1933.

Sudhalter, Richard. "'Doc Cheatham: Good for What Ails You' Liner Notes," 1977.

Sydney Morning Herald. "John Amery on Trial for High Treason." July 31, 1945.

Teachout, Terry. *Pops: A Life of Louis Armstrong*. Houghton Mifflin Harcourt, 2009.

Ullrich, Volker. *Hitler Ascent: 1889–1939*. New York: Alfred A. Knopf, 2016.

United States Holocaust Memorial Museum. "Documenting Numbers of Victims of the Holocaust and Nazi Persecution." Blog. Accessed November 6, 2018. https://encyclopedia.ushmm.org/content/en/article/documenting-numbers-of-victims-of-the-holocaust-and-nazi-persecution.

United States Holocaust Memorial Museum. "Kristallnacht." Blog. Accessed May 28, 2019. https://www.ushmm.org/wlc/en/article.php?ModuleId=10005201.

US Department of State. "The Atlantic Conference and Charter, 1941." Accessed October 30, 2018. https://history.state.gov/milestones/1937-1945/atlantic-conf.

Variety. "Foreign Show News: Josy Baker Concert." April 3, 1935.

Webb, William Joseph. *William Joseph Webb: Internment Camp Journals. Period 26th July 1940 to 31st December 1942. At Laharie Camp in the Landes and St. Denis Military Barracks*. British Imperial War Museum, London, n.d.

Wiggins, Edgar. "Across the Pond." *Chicago Defender*, May 8, 1937.

Wiggins, Edgar. "Across the Pond." *Chicago Defender*, November 20, 1937.

Wiggins, Edgar. "Across the Pond." *Chicago Defender*, December 17, 1938.

Wiggins, Edgar. "Across the Pond." *Chicago Defender*, January 20, 1939.

Wiggins, Edgar. "Across the Pond." *Chicago Defender*, February 4, 1939.

Wiggins, Edgar. "Across the Pond." *Chicago Defender*, February 18, 1939.

Wiggins, Edgar. "Across the Pond." *Chicago Defender*, March 4, 1939.

Wiggins, Edgar. "Across the Pond." *Chicago Defender*, May 13, 1939.

Wiggins, Edgar. "Across the Pond." *Chicago Defender*, June 24, 1939.

Wiggins, Edgar. "Jo Baker Refuses Offers to Come to U.S.: Fears Home Folks Would Criticize Her Dancing." *Chicago Defender*, April 13, 1935.

Wiggins, Edgar. "John Lewis' Modern Jazz Combo Awarded Music 'Oscar' in Europe." *Chicago Defender*, August 4, 1956.

Wiggins, Edgar. "Louis Armstrong O.K. on Air." *Chicago Defender*, December 22, 1934.

Wiggins, Edgar. "Mme. Caterina Jarboro Leaves Paris for Six Months Tour of Europe." *Chicago Defender*, November 21, 1936.

Wiggins, Edgar. "Montmartre: By the Streetwolf of Paris." *Chicago Defender*, September 29, 1934.

Wiggins, Edgar. "Musicians Jilt Leader One Hour before Dance Date." *Chicago Defender*, January 7, 1939.

Wiggins, Edgar. "Paris Night Life Returns to Old Form, Says Wiggins." *Chicago Defender*, January 27, 1940.

Wiggins, Edgar. "War Scare Blamed for Poor Business." *Chicago Defender*, October 22, 1938.

Winnipeg Tribune. "Amery's Son Faces Trial for Treason." July 30, 1945.

Winnipeg Tribune. "Nazis Didn't Look up Chimney: Well-Hidden Radio Kept British Internees up-to-Date on the War." September 29, 1944.

Winnipeg Tribune. "Winnipegger Tells of Life in Nazi Internment Camps." December 7, 1942.

Wood, Ean. *The Josephine Baker Story*. London: Sanctuary, 2000.

Zwerin, Mike. *Swing under the Nazis: Jazz as a Metaphor for Freedom*. New York: Coooper Square Press, 1985.

Index